I'VE WALKED MY OWN TALK

I'VE WALKED MY OWN TALK

One Man's Walking and Working for Charity

JOCELYN WIJS-REED

PARTRIDGE
A Penguin Random House Company

To order additional copies of this book, contact
Toll Free 800 101 2657 (Singapore)
Toll Free 1 800 81 7340 (Malaysia)
orders.singapore@partridgepublishing.com

www.partridgepublishing.com/singapore

CONTENTS

I dedicate this book to my late daughter Zoë Reed, whose courage and love both shaped and inspired my life. God bless and keep you, my angel.

I also dedicate this book to my mate Colin Walker, who helped me make the journey of the last 30 years of my life and who was the Founding President of the Zoe Reed Little Bridge House Association.

Best wishes
God Bless
Nigel Reed

Nigel & Jocelyn's Web Site
www.walkyourowntalk.yolasite.com

FORWARD

The emotional part of our lives that is nurtured through our early childhood, can, I believe, be frozen. When something so desperately needed, as an outward display of affection and love, is missing a child will fail to thrive. For over forty years my emotional growth was frozen, frozen as firmly as any iceberg due to exactly that.

However, the good news is that a steady rise in temperature can melt the oldest block of ice. For me, that rise in temperature was a child's unconditional love. That child was a little girl named Zoë, my late daughter. Her courage, love and self-belief freed me from an emotionally frozen life, and as a result I have been able to grow as a member of this wonderful human race. She had the ability to wake each morning, aware that she had a life-limiting illness, yet still make the choice to be positive, happy, and optimistic about her future. Zoë helped me realise that each one of us has the ability to overcome any adversity by choosing to be positive and happy. My life had changed forever.

Nigel Frank Reed

PREFACE

"Begin difficult things while they are easy, Do great things when they are small. The difficult things of the world were once easy. The great things were once small. The thousand mile journey begins with one step". (Unknown)

This book is the result of keeping a promise to my dying daughter Zoë Claire Reed, who sadly passed away in March 1994 from a combination of asthma and cystic fibrosis. On her death bed I made a promise, a promise that was to see me walk halfway around the world to raise awareness of cystic fibrosis and other life-limiting illnesses.

I walked a total of more than 20,000 km in 10 years, and every step I took was for children with life-limiting illnesses. I crossed the United States of America, walked half the length of England and covered over 11,500 km throughout Australia. Lions International, the world's largest service club organization, supported me throughout my journeys. They leapt to the aid of a father who was trying to keep a promise to his dead daughter. I was inspired along the way by so many courageous and inspirational people, both young and old, who helped me on my journey. While speaking to Lions Clubs and children with life-limiting illnesses and their families, I slowly became convinced that I should share my story with as many people as possible in the hope that I could inspire others.

This book is the vehicle for sharing my story. It shows how I survived and grew out of the depths of despair and grief. As a result, my life has been changed forever. So can yours! Just open your heart and let my story strengthen your soul. For I believe that we all have the seed of greatness nestled deep within, planted by a God of love. This is a journey of discovery, wonderment and enlightenment. It is the tale of a pilgrimage that continues to unfold to this day.

In these times of economic rationalization, youth suicide, high divorce rates and high levels of personal and business bankruptcy, it is hard to quantify the effect that grief is having on the broad community. There have been thousands of books written to help us achieve success, but few to show the way through the darkness of grief. Helen Kubbler Ross has been our shining light; maybe, in some small way, this father's story will also help others. That is my hope. History shows that a crisis can often be a wakeup call that inspires everyday people to achieve wonderful and remarkable things.

Nigel Reed (Zoë's Dad) formerly Brisbane Queensland now living at Mount Maunganui New Zealand.

INTRODUCTION

He cannot yet express all his needs. He cannot tell you how much he craves for the warmth of his mother's body, for the security of her presence, for the soothing voice and her special touch. Where these are absent, the baby suffers, and the deprivation will almost inevitably show up in later life.

Marilyn Bonham, Physiotherapist

Sitting on the Olympic bus that carried all the Torchbearers for our particular leg, I looked at all those people who, like me, had been given the privilege of carrying the torch on its journey to the Olympic Games in Sydney. I wondered about their lives and what stories they had to tell. It wasn't long before I got my answers, as we were asked to share briefly why we had been chosen to carry the torch. These were everyday people who had made a difference in their community; the elderly, the young and even some who had disabilities. Very often we pay many hundreds of dollars to listen to motivational speakers whose lives are far less inspiring. I could do little else than sit in awe of the people I was sharing the day with.

For a brief period in time, my mind drifted back to my childhood, and as if I was dying, suddenly my life was flashing past. As a little boy walking home from a movie about the late great Jim Thorpe, I remember running down Curzon Street imagining I was an Olympic runner. I never became an athlete, but here I was carrying the Olympic Torch for a nation 9000 km away from my place of birth in Long Eaton Nottingham England.

A quote came to mind: *"Every journey starts with the first step"*. I had believed for many years that my journey started in 1987 when I lost my home and business. I now understand the first step was in 1944 the year of my birth, fifty years before my daughter's death.

The only way I can understand and grow from the challenges of my early years is to believe I chose them and that my soul needed these experiences to grow. This story is about that growth.

Between 1990 and 2007 I have been privileged to walk 30,000 km all over the world, raising pledges of millions of dollars while also raising awareness worldwide for children with life-limiting illnesses, diseases like Cystic Fibrosis (which claimed my precious Zoë), Muscular Dystrophy, Battens Disease and many other lesser known ailments.

My first 45 years, however, were far from being positive. In fact, they were filled with self-pity and a clear lack of direction. Unresolved grief played a large role in my early life, and in 1998 it finally overcame me. It was as if my spirit finally surrendered. Even though I had founded the organization that would build Zoë's Place, Queensland's first children's hospice, I suddenly found myself breaking down emotionally almost every day. The disintegration continued until I found myself living on the streets of Dover, England. For three months I wandered from town to town along the south coast of England, sleeping wherever I could find a dry spot to shelter from the rain, snow and wind. The shelter of my tent at times felt almost like I had returned to the womb, warm and secure. I had no desire to venture out. However, I realized that I had left people behind and that knowledge weighed heavily on my mind. I knew the day would come when I would have to leave the security of that tent and find help.

Finally, I decided enough was enough. I went to see a doctor in Dover who diagnosed my emotional breakdown and he directed me to a youth hostel. Not knowing Dover that well, I got lost and wandered instead into a YMCA Emergency Access hostel, a crisis centre, a place where people who had lost hope could go in search of support. In a material sense, that support came in the shape of a mattress on the floor and a breakfast of Kellogg's corn flakes. But what it offered in an emotional sense was even more valuable. It was there that I finally surrendered in the presence of a total stranger, the Manager, sharing with him as much of the story as I dared, a story that until that moment had been stored deep within my memory.

Through a stream of tears, I told him my tale. The last straw in my emotional load had been the news that little Lizzie, my daughter's friend, who also had Cystic Fibrosis, had died. Her death came during the same weekend that Princess Diana was killed. It was also the weekend when the Zoe Reed Little Bridge House Association was holding its first annual General Meeting. Shortly before, I had married for the fourth time, and for some reason I had begun to feel the pressure and responsibility in caring for someone else's children. Was I fearful of failing and losing another child? Was it the belief that if anything *could* go wrong it *would* go wrong for me?

I told him I had reached a point where I was crying like a child daily. It was as if the emotionally starved child within me had taken over. My tears were followed by palpitations, hot sweats and anxiety attacks. I believe it is called the fight or flight syndrome. Well, I never was a good fighter, so when it all became too much, I decided to visit a friend in Melbourne to ask for advice. On the way, I made a call to my new wife to try and explain myself. Her response to me tipped me completely over the edge. She wasn't impressed with my fear and sadness and rage. She had every right to feel that way, but I wasn't in the mood to listen to what she had to say, so the mobile phone went out of the window. I drove to Sydney Airport, instead of Melbourne, and boarded a plane to England. That, I explained to him, is how I had found myself on the streets of Dover.

Just to share this part of the story with him was an instant relief. In the safety of my tent, these same thoughts had eaten away at my very being. Over the next twelve weeks I shared more and more of my feelings with anyone who would listen. This proved to be very therapeutic, and I wondered why I had not had the courage to do it sooner. I now believe it was fear of rejection. What would people think of me, a grown man, so sad and confused that he needed to cry? I gradually came to understand that it's okay not to be strong all the time. If you can be happy with whom you are other people's opinions about you do not matter. I also figured out that I had tried to keep the grieving process at bay by founding Zoë's place and raising funds for it.

I lost five people in one year; first my step-brother Maurice, then a few weeks later my daughter Zoë, then my good friends Barbara and Byron. It felt as if I was in shell shock. But the worst was about to come with divorce from Erika, Zoë's mum. I loved her more than anyone. I truly felt like giving in. But I was taught to believe that in times of hardship and crisis we should look to help others. If we, in some way, can provide proof that hope exists for others less fortunate, then not only do we help them, but we also help ourselves. I hoped I would learn from others how to grow and cope. By walking for sick children and attempting to raise funds for a Respite Centre, I was helping families experiencing similar problems to my own. And just maybe their example would help me survive.

What had surfaced over those months was grief, but it was not just over the deaths of my daughter, brother and friends, and the loss of Erika; it was the unresolved grief associated with the loss of my father and mother. It had lain dormant in my innermost thoughts, just waiting to surface and bite me. Grief had also affected many of my decisions in the past and was responsible in many ways for my early journey's path.

As I recounted my tale to others, a question came to mind. How could I have a successful relationship if my self-worth depended on others? Surely, until I loved myself I could not truly love someone else; my need for demonstrative love from others eventually seemed to drive them away and, in the end, reinforce my loneliness.

This was the other lesson I learned: until I was able to resolve the childhood issues that haunted me into my adult life, no matter how successful and secure I thought I was, I would not be able to handle life's unavoidable challenges such as loss, grief, death and change. It seems we in the Western world will do anything to avoid any discussion relating to these subjects.

A common phrase during my childhood was, "little children should be seen and not heard." When I was confronted with one of life's challenges, as when I was confronted with grief, I ran. But thanks to the help of my many friends at the `Y', many of whom had also run, I discovered something special; I was a child of God and he loved and cared for me. It was okay that my father had died before my birth and that my mother chose to give me away, for God was there for me. But I also needed to let go of my past. And the only way I could free myself was to totally and unconditionally forgive myself and set adrift the mistakes and failures of my early life, then totally and unconditionally forgive others for their errors and mistakes in dealing with me.

I remembered a passage I had read in a church news letter, while walking through Ohio when I was crossing the USA in 1995: *"God is not protection from storms but perfect shelter during storms."* So he would not protect me from the challenges of life, but his example could offer guidance through life's stormy passages. I came to understand that even though I had chosen a new path, I would still need his guidance to grow and cope. Once I accepted this, I was able to confront the ghosts of my childhood. Over the next ten months I was even able to help those who had helped me, by working as a night manager with the YMCA.

As I mentioned earlier I have always believed that when confronted with a crisis, we have two choices, fight or flight. John F. Kennedy, when faced with the Berlin Crisis, was heard to say: *"We must never forget that the word **CRISIS** in Chinese has two hieroglyphics, one stands for Danger the other Opportunity. Be aware of the Danger but seek out and embrace the Opportunity."* No matter how desperate we feel, out there in our community are those who are far less fortunate than we are. By offering food and shelter to those that are in need, the YMCA gave me time to reflect on the decisions I had made, and made me realize that I could seek help and rebuild my life.

In Dover there were seemingly more destitute people than in most places I had visited, for it is the gateway to Europe. In cities and towns all over the world, however, there are people in need of help. The lingering memories of those broken souls, the display of courage by sick children, and the lessons I continue to learn by associating with other people who have been challenged by life's experiences; all of these things make me want to help others less fortunate. I am positive that out there in those towns and cities someone like me is in trouble, or in need of help.

Here's a story I like to think about:

'An elderly Gentleman was walking along the beach on the east coast of America. He had noticed the beach was covered with starfish but something else had attracted his attention. It was a young boy who was throwing them back into the sea one at a time. On reaching the boy, he gently asked, "Son why are you throwing them back? There are too many of them to make a difference". The young boy replied (as he cast another starfish back into the sea), "It does for that one, mister".

May God bless, keep and guide you on your journey of discovery, for now I will share my journey with you.

MY YOUTH AND EARLY YEARS

"Too many people overvalue what they are not and undervalue what they are.
Malcolm Forbes

There is an old boxing adage that can be applied to the first forty-four years of my life: "It isn't how many times you get knocked down that matters, but how many times you get up!" But we need to discover how to duck along the way so we can avoid being caught by the same blows. I guess I was a late learner. As I saw it, being born on April Fool's Day 1944 and being called Nigel wasn't a great start, but when I discovered my father would not return from the war and my mother had chosen to give me away, I had no doubt that I wasn't worth too much. Though I tried as hard as I could, I could not convince my grandparents to adopt me. I have heard people remark over the years, "Well, the same thing happened to young Tommy Smith and he went on to become a doctor and build a life for himself." That's ok, but hey! We are not all the same, or I hope we are not. What I wish I had understood back then was this: It is a matter of choice. Sink into the pool of self pity or alter your attitude and choose a better life. But some of us need help to make the best choices.

For me, the only thing I wanted was to belong, to have a family of my own and prove I had some value. I guess that back in the forties, family things like adoption, sexuality and death were seldom talked about. A generation of parents said, "Little boys and girls should be seen and not heard". This made things like the death of a parent and reasons for adoption hard to discuss. So the little boy in me never got to ask, "Why me"? I was in my forties when I came to my own conclusions, be they right or wrong.

For background, let's start with the relationship between my grandparents. It's a bit confusing. You see, my mother lost her mother, then my father lost his father, then the two remaining spouses married each other before my parents got married. Formerly unrelated persons, my parents instantly became stepbrother and stepsister. There was tremendous family concern when the stepson fell in love with the stepdaughter because, although not related by blood, they were bonded by their parents' marriage. So my mum and dad's marriage was sanctioned at a Registry Office, since no church would marry them. What was to become of Nigel, who was steadily growing as an unborn baby?

Soon after my father's failure to return from the Second World War, my mother asked her father to raise me because she wanted to remarry. Her request, coming so quickly after my father's untimely death, and it divided the family because he objected to this arrangement. The family was estranged from then on; not only did my father's siblings reject my Grandfather (their stepfather), so did my own mother, his only daughter. She refused to speak to him. I remember one day he walked three miles to visit my mum and she wouldn't even answer the door. He went home in tears and heartbroken. I was too young to really understand, but I do remember feeling sad for this old gentleman. Now, having lost my only daughter, I understand his grief. She was his only child.

In earlier times, due to my grandmother's efforts, I can remember occasional visitations to my mother's house. As I grew older, I made my own efforts to visit my mother. My mother's new husband, my stepfather, occasionally came to see me. As a couple, they had no other children and were very comfortable financially, yet they never contributed to my upbringing in any way, emotionally or financially. My mother came to my first wedding and, apart from having a meal with her four years after that; I have never seen her since. My mother and her husband chose to leave England four days after I last saw her, without telling anyone of their plans. I believe they lived for many years on Guernsey but that's all I know.

The constant talk of my grandfather's violence left me feeling fearful of a pending good hiding. Yes, he had been violent in the past but I never encountered any violence that was directed towards me. It just never happened. I only saw his mean side on one occasion, directed toward my grandmother, and after it happened I asked my grandmother to leave him. Her reply confused me even more. She said, "Do not ask me to choose between your grandfather and you". He loved his grandchildren and they loved him. Sitting on his knee as a child, I sensed that he was lonely. I remember how I sat there as he polished his medals earned in the First World War, a war that had molded him into a committed socialist, a friend of the underdog.

He told me how he had drunk some of the officer's rum ration, as he drove the ration carriage led by six horses. Then how he had fallen off the carriage on arrival at the Officers Mess, and for his indiscretion he received field punishment No 2; crucified on a gun carriage wheel for 3 hours a day. He never forgave the privileged class, as he called them. For the remainder of his life he would take on the Tories, the Conservatives, anyone he saw as the privileged class. I watched as he would cry when the various national Labour Party Governments were defeated. At a personal level, he was proud that he had won the local election twice and was elected Chairman of the Council (Mayor) by the largest margin of his day. I often wonder if his photo hangs along those of the Tory heads of council that proudly adorn the corridor's in Long Eaton's Council Hall.

What did I miss? How bad was he? He adopted six children and worked tirelessly for his community. He was head of the Council twice and President of the British Legion for many years. Accused by some of the public of favouring his adopted family, scorned by the family he had taken in for spending so much time helping others, he just couldn't win. I am proud to say he raised me. One of the greatest compliments Erika (Zoë's mum) paid me was that she saw my grandfather's influence in my later life. I now believe that his life was dedicated to serving his fellow human beings and that he set the example I would follow in later life.

"Anyone can be great because anyone can serve, you do not need a college degree to serve or to be able to make subject and verb agree to serve, just a heart full of grace and a soul generated by love."

Martin Luther King Jr.

The other sides of the family were wonderful to me, especially my Gran. I owe her so much, and I do believe my granddad was hard on her. She was the best mum anyone could ask for, hard-working and very loving in her own way. I must say I do not blame anyone for my inability to achieve as a young person. The prevailing attitude of that time, the idea that children needn't be listened to, led to my inability to heal my grief and take control of my life. I have now learned to embrace those unspoken words, for they contributed to my journey.

As a school kid, things were never easy. I was embarrassed by my family situation. Even back then, my lack of confidence was showing. I remember one incident when my stepfather took me for a driving lesson. When I found it difficult, he said I would never pass my test. I guess I believed him, for although I drove (risking prosecution for not having a license), I did not take my test until I was almost fifty. I am sure Erika would say this contributed partly to our breakdown. It was seen as a lack of responsibility. And it was.

Why can't parents think twice before they make flippant statements to their children regarding their abilities? My step father's off hand judgment haunted me for years. I saw numerous cases of this in the YMCA emergency access in Dover. Dozens of broken souls shattered by a careless word. There were people of all ages running from their pasts and unable to confront issues that should have been resolved in their childhood.

I have often thought that I should have changed my name to Littlemore, for my school reports always said the same thing, "With a little more concentration, with a little more effort, Nigel could achieve so much more".

But hey! Who cared? Not I. For by now I was dancing the night away to the Beatles. Even that was a challenge. It took me six months to pluck up the courage to ask a girl to dance. Talk about reluctance! Finally, Sandra Wells, someone I had liked from afar, dragged me onto the floor and Eureka! For a while, things changed. I had finally found something I was good at. I even contemplated a career in the field of dance but "only queers danced on the stage," I was told. I had heard the story of Duggie Squires, the choreographer for the BBC, who used to live just around the corner and I wondered if I could be like him. But I dared not ask questions about it for fear of what people would think, and the only thing I knew about goals was that they were the things that were scored when playing football at West Park with your mates.

I later read somewhere that everything started with a day dream, even creation. How I wish I had read and understood that sooner. I knew nothing about how to achieve a dream. I expected to spend my adult life in the steel mills like my father's family. So having left school with no clear direction, for one year I drifted from job to job as a furnace worker, painter and steel worker. When anyone told me I had done something wrong at work, I quit.

However, things changed the day my Dad's youngest brother, Stanley, returned from Hong Kong. Blonde, six foot, bronzed and dressed in his army uniform. He had been my mentor and friend, almost a father figure. I had waited in anticipation for his return from national service. His first night home we sat around the gas fire in the front room (which was reserved for special occasions) and we talked of that wonderful far off place, Hong Kong: The attractive girls, the drinking sessions. These were things he never told our shared mother about, but I had also watched as the family welcomed him back with open arms. To me it was a demonstration of love. Would they do the same for me, I wondered? So from that day, the stage was set. A military career was for me! I wanted some of that excitement and the warm feeling that would come from being welcomed home.

THE MILITARY

I discovered that the only way I could join the military at the age of 16 was to become a boy soldier. This meant getting my Granddad to give his consent. So I took myself off to the recruitment office that was situated eight miles away in Nottingham, filled in the forms, took the exam, and, to my surprise, passed. I then jumped on a bus and headed home. I planted the form firmly in front of my granddad and he looked me in the eyes and said, "Are you sure"? I just nodded. He shook me by the hand and congratulated me. I saw pride for me in his eyes, something I had never seen before. 1 January 1960 was the first day of my army life. I was on a train to North Wales when I met a six foot giant who was shaving four times a day at age 15, Spud (Fredrick) Murphy. Spud became a good friend. It wasn't a hard decision for me. After all, who would argue with me when I had him on my side? After the army it was another thirty-odd years before we were to meet again in Australia in the year 2000.

We were greeted by Sergeant Williams of the military police, a giant of a man in a red peaked hat. As we stepped off the train, we saw a sign saying Tonfanau Junior Leaders Camp, North Wales. It sure did look like a bleak place! There was heavy cloud cover and it was windy, very grey and overcast. Suddenly, in a loud, almost melodic voice, he captured our attention, as he would on many occasions over the next 12 weeks. He said his first words. "Gentlemen, I know what your first letter will say: *"Dear Mum, he's a bastard! She will reply, So are you son, but don't tell your father"*. I asked myself, was this military humour, or had he read my birth certificate? The first term as a trainee was hard, but I enjoyed it, and my relationship with my Grandfather improved out of sight. Once he signed my papers to enlist, it seemed I had won his respect. My wonderful Gran Ethel was also so proud. What upset me was that no one from the family came to the railway station to say goodbye except Mike Severn, my oldest mate.

My military career went along well. I never achieved any rank during my time as a boy soldier, but I improved my education and learned how to care for myself. I also attained the Silver Duke of Edinburgh award. The first hint that I had a problem buried deep in my subconscious came when my Uncle Eddie died of a heart problem. It brought back issues relating to the loss of my father. Once again, the family chose not to discuss the loss. So, having taken compassionate leave for the funeral, I returned to Osnabruck, Germany, where I was stationed. I was missing Eddie a lot. He had been a good friend to me. What I could not understand was how this outwardly healthy young man of 40 could die. But no one wanted to discuss this with me. Life seemingly just went on as normal for all but Betty and Marie, his wife and daughter. I now believe that it had far-reaching effects on Betty's health. I just wished I had found someone who I felt comfortable talking to, so I could have told them how much he had meant to me.

One thing I began to understand was that as a member of a fairly large family, almost a tribe, it was inevitable that death would become a fairly familiar visitor. Next to go was my grandfather and sadly, no one had told me of his impending death. I never got to tell him how much I loved and respected him. Was this as a result of the family's dislike of him? No one chose to discuss his death, even his daughter, my Mother! She never even came to the funeral. Considering the number of people who he had helped, it was a poor farewell. Erika later said, "It did not matter how many came. God knew the good he had done".

It seemed that in the Army I had found a life I was suited to. Although I didn't attain any rank in boy service, it did give me an understanding of what the army required from you if you wanted to climb the ranks. Volunteer for everything! Shout the loudest when they called out for volunteers! And when they said "Jump"! all you asked was, "How high"? With those words of wisdom under my belt, I launched myself full bore at my army life. Very quickly I climbed the ranks. Lance Corporal, then Corporal, and with the rank of Sergeant on the horizon, suddenly out of the blue, the old self doubt crept up behind me and bit me in the bum.

After having been deployed to Germany to train on tanks I felt something inside me wanted a closure on my father death and Germany was where he was shot down during the Second World War. A grave! A body! This would at least prove he had lived. So as a way of doing this I made up a story. I said that I had found his grave stone in Hanover Germany, where they believed he was shot down and killed. I wrote to my Gran and told her. Not expecting her to want to fly over, I was caught out. I still regret to this day causing that wonderful lady any pain, but I so desperately wanted to find something of him.

Although I had total belief in my abilities as a tank commander, a rather strange sergeant called Taffy Cox had a different opinion of me and he shook my confidence. As a result one night on the Saltau ranges in West Germany, with a dozen or so Heineken beers under my belt, and after a lot of posturing and swearing, we had a rather short, sharp attempt at fighting. In retrospect it was more like two old chooks flapping their wings.

I 'went walkabout', AWOL as the army refers to it—my old escape of running. I did not get far before I collapsed in a ditch and fell into a drunken sleep. At about 9:30am the next morning I awoke to find myself damp and cold with a throat feeling like I had swallowed a sand bucket, or at least its contents. In good military fashion, I gradually lifted my head, unsure of my exact location, for Saltau was the tank firing ranges for NATO. Immediately I thought, "Shit, I'm in trouble now". As it turned out, I had got that right.

As I gingerly lifted my head above the horizon, I saw a line of soldiers. I was intrigued as to what they were doing, so I wandered over to the nearest guy and asked, "What are you doing? Can I help"? His look should have warned me. He replied, "You stupid arsehole, we're looking for you". At that, a sergeant came over, arrested me, and had me transported to base camp. I was immediately placed sitting crossed-legged under a tent. I could not help but see the comparison to my grandfather. I only hoped I did not get field punishment number two. The next thing I remember was Left! Right! Left! Mark Time! Halt! Those commands came from the mouth of someone considered by many in the army to be more powerful and less forgiving than God, the Regimental Sergeant Major. Within 3 minutes I lost my rank. The Colonel was Acting Brigadier and he was able to strip a non-commissioned officer of his substantial rank. On top of that, I received 21 days in the guard room and was posted to another squadron.

Soon after that, I purchased my discharge from the army. I came out on the same day as my nemesis Peter Why. Pete and I had been mates of a kind for a while. Although he seemed to be able to beat me at most things, we had remained mates anyway. Sometime later, in fact about twenty-five years later, he would inspire me beyond belief. In his typical way he helped change my life. To leave the army before your due date in those years you had to purchase your discharge. The cost was two hundred pounds. As usual, I had little cash, so it was my Grandfather who gave me the two hundred pounds required. I believe he was disappointed in me for not staying on and building a career, but he was there when I needed him. When I found out he had given me all he had, I had no choice but to give it back. I chose to go back into the army and after 18 months I re-enlisted. I had found it hard to settle in civilian life, so I returned to my old regiment, The Royal Dragoons, now based in Detmold, Germany.

I very quickly got my rank back as a result of a friend and Sgt Major called Jim McKay. Jim, in his own way, inspired me. One day I was sitting up in a squadron bar called The Rainbow Bar. A few guys were joking about who would win the 100 yard sprint in the regimental athletic meet, when suddenly there was a voice from the next table. It was Jim. "I could beat you all, without a problem". To say the guys were amused would be an understatement. Jim, although a very tough guy, was in his mid-thirties and enjoyed a few drinks. So without much ado, Bobby Moon and Stan Thompson took him on. Some months later, they all lined up and to everyone's surprise, Jim blitzed them. Little did we know he had been an army champion in his days? Old Jim had a real good year. He won the battalion relay final for us, to the great surprise of everyone who had not witnessed that wonderful day months earlier. An old dog taught the young pups how to win, and how to win in style. All in all though, the army was good for me. It gave me a sense of belonging, and in some ways, a family.

However, I still felt lonely. So much so, that I actually attempted suicide. As I look back, it was like a bungee jump without the elastic band. I must have looked silly, tying the rope of the flag pole around my neck, then climbing to the top of the pole and jumping off. All I know is, the rope just ran through the pulley and I ended up with my feet firmly planted on the ground. When I landed, all my mates leaned out of the window, had a good laugh, and applauded my show. I don't blame them. It must have looked pretty stupid. I suppose the amount of alcohol I had consumed did not help either.

Not long after this, I decided to transfer from my tank regiment, which is now known as the Blues & Royals, (the same regiment of the young British royals, Princes William & Harry) to a mounted squadron to ride a horse behind the Queen in London. I got part of my rank back, and things looked a little better.

AFTER A SINGLE LIFE

Not long after my army transfer back to England, I met my first wife, Janet. After a short courtship, we decided to marry in England and then go back to Australia, where her family owned a hotel. Our wedding took place in London's Cheyne Place in Chelsea. It was the first and last time I would see my grandmother and mother standing together. Although I was disappointed that my grandfather, sadly, could not be there, I was very happy that my uncle Stanley (against doctor's advice) had come. He had been like a dad on many occasions and I was able to relate more to him as a father figure. He was the same age as my mates' Dads.

"Come to Australia, my father owns a hotel", Janet had said. So with having left the Army, I landed in Townsville in February 1972 in a blue pin stripe suit and regimental tie. After a 30 km drive in a Holden Ute I arrived in Giru, a sugar refinery township, with about 100 houses, a service station, general store and the pub. On my first night tending the bar, I was greeted with, "So you're the Pom that married the Wog". The scene was set. But to be honest, those were great times. Now firmly entrenched behind the bar of the Giru pub, I began to feel safe and the future looked rosy. I had a new home and for once money in the bank, although much of it was due to the generosity of my in-laws.

But their generosity was a double-edged sword. After a holiday in Brisbane, where Janet and I stayed with my old army buddy, Pete Why, and his wife Barbara, we arrived back to work at the hotel and were promptly asked by the in-laws to have separate days off each week from this point on. I was not prepared to do this; I felt that being married meant being able to have time off together. It was as if my in-laws were simply taking control over my life and my marriage. I am sure that my wife felt it was okay, as that was how she had been raised, but for me, it was devastating. While I appreciated the help they gave,

I needed to be more independent of the family. At the same time, I also appreciated the fact that Janet was an only child and felt the family pull very strongly. There came a time when my father-in-law wanted to leave the hotel at Giru and I discussed with Janet that I would like to take the lease on. It was clear that I would never have her support in business because she knew from experience how much effort her parents had to put into the hotel and she didn't want to have to work that hard. I then asked her if she would like to move to Sydney to live. She said, "Don't ever ask me to choose between my family and you". It was clear she would never leave her family, just as it was clear I would not be happy under their control.

So I quit the hotel and went to work in the sugar cane industry as an off-sider on a sugar cane train. It was many years later, while doing charity walking, that I was to meet up again with the man, in the Giru hotel, who had chosen me from a line of blokes to be his off-sider. I ended up working double shifts and extra days to prove that I could take care of my wife and household, so that we could have money in the bank and exist on our own. Shortly after that Janet and her father arrived home one day with the deed to a section in Townsville they had just bought. This was to be where my new home was to be built. I had no say in where I was to live if I wanted to stay married to Janet, but I appreciated the fact that owning our own home was a great opportunity. So I chose to stay, hoping that maybe someday things would be different and the in-laws would begin to back off. After our house was built, we moved to Townsville and I went to work at the Copper Refinery. Once again, I worked hard so as to provide for my wife and myself.

One day, out of the blue, I received a phone call that shook me to the core. Stanley, my dad's youngest brother, had been diagnosed with lung cancer. Why him? For years he had battled spondylitis of the spine. He had gone against doctor's advice and come to our wedding in a wheel chair. It had meant so much to have him make that journey to our wedding. Was I to lose someone else? Stanley was my mentor, friend and father figure. He was far too young and I loved him so much. I was devastated and, without thinking, instantly knew I had to go and be with him. Janet arrived home shortly after that phone call and an argument occurred as I had made the decision of going without discussing it first with her. In retrospect it seems strange; even though we had plenty of money in the bank, her father paid my fare and wanted to pay hers as well, but she did not want to go. Soon, Janet and I calmed down about the situation and I left to visit Stanley in England, thinking that all was well in Australia. I made it back to England and spent four weeks with Stanley. While I was there, I saw my birth mother for the last time. I took her out to dinner and for the first time ever we spoke of my father. It was a strange evening, and the strangest thing I remember about it was that I was told that I had hands like my father's. Stanley and the family could not understand the need I had to meet with my birth mother. Stanley and I fought verbally about it and it amazed me to see that, even as he was dying, he still had so much hate for her.

Stanley was still alive when I left to go back to Townsville. Within 20 minutes of setting down on Australian soil, Janet announced that she was leaving me. This announcement, coming so soon after seeing Stanley and my mum, was almost too much for me. I had never experienced such a sense of loss. Janet was shocked at my reaction, believing in some way that I wanted the marriage to end. After some discussion she mentioned trying again, but my thoughts made me wonder how she could swing from not being in love to trying again. We had been married for five years and all for what. I was confused and troubled and decided against it. I went to stay at a motel and met up with Barry Keogh, a bloke I met while working at the refinery, who had become a good friend. He was concerned that I shouldn't be alone at this time and we had a meal together.

Janet and I arranged our affairs over two days and all at once I was separated. I flew back to England to see Stanley before he died. It was only a fortnight later, the night he died, that I found myself walking alone, grieving for both him and Janet. I encountered Fred, Stanley's elder brother, and I put my arms out to hold him. All he did was push me gently aside, and his reaction surprised me. He did not want to discuss Stanley's death or my separation. Two losses in such a short time! For me, divorce was almost as painful as the death of a loved one. But again, someone I loved and trusted refused to talk about the things that weighed me down. I stayed on in England and for a time stayed with Betty, my father's sister. My ex-wife Janet sold our house in Australia very quickly and sent my share of the money. I will always remember Janet's honesty in making sure that I got my rightful share, and I thank her for that. I took my Grandmother for a holiday, bought some nice clothes and decided I would try some sort of work training.

After a discussion with an old friend who had her own hairdressing business, I signed up for a hairdressing course. After a couple of weeks we had to design a hairstyle on our dummy head. I didn't have a clue what to do, but I got a rave report for being creative and to this day I am not sure why or how it all happened. After a few weeks I realized this was not what I wanted, so I got a job working for the Post Office delivering mail and, as usual, worked extra shifts. For what seemed like a long time, I would find myself in tears, especially in the evenings. Betty said to me one night, "you have to move on Nigel". Betty's husband had died very early on, so she knew what it was like.

After about 18 months I met the lady who was to become my second wife. Jane was a registered nurse with a twin sister, Elizabeth, who was also a nurse. Jane and I eventually married and, after many discussions, we moved to Australia and settled in Brisbane. I remember being told by Jane's mother that I had a responsibility to Jane's sister Elizabeth. At the time I wasn't sure what that would mean. Jane and I very quickly found employment and life was good. We eventually bought a house on the south side of Brisbane. Sometime after that Jane's twin Elizabeth came from England to live with us. My wife Jane was the softer personality of the two. Elizabeth was able to manipulate any situation to her advantage and managed to talk Jane into seeing her point of view. The second morning Elizabeth was with us there was a strange man in our bathroom, obviously coming from her room. This set the pattern for things to come.

When Elizabeth came into our lives and our home, things very quickly went downhill. Jane and I discussed selling our home, buying a caravan and traveling around Australia. We were both keen on the idea, so we bought the campervan and put our house on the market. It sold very quickly, and Elizabeth decided she would have to come with us. Elizabeth's influence over Jane was powerful. One night shortly before we were due to leave, an argument ensued. I have no recollection what it was about, but I decided to go to a friend's house for the night just to let the air settle. The next morning I went straight to work from Pete's. At about 9.00 am I received a phone call from my good friend Colin Walker, who lived across the road. He asked, "How long since you have been home"? When I said "yesterday" he said, "Get home quickly there is a furniture truck at your house". By the time I got permission to leave work and cycled home (a half hour trip) I was too late. I arrived home to find the house stripped of everything except a black dust bin liner in the middle of the lounge floor with my clothes and personal effects in it and odd bits of stuff lying around. The dog was also gone. They had taken the TV aerial and curtains, which were supposed to be fittings sold with the house. I quickly went to the bank but I was too late. Jane had cleaned out the account and taken all the money from the house sale. They even returned the camper van and took off with the deposit. I sought legal advice, but I had no money left to find them or fight for what should have been half mine. Was it planned or did they decide after the argument? Who knows?

There was a time whilst Jane and I were still living in England when I had defended Elizabeth and Jane against a charge of theft at the hospital they were working at. They had been accused of pilfering. When I went through the empty house that day I found nurse's scissors in a drawer with other people names on them. I guess its true; once a thief, always a thief.

It is funny how life revolves around. Later on, when I was working at the Sheraton Hotel, I met a chap who knew Jane and Elizabeth. He told me that they bought a house in the Perth area on an interest-free loan and sold it for a large profit at America's Cup time. He gave me their phone number and I rang them to let them know that

I knew all about their dirty scheming and knew where they were. But that's all the satisfaction I got. Once again I had been knocked down; another loss, another betrayal.

I returned to England and took up a position as a Bar Manager at the Croft House Health Club. It was not long after starting as Bar Manager that I saw a little MG sports car drive up and out of it stepped the most beautiful lady I had ever seen. Her name was Erika and she was to become my third wife and the mother of our only child, Zoë Claire Reed.

A CHILD IS BORN

It is pretty hard to find what does bring happiness.
Poverty and wealth have failed.
Kin Hubbard

I read somewhere that once a child enters your life, it is never the same again. Without any question that is true for me. October 1982 was the month Zoë Claire Reed was born. It was the happiest day of my life! It seemed for once I would achieve my childhood dream to have my OWN family. Happiness had finally arrived. In terms of the universe it would be no more than a fleeting second, but in human terms it lasted for eleven wonderful years.

The time prior to Zoë's birth was the happiest of my life. I fell in love with Erika at first sight. That she was interested in me seemed unbelievable, but it was true. We spent many happy hours walking our two dogs Timmy and Toby through the woods in and around the Horse and Groom public house, which was a pub we took over when I left Croft House Health Club. We were completing our hotelier's course when Erika first started to feel morning sickness. Neither Erika nor I had any idea that it was as a result of being pregnant, but we soon found out. I was so happy that when we visited Erika's parents I just could not wait to tell them the good news. "You are going to be Grandparents"! I shouted as we entered their house in Romford.

Erika had told me when we met that she had lost a baby brother to Cystic Fibrosis. I had to admit that I knew nothing about the illness, so we decided to get some medical advice. It was explained to us that CF was genetic and that both parents had to carry the defective gene for a child to be born with the disease. We were told that our odds for having a CF child were about the same as our odds of winning the lotto. With that newfound information, we considered our chances and decided we did want a family. Little did we know though that things were about to change forever. The day was October 7th, 1982. We had just finished a long day and both Erika and I were tired. The moment we got into bed, Erika proclaimed, "My water has burst"! Zoë Claire Reed wanted to be born. I managed to get Erika to the hospital but then had to go back to the hotel. There was no one else to look after it. The next morning I received a phone call from the hospital telling me we had a daughter, but that I should get there as soon as possible.

As I walked into the ward the look in Erika's eyes told the sad story. They had taken Zoë away! Erika looked at me and said, "Zoë has Cystic Fibrosis Nigel, I know, I just know". She was not wrong! Zoë had a distended bowel, which is a sign of possible Cystic Fibrosis. The bad news then got worse. During the 20 mile journey to Hackney Children's Hospital (the only hospital close by that had a doctor who specialized in Cystic Fibrosis), Zoë's bowel burst. As I followed the ambulance in my car, my thoughts went back to the day Erika told me how she had lost a brother to this terrible illness. We had taken medical advice to understand the odds, and thought we were safe. According to the genetic counselor, Cystic Fibrosis was about as likely as winning the pools. Yes our beautiful little girl had the illness we so dreaded. What a journey her life would be. What a legacy she would leave, not in England but 9,000 km away in Queensland Australia. Little did we know that in the future her short life would affect sick children and their families throughout Queensland, Australia?

But what is Cystic Fibrosis? It is a genetic disorder that affects one in twenty-five people throughout the world. When two people with the defective gene have a child, they have a one in four chance of having a child with Cystic Fibrosis. Cystic Fibrosis is a life limiting illness that affects the pancreas. Initially, this means the child has to use pancreatic enzyme supplements to digest food. Then as the child gets older, the lungs produce mucus that is far more adhesive than that of healthy children. Consequently, the children have to have up to two hours of physiotherapy daily to attempt to drain the mucus off their lungs. With the help of heart and lung transplants the young sufferers of today are now surviving into their late twenties and early thirties, though this was not the case with our little Zoë.

As I watched them take her into the hospital, I was convinced that Zoë smiled at me, as if to say "I'm okay Dad!" (I heard her say those words many times over the next eleven years). It took three weeks for her to recover from the surgery on her bowel and Erika and I spent many hours beside her bed. Initially, we kept the news from Erika's parents because they were on holiday in Hong Kong, and we didn't want to worry them. We knew it would bring back too many painful, sad memories of their little son. But once we told them, they were great. Even GT, Erika's wonderful Grandmother, rallied round. It was a time of confusion, disbelief and immense inner pain, equal in every way to the way we all felt in those final hours when she lost her battle to stay alive.

Today I take strength from the belief that we all choose our own life's path. I believe each choice brings us a little more wisdom, and wisdom brings us a little closer to contentment. But back in 1983, things were different. I was close to despair. Why was this happening again? Was I once again to lose a precious loved one? Please, not my daughter! The only thing that saved me from the abyss was Erika's strength. When I was consumed with pain, she became the strong one. She was a survivor. I began to curse my weakness, but still I felt helpless, sad and lost. Then I'd start to wonder: Does Erica deserve someone stronger than me?

Although we were there for each other in those early years, without our friends and Erika's family it would have been much, much harder. We must never forget the value of friends. They can be a strong source of support when things fall apart, even though they have their own troubles. Some of our friends and family found it hard to be there for us. Without Erika's parents, GT and a few loyal friends, such as Ernie and Sandy (Zoë's Godparents) we may not have survived even the early days; nothing prepares you as parents for that initial shock. "Not our child"! "Surely not Zoë"! we said to one another.

Shortly after the operation to repair her bowel, I remember the surgeon saying, "It is up to her now, her desire to live." Desire to live, I thought. She looked so fragile with her little head shaven. The doctors had to fix the drip needle to a part of her body she could not disturb because in her restlessness she would constantly pull the needle out of her arm, sending off the alarm. The nurses said it was "accidental" but I wondered about that. I was convinced it was her developing a sense of humour, or maybe even wanting to make a decision about her own life, even at that tender age, for it seemed every time we stepped away she would say to herself, "I'll get those two!" and the alarm would go off. We would dash to her bedside praying she was ok, only to find she had set it off by turning in her little white cot. But it was the tiny grin on her face that convinced us she was having some fun with us.

Our Zoë survived and we took her home to the Horse and Groom Public House. She caused quite a stir, when the regulars saw her. What an adorable little mite! Even the brewery sent us a bunch of flowers. However, when news filtered through to the brewery that our little girl was very ill, the pleasantry was very quickly replaced with a notice to quit our job. Then that was followed by what is pleasantly called in the pub trade a "lock out." This is where you are kept upstairs by changing the locks and a new manager is running the downstairs. Thankfully, Erika's Gran (GT, as she was affectionately known) had moved out of her flat in Hackney London, and she allowed us to live there. Erika drove to Romford in an attempt to drag the Sales Director out of his office for an explanation, but he did not have the courage to confront a grieving mother's anger. For we must not forget that you do not just grieve at the time of your child's death; you also grieve when your child is diagnosed as having a terminal illness. The grief starts and never stops. Erika had stopped me from going in case I found myself charged with grievous bodily harm. I often think about what I may have done, had I confronted the Director of Sales that day. Anyway, it was to no avail. We found ourselves living in Hackney, East London.

In the early eighties, Hackney wasn't the most desirable area of East London; graffiti and riots were commonplace. The next eight months were hard for both of us. We had a very steep learning curve. Overnight we had become caregivers as well as parents, and sadly there were no courses to train you for this new role. It's hard enough learning to be a parent and coping with the normal challenges, but every runny nose, sneeze, rash or temperature change creates a different stress when your child is terminally ill. It was heightened for me the day I saw a London bus advertising the need to support Cystic Fibrosis. The words read, "Even the common cold can kill this child." Wow! Talk about panic! I was off to the hospital. My first question was, "Does that mean we should always wear a mask so she has a better chance of survival?" Sadly, the answer is that one cannot be wrapped in cotton wool, because if you don't pass on the germs, someone else will. Erika would comment later to me that it was the worst period of her life.

Although we had been told that Cystic Fibrosis did not mean a life of physiotherapy and drugs, we soon learned how far from the truth that statement was. Maybe they said this to save us from too much pain and panic in the early days. But from day one we did physiotherapy massage twice a day, starting with our index fingers and progressing to a fully cupped hand. Then as Zoë turned red coughing, it would be panic again! Would she choke? We eventually realized that coughing is the desired outcome of the massage. But when you see a three month old child red in the face with eyes bulging, it's scary, believe me!

It was during this period that we both became aware of the need for support, but search as we did we could not find anyone or any place that provided respite care. We called organizations set up by other parents, but such groups were few and they were scattered around the United Kingdom. We were disillusioned with the level or lack of support available. All we wanted was just some time out to pursue a little bit of a normal life. Although family and friends were supportive, they were uncomfortable with the responsibility of total care of a sick child because of fear of the unknown. "What would we do if she started to cough"? "How much medication do we give"? All in all, we were very much on our own. Erika's parents provided help whenever they could while we lived close to Romford where they lived, but when we moved to the north of England their support was largely unavailable.

We had not thought about the effects of grief and no one had ever mentioned it to us. We did not have time to read or research. Helen

Kubler-Ross had not yet written her book on death and dying. Much of the community really did not understand the ramifications of grief in the broader community. As I had encountered in my own family, it was unusual when someone discussed grief and its impact. Funny, now as I look back I think of how the collective joy at the end of the war may have shrouded the collective grief of parents left childless and children left parentless through death. It is so hard to quantify the effect unexpressed grief has on the whole community. It can surface many years later in siblings, parents and extended family as time lost from work due to depression, suicide without explanation, low self-esteem and risky behavior, broken marriages and homelessness.

Without much support we could only try our best, like other families had before us. It was frustrating that we couldn't find respite because it was so obvious that respite was desperately needed. Parents with terminally ill children need support. If they could only get it, they could provide a better quality of life for their sick children because a well-needed rest would lessen their extreme level of stress. I will never forget my reaction when another father told me of the high divorce rate in families that had a child with a life-limiting illness; 70%! What immediately went through my mind was "surely not us". In a bid to relax whenever we got the opportunity, Erica and I would walk along the canal bank and she would listen to my stories of life overseas in Queensland, Australia and those welcoming red roofs as you fly into Brisbane. We were both convinced that Australia would be the best place to raise Zoë, but for now her very survival was uppermost in our mind.

Both of us found work in early 1983, me as a night security officer and Erika as a legal secretary. We became the proverbial ships in the night, with me dashing off to work nights and Erika away during the day. We continued to search for a better schedule and were eventually successful at getting a position with a company called Scottish and Newcastle Breweries, as a Pub Management Couple. The offer came after we applied to go to Australia, but our first application was turned down because Zoë was seen as a disadvantage to the Australian community. They turned down both Erika and Zoë, but not me! A strange decision, we thought. What kind of man would leave his wife and his sick child?

So we took the position offered by Scottish and Newcastle. We hid Zoë's condition from them for fear that they would view our employment as being unworkable, as our previous employers had concluded. Nothing could have been farther from the truth. The new position meant a move to the north of England to Ormsby, in Yorkshire. The pub was called the "Fountain Hotel." This was one of the happiest and most financially rewarding periods of our marriage. Although the job was initially stressful because of the violent nature of some of the locals, Ormsby proved to be a very supportive community. From the moment we were accepted, the local people took great care of us. However, even though we were both happy and coping fairly well, we still had a burning desire to move to Australia. So once again we sent off our application to emigrate. We thought that the warmer, dryer Australian climate would be much better for Zoë.

Although Erika had to wear many hats (mother, caregiver, wife and pub manager), she did a wonderful job of it. That bar quickly became her domain. She was the first publican's wife in Ormsby to compete in the two pub races on Boxing Day. As a result of Erika's hard work, Zoë remained relatively healthy during this period and had only one close call. Having heard nothing from our second application, Zoë's close call was enough to convince us to try again. One day shortly before Christmas, I saw a letter with the Australian Embassy stamp on it. I remember thinking "Don't get your hopes up!" for it had been weeks since we had sent off the third application. But, much to my amazement and relief, the letter said we could go! I ran in and told Erika and we both cried with joy. Our dreams had come true. Erika and Zoë would finally see those red roofs of Brisbane.

We chose the right time to tell our Area manager, a wonderful guy named Rob Wheatly. He almost offered us the earth to stay, but our minds were made up. We were going to start a new life. We had a little money saved and some furniture (not as much furniture as we would have liked; during our stay in Hackney our storage shed had been broken into and much of our property was stolen. I don't think Erika ever got over the loss of her Elvis and Tom Jones records, only joking! But, really, all the stuff we lost didn't matter because we knew we were on our way in March to a new life!

AUSTRALIA—A NEW LIFE

"A marriage without conflicts is almost as conceivable as a nation without crises" Andre Maurice

Zoë had handled the journey well. We had been concerned about her already damaged lungs and had consulted doctors before we left. One thing we very quickly had learned was that not too many doctors in the United Kingdom knew too much about Cystic Fibrosis. So we took the chance and flew out to a new life and hopefully a better chance of survival for Zoë. We were met by Tony (an old army buddy of mine) and his wife, Liz. They provided us with accommodation in those early days. Our arrival this time was unlike my first arrival in Australia in 1972, when I arrived in a blue pin stripe suit only to be driven 30 km into the Queensland bush to the Giru hotel. This time I knew what to expect, or so I thought!

All the challenges experienced in the UK regarding respite and grief existed here, but the good news was that the Royal Brisbane Children's Hospital had a reputation for being the finest hospital for the treatment of Cystic Fibrosis. Looking back now I can see that a new way of viewing life's challenges was developing in me. It was coming about as a result of my passion to save my daughter, though it wasn't to surface for a few years. It came about because of the courage of my young daughter and her friends at the hospital, and how they dealt with their condition. Even as young children they displayed maturity beyond their years. Quite often in later years they became the adults in the family when their parents found coping difficult. Very often parents separated early in the relationship, if not physically then most certainly emotionally, like the father we knew who chose to drive his long distance rig day after day to avoid confronting his little girl. I got my first chance at employment at the Sheraton hotel, the first truly international hotel to open in Brisbane, though it was still very much under construction. They needed an Assistant Beverage Manager, so

I sent off my resume and, to my surprise, I got an interview. I knew that the only way I was going to get this position was to bluff. During the interview, when I was asked why I thought I could do the job, I said that as Mess Caterer of the Household Cavalry, I had catered each month for the Queen. A slight stretching of the truth; all I had been was Corporal's Mess Caterer. (I had ridden behind the Queen on a couple of occasions while in the Household Cavalry, but I was sure Her Majesty would not have written me a reference). Apparently, my truth stretching got me the position and Erika and I celebrated with a bottle of champagne.

In the first months, like any other person in a new country, we looked around for the right area to live, and for work that would provide food for the table. We settled on the south side of Brisbane at Rochedale, and then we applied for as many jobs as possible that would provide a better income than the Sheraton, but always had to take into consideration Zoë's health and our accessibility to the hospital. At this time, her condition was quite manageable. We almost got positions as hotel managers at Karumbin in the Northern Territory. Thankfully, we failed; it rained for half the year in the Northern Territory! Watching the person who interviewed us nonchalantly pick his nose was disgusting, especially for a Romford girl like Erika. Was he trying to warn us of things to come? Who knows?

For the first couple of years that we were in Australia, there were many check-ups with our family GP. We were advised on all the necessary enzyme treatments and physiotherapy. It was a constant round of medicine, physiotherapy, working and trying to squeeze in all the other things a family does. Even so, life was good. I had started to believe that we would be able to beat this challenge, and we needed to ensure that Zoë believed it. I took the stand that the only way she could fight this terrible illness was if she understood the severity of her condition. This decision would at times challenge other parents' beliefs, but we must all do what we feel is best.

As time passed Zoë's condition became more challenging. The physiotherapy was now full on, using our whole hands. She was taking about two teaspoons full of pancreatic enzymes with each meal. This was sprinkled on her food so she could digest it. The only problem with the powder was, if she did not digest it all, it would pass through her system into the nappy where the undigested enzyme would literally eat into her exposed skin, leaving her bottom red and raw. Thankfully, it wasn't long before the medical profession developed a capsule that improved things for the children and parents by making it easier to gauge the correct amount required. In Zoë's case, it was three capsules per meal. Already she was taking upwards of twenty pills a day between the antibiotics and the enzymes, plus she needed two hours of physiotherapy and various treatments of Ventolin each and every day.

In spite of everything we did, it wasn't long before her first visit to hospital. This proved to be a very difficult period for Zoë, who was now a little older and able to understand some of what was happening. We learned that she also suffered with Asthma. Again, I remember asking God why our little girl had to have so much to battle. In hindsight, I have come to realize that in comparison to other children she was truly one of the lucky ones, for she could laugh, run, swim and dance when she was well. There were so many other children who would have loved to do those things, so many other parents who would have loved the chance to enjoy those simple pleasures with their ailing children.

It was very hard to leave her at the hospital. Each night we would try our best to tiptoe out of the ward so as not to wake her. Erica and I would leave one at a time, but Zoë would open her eyes just as the last one got to the door and start to cry. She must have been so scared. I have no doubt she remembered being in hospital when she had a nasty encounter with a needle as the nurses tried to find a vein for her canula. All I could hear were screams coming from the anteroom. I decided to go in and found her in near panic and those around her not much better. I asked them to leave, sat down next to her and in no uncertain terms told her that she needed the needle to survive. Her reply was typical of our daughter, with tears in her eyes, she said, "Ok Dad, but can I shout ouch and hold your hand"? I obviously said yes and from then on that is what she did. Mind you, the "Ouch" was almost deafening and very often she stopped the flow of blood to my hand. All in all, though, she was a very courageous little girl.

It was about two days after one of her admissions that I first saw the love that these children have for each other, and the courage that was slowly affecting how I viewed life's challenges. Scott was about 14 and, like Zoë, had Cystic Fibrosis. Scott had watched our nightly challenge getting Zoë to let us go home. One evening he approached us both and politely asked if he could hold her hand and take care of her as we left. We agreed and were amazed when she calmly agreed for us to leave. For the next week Scott was never away from her side until one morning when he just wasn't there. As we sat outside contemplating things, we saw his mum in tears. When we asked why she was weeping, the reply shocked us. Scott's lung had burst and he was not expected to live. That was our very first exposure to the reality of a Cystic Fibrosis death.

This wonderful young man had taken time out in those last days of his life to care for our little girl. We both cried that night for both Scott and our own daughter. Grief is always a close companion when you have a sick child. We realized that one day the weeping parents were going to be us. We wondered what impression Scott's death had made on Zoë, but we never found out because she never brought it up. She lost more of her friends as she grew up but she never asked what was going to happen to her. She just took life one day at a time. Zoë was only about five at the time and she seemed to already know what was to happen. That's a lesson we all should learn. Live for the moment!

Our luck changed for the worse again, with me having to give up my job through a back injury. It must have been hard at this point for Erika to feel secure, for by now my inner voice was sending out some very negative messages. Having applied for job after job to no avail, I started to panic and in the end, out of desperation, I took a job with the AMP Society, Australia's largest insurance institution. Sales! As if my self esteem needed this. Already it was as shaky as a kookaburra's nest in a force nine gale, but we needed the money so what the heck, I knew I had to try it. Who knew what the outcome would be? With only one little old car, Erika was beginning to feel more isolated, so I asked if she would do some door knocking for me. I knew she was a far better sales person than I was. I thought this would help her, by letting her mix and take time out from being a carer. For a while this did help, or at least I thought it did. But Erika and I seemed to be losing our way as a couple. Sadly, our sexual life was now non-existent, and I had become too frightened to approach Erika for sex, for fear of rejection. Sleeping next to my beautiful wife night after night became very difficult and any time we discussed it we fought, so it gradually became taboo to discuss. Erika seemed unable to explain her feelings towards me. Later on we had several discussions on this topic and she was able to explain that all her energies and thinking had to be focused on and with Zoë. Her own life had to take a back seat. We continued on as parents, providing Zoë with so much love it was hard to imagine the struggle we had at loving each other. Zoë absolutely radiated love from every angle. We would never allow our own shortcomings to affect her in those early days, or so we thought.

About 12 months after Scott passed away, another of Zoë's friends, Enika, would also lose her battle for life. She, like Scott, was just 15 years old, and although much frailer than some of the children she was very bright and in many ways a role model to the younger Cystic Fibrosis children. She had spoken to her parents about her pending death, even planning the funeral down to what she wanted to wear. My lasting memory of Enika is of her father, Alan, carrying her daily to the Expo where she had a legion of friends and admirers. The year was 1988. I wonder to this day what Zoë felt, as a child who had the same disease, watching her mates die.

I do know these deaths challenged all our hope for our daughter's survival. For Alan, like others before him and those to come after, his battle was not yet over. Shortly after that, his wife was diagnosed with cancer and died not too long after. I have often wondered whether the huge void that's left when a precious child you have constantly cared for and loved, and then watched die, creates a stress that triggers a cancer in some of us. There are still so many unknowns in the daily battle that I associate with caring for a sick child.

On one occasion we drove to Melbourne to visit Erika's aunty for her daughters' wedding. As we prepared to leave Melbourne and head for home, we visited a bank to get some funds out for the drive back. And guess what? Insufficient funds! Here we were, sick child and no funds to return home. I never had much spare money since we left the pub trade, but I had bought Erika a nice gold bracelet. Sadly, it was the first thing to go. We barely got one third of its value, but at least we were able to get home. There were many times when we waited for our commission to come through and were disappointed because someone had cancelled their policy and AMP would very quickly deduct it from the commission. Commission only is not the best way to earn a living when you are trying to build a new life thousands of miles from home.

It wasn't long before it was our turn to sit beside our daughter for the second time as she battled for her life. This time it came right out of the blue. Suddenly, when all was going well, she developed a blocked bowel and was rushed to the hospital. Apparently, the spot where her bowel was joined during her first operation developed a blockage. The major concern was the condition of her lungs and the problems associated with giving her aesthetic. We had experienced something similar when she trapped her finger in a sliding door. The hospital had been hesitant to operate because of her condition. So, as on many other occasions, all we could do was pray. The doctors decided to starve her in the hope that this would free the blockage, so it meant being patient and waiting in the hope it would work. Zoë, although ill, was only concerned with one thing: Food! But food was a life-threatening thing to her at that point. She looked at the doctor and the nurse, then Erika and me, and said: "Can I have some strawberries and cream sweets"? The doctor was won over and agreed, but only if she understood she could only have one per day. The look on Zoë's face said it all. Heaven! A sweet to eat! She thanked us all and gradually devoured her overdue daily sweet. When we returned to the ward the next morning the place was buzzing. There was concern over some red liquid in Zoë's drip. For a few moments the nursing staff was concerned that there was a burst bowel, but they had underestimated our daughter's appetite during the night. She had gone on a sweet raid and had consumed all the sweets. The red liquid wasn't blood, but the strawberry component of the sweet. She just sat there with a very contented look on her face. And believe it or not, the sweets freed her blockage and we lived to fight another day. Zoë was about eight years old then.

During this period Zoë started going to Slacks Creek State Primary School. Little did we realize this would be the only school she would attend? It was the second love of her life and, thankfully, we never had to battle to get her to go. She wasn't an exceptional student but she always tried her hardest. Her condition initially caused some problems with her grades due to her extended visits to the hospital. Usually, about three times a year the hospital would take her in for what was known as a "Top Up". This was an opportunity to build up her weight so she could keep up the fight and save herself from frequent lung infections.

I wondered about the continual treatment with steroid-based medications that caused her to put on weight due to water retention, a side effect of this type of treatment. But we wanted her to have the best chance of survival, so we needed to place our faith in someone, and the medical profession was all we had. Some families chose another path, to stay out of hospital as much as possible to avoid cross infections and to protect their children from what they saw as the negative side of this terrible illness. They had some success I must admit, but alas, the illness always had the final say. Zoë continued to enjoy school. As far as we knew, the other kids accepted the dozens of tablets she took and her constant coughing. She never complained about the way they treated her.

I had decided that, since both Erica and I worked, one of us would always be there when Zoë got out of school. She would not become a latch key child as the quality of her life was too important. This meant ships in the night again because I got a second job, working nights as a cleaner. The training I received in the early part of my military career on how to polish a floor would finally pay off. It was during this period I became interested in personal development, reading as many books as possible. But the more I read, the more I became confused. Although I almost became a book addict, it made no difference in my performance. I drew my strength from my daughter's love.

I looked forward to her smile when I picked her up from school. She would say "Hi Day"! Day was her way of shortening Daddy. My visits to her school were always a positive experience. I'll never forget the day of the Sports Carnival. Zoë had been selected to race in the 100-metre dash. She had come through the heats and made it to the finals. She lined up against some young, naturally gifted kids and came in last. She ran over to me almost in tears and said, "I got beat, Day"! I replied, "No my mate, you are the winner. Don't forget that you only have 46% lung function and the others have a normal lung function. You are a winner". Her whole life was about beating death. She probably knew that she was never going to win races. The lesson I learned on that day was a simple one: ***Be prepared to go the distance, for it's your contribution to life that matters. Be aware that others are watching. Your courage may help them.***

Some months later at her school camp, while sitting around the campfire one night listening to the children chat, I learned first-hand how her mates treated her. It was terrific! But the best was yet to come. On the last day, the kids were to climb a high mountain. In terms of climbing it was not the greatest challenge (although a couple of teachers couldn't go the distance) and most of the kids climbed it fairly easily. For Zoë it was a difficult endeavor but, true to her courageous nature, she got there. Once again she was last, but she got there. We had a saying, Zoë and I, that dynamite came in little packages, and those who were negative were "dumbamite." She was the opposite of dumbamite. She was always willing to go the distance. As we both reached the summit, all her friends stood cheering their little mate. I will never forget the pride in her eyes. My pride felt like the heat of the sun. A warm glow completely engulfed me. She was my hero!!! She was willing to go the distance and pay the price. Sometimes the price was high, but when she reached her personal summit the feeling of accomplishment was beyond measure.

By now another little girl had been born with cystic fibrosis and had become Zoë's mate. Her name was Lizzy. She had an even more challenging start in life for she had lost part of one of her lungs. This time it was Zoë's turn to look out for someone. It wasn't long before they were inseparable. Zoë was about four years older than Lizzy, but the age gap made no difference to them. It was as if they were inseparable sisters. We would arrive at the ward and see them arm-in-arm dashing off all around the hospital. During breathing tests and blood tests Zoë would hold Lizzy's hand, just like I had held hers in the early days.

Although Erica and I were each focused on keeping Zoë well, we seemed unable to resolve our own personal issues. As hard as it was for me to go without intimacy, I am sure that Erika was going through the same thing. Our early courtship seemed like a romantic movie we'd once seen. We came to a point where we decided to make one night a month our "date-night" so we could enjoy dinner out and gain back some intimate time. Instead, we found that the dinner table became the place to air all the issues that never surfaced whilst Zoë was present. It was obvious that if our marriage was to survive, we needed more than one night per month free from the intense pressure of caring for a child with a life-limiting illness. We needed time to walk along a beach or sit beside a river and just *relax* to maintain some feeling of romance. More than a three hour dinner date once a month. We needed to feel easy in each others' company again. Then maybe we could sit and discuss our concerns and issues, especially the emotional pain that was driving us further and further apart.

Convinced that this was what I needed to do, I decided to become a member of the Cystic Fibrosis Association Committee. Like many similar well-established organizations that start out with every intention to help both children and families, it seemed to me it had lost its direction. I believe this happens frequently when the original visionary has left and other people take over the organization. Their mission often shifts to what they believe families need, instead of what the families themselves need and want. Little did I know that later in my journey, I would see the very same thing happen to me! I remember an occasion when the father of a little girl who had passed away asked the committee if he could help other families in any way. A member of the committee replied, "I do not want to speak to him. He represents the negative aspects of the illness". I was shocked. Were we all not eventually going to be the negative side of this illness? At the time I was not sure how he could help, but I now feel it was a cry for help. He needed to feel that his daughter had died for something! To this day I do not know what happened to that father. I know that as an organization we let him down. I only hope that he survived the trauma of losing his child.

Finally the committee decided to build or purchase a building for a Respite Centre. A very prominent Brisbane business identity was recruited to chair the Capital Fundraising Committee and after much publicity, a Campaign Manager was recruited. However, I didn't see the level of commitment and passion required to ensure that the campaign would be a success. When the first attempt to purchase a building failed, the project stalled. Since Zoë had been involved in the media campaign, I decided to confront the chairman and see what he planned to do next. On entering his office, I noticed that he proudly displayed behind his desk a photo of four young Cystic Fibrosis children. My daughter was one of them. Sadly, two of the other children had already passed away. My opening comment was, "Do you know how many of those children are still alive"? His reply was, "No". I said, "If they were your shareholders, you would have been asked to leave months ago". To his credit, he admitted to being embarrassed and sometime later he stepped down from Fundraising for the Cystic Fibrosis Association. He was not the right person for the position of Capital Campaign Chairman. The success of any campaign hinges on the chairman having both influence and affluence, and the courage to use both. Later in my journey I was to encounter such a man.

Shortly after the Fundraiser resigned, we lost another wonderful young man to Cystic Fibrosis. David was tall, intelligent and handsome, the favourite of many of the younger kids. He had worked diligently for the cause, but when he reached 21 years of age he decided enough was enough. He wanted to lead a normal life. What would make a young man decide this? Well let us look at his life up to that date: 250,000 pancreatic tablets to digest his food, 1000 antibiotic tablets to stop infections of the lungs, daily doses of inhalers (Intal, Becatide, and Ventolin etc.) and 21,000 hours of physiotherapy. He had watched 10 young friends die. Life for him was a nightmare, so he stopped taking everything that kept him alive and said, "enough is enough I want to live like normal people live". He died 12 months later. What a price to pay for normalcy. Whenever I feel under the weather and have to take medication, I look back on David's short but courageous time on earth and thank the Lord for my normal life.

Back then the Cystic Fibrosis Association used to send children to the Lions Club's Camp Duckadong for a week. It was an opportunity for some R and R for parents and a time for kids to be with their peers who had similar needs. Zoë told me later that while there was plenty of laughter, it was also a time to talk about their own mortality and remember their friends that had gone on before them. If there is a place after life where we all meet, I know for sure that these mates will have prepared it for each other. They will be waiting to greet them, each and every one sitting at the right hand of Jesus.

Throughout this time, Erika continued to do work with me. Her ability to cold call on potential clients convinced me that she should be selling insurance in her own right. She soon became an AMP agent and I resigned my agency and put any business I could through Erika's agency, enabling her to achieve "blue ribbon" status in sales. After working all night, I often went with her on appointments to help out, only to fall asleep in the car. It was difficult living on commissions, but most of our fellow workers were great and supported us. Zoë was often seen on our agency manager's knee telling him a story. But insurance was ultimately not for me. All it led to was heartache and a loss of assets for me, though Erika continued to do quite well. The secret to sales is Persistence! Persistence! Persistence! Although I didn't succeed at selling insurance, I thank AMP for opening the window of my mind, making me receptive to ideas and attitudes that have helped me along my pathway. I will never forget my friend and then insurance agency manager Tony Miller asking, "What would you do if your daughter's life was being challenged"? Although those words did not motivate me to sell more insurance, as he thought they would, they made me realize that my daughter's courage could be a source of motivation and passion that would ensure I would go the distance when I found a direction.

Some months later we had a good stroke of luck. I had applied for a position as Manager of a hotel in Gladstone, Queensland. To my surprise, I was called up for an interview and offered the position on the spot! I asked the owner if I could use the phone to tell Erika. This could be a chance to rebuild. What happened next was equally amazing. It turned out that Erika had just been offered a position as State Coordinator of an AMP subsidiary company called Parent Craft. We discussed which of the two positions was better and, after making a trip to Gladstone, decided Erica's opportunity was definitely better. Although I was disappointed, I was determined to support her in her new position. The main consideration as before was Zoë being picked up from school. So, as well as selling some insurance, I picked up my trusty broom and dustpan and rode off every night to a cleaning job, leaving me free to pick Zoë up from school.

We then got a letter from Erika's parents saying they were coming over to Australia to live. I got on fairly well with Erika's parents. There were a couple of occasions when we did not see eye to eye, but all in all I was pleased to hear they had made a decision to come over to Australia to live. During the same time period, the world was rocked by a stock market crash on October the 8th, 1987. AMP was struggling as an agency, both with finding clients and retaining them. Financial fear was everywhere. As AMP agents, we were prevented from offering advice to our clients other than sit tight and to hang on to their investments. But many people panicked and withdrew funds, eventually losing up to a third of the value of their investments. Although history clearly demonstrates that when the market falls it always comes back higher, it is hard to remain confident and positive when it is all you have in the world.

Besides lack of income, we had a more worrying crisis. Zoë was once again fighting for her life. In sales, if you don't sell you don't earn. We spent more time beside Zoë's hospital bed than talking to prospective clients. For me it was so much harder this time, for it was obvious that both Erika and I were trying to cope as individuals rather than as a couple. One day when I arrived home, Erika told me there was no food in the fridge. As a man and father, nothing has ever affected me more than not being able to provide for my family. The only answer left was to visit a lifeline charity food store. The feeling of failure burned in my stomach as I drove to Brisbane in the hope that I would qualify for some assistance. The procedure to obtain help is humbling, for you have to explain how and why you have arrived at this position. I must have fit the requirement because I left with food and a petrol voucher to get me home to Beenleigh. I gave Erika a bag of food that I'd almost had to beg for. How do you look a wife in the eyes when you know she has already lost her respect for you? If I thought that was hard, it was to get even harder. We lost our home and had to go searching for a home to rent. With the words *"It isn't how many times you get knocked down that matters, but how many times you get up"* ringing in my ears, I prayed for help. How long could I go on before becoming punch drunk? Life's body blows are harder than any physical beating I have ever taken, and also a lot harder for the mind, spirit and soul to get over. But they do. *"Some times the most beautiful sky can only be seen from the deepest hole."* However little did I realize that this was the start of a new direction in my journey and that in fact there is a way to repair the damage done to all those things that make up a human being?

Zoë was battling for her life during all this, never giving up, asking why or feeling sorry for herself. As I look back now the other lesson Zoë and all her friends have taught me is that we as human beings have the ability to choose. We wake each morning with the ability to say every day is a good day and make the most of it. For terminally ill children, every day could be a crisis, every day could be their last, but they choose to get on and live to the maximum. One day as I was leaving the hospital, I felt the need to visit a small chapel opposite the Brisbane City Hall. What led me into that church, I now believe, was God answering my prayer for help. In complete and utter despair, having reached a state of mental and emotional breakdown, I turned to God.

As I knelt with my head bowed in prayer, I said to the Lord. "I am at the end! As you know this is the first time in many years I have knelt before you and asked for your help. My family needs you and I believe you and you alone can help. My daughter is once again fighting for her life and my wife no longer respects and loves me. Please help me save my daughter and my marriage". What happened next was a miracle. With my eyes closed I saw the number 23. It was like a neon light as it burned brightly before me. What did this mean? With goose bumps all over my body and my eyes rapidly filling with tears, I sat back on the seat and just stared at the spot where I had seen those numbers. Finally I decided to look through the Bible. It wasn't long before my eyes fell upon the 23rd Psalm. As I started to read, I began to see a blueprint for our lives. Here was David's story. If ever someone who had fallen from grace had been able to lead a successful life, he had. Could I go on and do something similar?

I walked away from the chapel. Emotional and still in tears, I decided to walk through the botanical garden to try and get an understanding of what had happened. On reaching the gardens I sat on a bench and stared between my feet. On the floor directly in front of me was a cloth badge and on it was written the words, "Jesus is the Way". I got goose bumps! I drove home like a mad man. Finding it hard to contain myself, I was gibbering like a wreck to Erika. Having had so much happen that was negative, it was hard for Erika to have any faith in my newfound optimism but I felt as though my life had changed in just an hour. Over the following weeks I decided to read about this psalm and the young man Jesus. Here is a man who was born in an obscure village. The child of a peasant woman! He grew up and became a carpenter until he was thirty and then for three years he was an itinerant teacher. He never wrote a book, he never held office and he was never able to own his own home. He never went to college, and he never travelled, except in his infancy, more than 200 miles from the place of his birth. He never did one of the things that usually accompany greatness. He had no credentials but himself. While he was still a young man the tide of popular opinion turned against him. His friends ran away. One of them denied him. He was turned over to his enemies. He went through the mockery of a trial. He was nailed to a cross between two thieves. His executioners gambled for the only property he had on earth, his seamless robe. When he was dead, he was taken down from the cross and laid in a borrowed grave through the courtesy of a friend. Twenty wide centuries have come and gone and today he is the centerpiece of the human race and the leader of all human progress. I am well within the mark when I say that all the armies that ever marched, all the navies that were ever built, all the parliaments that ever sat and all the Kings that ever reigned have not affected the life of man upon this earth as powerfully as he has. **THIS ONE SOLITARY PERSONALITY.**

From the moment I chose a new direction in life, my journey would never be the same. It would still remain challenging and would not be free from trauma, but I have come to understand that life challenges are the moments that we grow in both emotional and spiritual stature.

When the man is willing and eager, the gods will join in. Aeschylus

I was willing and eager to change my family's fortune now that I had allowed myself to be joined with God. In my family life, things did not get all that much better, but Zoë did survive to fight another battle. Erica and I always knew that life for Zoë would be a constant battle. We also understood the hard reality; the battle could never be won. The remarkable thing about Zoë was that each time she came out of hospital, no matter how close to death she had been, she seemed stronger and more determined to get on with life. As human beings, maybe we should assume that life-affirming attitude to help us get life into perspective when we feel down.

By this time we had found a place to rent and were trying to get on and build a life. Erika's parents had arrived and things were starting to look better. I took up a position as Club Manager for the Brisbane Caledonian Club. Even Erika now felt we had a chance. I still wasn't sure what I was meant to do with my newfound Christianity until one day in 1987 when sitting watching the television I happened to catch a thirty second advert for a Terry Fox Cancer Run. As I watched this 18-year-old boy run across the screen, I felt totally inspired. Terry was attempting to run all the way across Canada in order to raise one dollar from every Canadian to help those who were battling cancer. Sadly, Terry never finished the run. He was taken from the road after completing 3,339 miles. The cancer that had taken his leg had reached deep into his lungs. Sadly, even though he would have a brief period of remission and be awarded Canada's highest award for bravery and service, Terry never finished the race. But since his attempt, thousands of people worldwide have completed the race and raised far more funds for cancer than Terry would have ever thought possible.

Some years later when giving a talk about grief to some nine year old children, a young boy put me on the spot. As I shared Terry's story, he asked me if I would finish the run for Terry. I wasn't sure how to answer that one.

There is a purpose for our life far grander and more significant than perhaps we might ever consider.
David McNally

Then it came to me like a bolt from heaven. If Terry could do something like that on one leg, then as sure as hell I could do something on two. If he could run, I could walk. If he could do it for cancer sufferers, I could do it for Cystic Fibrosis sufferers and their families. Maybe we could attract enough support to build a respite centre. I was disappointed with the work of the high-profile businessman who had been recruited by the Cystic Fibrosis Association to build a respite centre, but maybe this was the way to do it; walk for the families until someone took notice!

One day during the filming of a video about Cystic Fibrosis at Channel 10, the Brisbane Television Station where Zoë had been chosen as one of the stories, I suddenly turned to Anna McMahon the presenter and said, "We need some publicity here. I will walk from Port Douglas to Southport, Queensland to raise awareness of Cystic Fibrosis". This was a total of 2000 km. The look on Anna's face said it all. Here I was 17 stone and unbelievably unfit, committing myself to walk 2000km.

TERRY'S EXAMPLE

"How to live a successful Life"

The more I thought and read about Terry the more I became convinced he had captured the spirit of Jesus. As I looked closer I saw a formula, a way of leading a successful life. Both Jesus and Terry had a dream, a dream that involved service to the community. It was obvious that they were passionate about it, because they were prepared to go the distance in a bid to see their dreams become reality. All they needed was a plan. The outcome of this combination of passion and plan was the development of their purpose in life.

Dream + Service X Passion X Commitment = Your Life's Purpose

As I looked into these principles, I started to understand that a successful life needn't be measured purely by assets, money and lifestyle.

During the first four years of Zoë's life, both in Australia and in the UK, Erika and I had been amazed at the lack of information, support and counseling available for families in a similar situation to our own. There was no place that we could take our daughter and no advice on how to be not only a parent, but a nurse, dietician and carer. Friends and family were not so quick at coming forward to help and we were not keen to hand over our sick newborn to just anyone. We had often thought that it would be of great value if there was a place where a family like our own could leave a child and take some time out to relax and recharge batteries. It was plain to us that for a child like Zoë to survive, the family had to be provided with support. So I collected my thoughts.

My Dream: It was simple. Build a respite centre here in Queensland. A place where families could find shelter when the battle became overwhelming. A place where we could leave our daughter knowing she was safely in the hands of people who understood her needs, but also people who understood ours. A place Zoë could go to. Not just when she was physically sick, but also when our family was emotionally overwrought.

The Plan: Drawing on the example of Terry Fox, I decided to walk for Cystic Fibrosis until, as in Terry's case, someone took notice. The route would be 2000 km, from Port Douglas to Southport, Queensland. In order to do it, I needed to get fit and put together a back-up team.

Faith: As someone who had only recently started to look to Christianity for guidance, I believed that what had happened in that small chapel in Brisbane was God getting my attention. In some way, he had a plan for me. He knew that I would not be able to complete my task without strong faith, so that's where the 23rd Psalm came in. It was the key to strong faith, the blueprint that provided me with the day-to-day strength to carry out whatever plan he had for me. So it is correct to say at that point my faith was at its strongest.

Passion: It is the fire in the belly that makes ordinary people into great leaders. Whether in the community, in business, or in relationships, passion is what makes you willing to go the distance. It also gives you the courage to pursue your dream when others say you are crazy. It gives you the strength to battle against all the odds. I was passionate about my daughter's survival and helping her and other children and families was a worthy cause.

A Willingness To Go The Distance: There was no doubt in my mind that where my daughter was concerned, I was willing to lay down my life, if need be. This kind of commitment is the crucial element to the success of any undertaking. History clearly shows us examples of people with commitment; people like Martin Luther King Jnr, Nelson Mandela, Mahatma Gandhi and of course, Terry Fox. It was now time to put my newfound plan and faith into practice.

WALKING FOR CHARITY BEGINS

Port Douglas to Southport, Queensland, Australia 2000kms October 1990

Walking can have a remarkable effect not only on the body but also on the mind and spirit.

When the mind, body and spirit are out of balance we have two doctors to call on—the left leg and the right leg. Hippocrates

It had been quite easy to say I would do all this walking, but the next day the full impact of my decision hit me. It was scary how out of shape I was. I weighed 17 stone and had not exercised since my army days. Even then, I did not set the athletic world alight. I knew I would need help. My friend Peter Why, who had left the Army with me back in the mid sixties, used to say on the rugby pitch that I confused people more than inspired them with my athletic ability. But who knew what could be achieved with my new found formula for success; planning and faith.

Every endurance walk offered up a different set of challenges, many of them relating to my own physical and mental state and others relating to other people's agendas and expectations. In order to accomplish the tasks at hand, I had to transfer my vision to others and get people pulling together in the same direction. I knew I needed a back-up crew and maybe even someone to walk with me. But who would be able to spare the time? Who would be mentally and physically capable of undertaking such a challenge? Erika was quick to point out that the best person for the job was Pete Why, my old army and rugby mate. Over the years we had remained friends and had also come to

Australia at around the same time. He was a fit and much focused sort of guy, but I wondered if he believed I could go the distance. Pete was quick to agree and we both started to train. There was no doubt that he had a lot of stamina and courage. To this day, I am convinced that his example of pure persistence enabled me to do the things I have done.

I decided to attempt 12 kilometers a day. It was not too hard to choose a route. Around Beenleigh there were plenty of woodland walks that had their fair share of steep hills. So with my new trainers on my feet and sunscreen on my face, I started my training program. I walked 12 kilometers a day and ate a low fat diet. It wasn't long before the solitude had a wonderful calming effect on my emotional state. Out there away from the hustle and bustle of everyday life I was able to talk aloud to God and ask him for the strength needed to complete my chosen task. What happened over the following weeks was remarkable. As the pounds fell off me, my attitude became more positive. My self-esteem improved as my trousers were becoming looser and looser. I dared to hope that my transformation into an achiever would impress Erica favorably, even though things had gone pretty far in the wrong direction by then. I am not sure what Zoë thought about all of this activity. She had once referred to me as a "white beached whale" at the beach but I now looked more like a slightly tubby Dolphin.

Pete and I knew it was important to have a good back-up team. During breaks and at the end of the day one needed to be able to relax and not have to chase down food or clean equipment. But finding three people who shared the same vision and could spare three weeks was proving difficult. I was lucky enough to enlist the help of two great guys: Marty, a friend of the family who thought the world of Zoë; and Mike, an old friend from Melbourne who had the ability to manage people and projects. (He had been my Managing Director at Croft House in England). Mike had been in a parachute regiment as a young man and he was a very strong, disciplined character. Unfortunately, the mixture of Pete and Mike was so volatile that on more than one occasion the walk was almost cancelled when they could not agree on something.

Pete and I decided to train together. On our very first session, we chose to walk to Tambourine Village, about a 25 kilometer round trip, along some very impressive countryside scattered with gum trees and woodlands that were full of wildlife. Everything went well for about 12 kilometers until Pete suddenly pulled up in front of me limping. He had burst a big blister on his foot and the skin had peeled back. He attempted to go on but the pain was too much and he accepted a ride back. It was our first and last training session together. After that, we just kept each other posted on our individual schedules.

During training, Zoë remained relatively well, although another one of her friends died. It was David this time. It always amazed me as to how she took each death in stride and kept on with her own battle for survival. By now, Zoë had lost three mates. Her medications and treatments had increased to 12 enzyme capsules per meal, antibiotics, nebulizer treatments, two hours of physiotherapy daily, plus school each weekday. On some days she would do a short walk with me, but with less than 50% lung capacity she would very quickly get puffed. I would often see her look up at me in the hope that I would say, "Let's take it easy". But no matter what, she stayed with me. Zoë always gave 150%. For children with Cystic Fibrosis, it takes a lot more effort to do the things we take for granted.

Looking for sponsors when you have not done anything like this before is like looking for a needle in a haystack. There just are not many people out there who will take a gamble on the proposed outcome. And so it was with the walk, until a fellow Lion spoke about someone he knew in another Lion's Club who owned a service station. I had previously joined Lions at the invitation of a very good friend, Colin Walker, but sadly (after the loss of our home and the time needed with Zoë) I had let my membership lapse. Colin talked with this fellow Lion and the man immediately agreed to help with a fuel sponsorship. He very kindly contacted fellow Ampol dealers to gain additional support and these Ampol dealers became our sponsors. The remainder of our equipment was provided by each individual. We were so lucky that Pete was self-employed, as he agreed to let us use his four-wheel drive. Erica also helped by identifying and recruiting a campervan owner who gave us a discount on a vehicle we could use for our accommodations. I had not truly understood the Lions organization I had previously joined. The Lions Club is a committed group of people worldwide who work hard to make a difference to people in need. It was founded in 1917 by an insurance agent named Melvin Jones. From a very humble beginning, it had grown into a truly international organization with over 1,000,000 members in 181 countries worldwide. It is the only service organization that has a seat at the United Nations, with commitments to provide help for the blind and the deaf. In addition, its project areas are Citizen Services, Education, Environment, Public Services, Recreation, Health, Social Services and International Services. It would also turn out to play a major role in my dream.

The day of reckoning arrived and we all met at our house at Windaroo. We picked Mike up at the airport and discovered that he could not complete the whole walk and would miss the final leg from Brisbane to the Gold Coast. Luckily, since we would be sleeping in our own beds over the last three days, we didn't need the campervan for that leg of the trip and could finish without him. As soon as we started packing the vehicles, sparks began to fly between Pete and Mike, so when it came time to choose our traveling companions, Pete made it quite clear that he was traveling with me and not with Mike. I remember dreading what the next three weeks might have in store for us.

The drive up was pretty stressful. Pete wanted to drive directly there, while Mike felt that we should have a rest halfway up. After a heated discussion between Mike and Pete, I stayed out of it and just tried to enjoy the scenery. Although Mike's organizational skills were important to the walk, his people skills were somewhat rough around the edges and it occurred to me that all four of us living under one caravan roof, was going to be difficult. Mile after mile we pushed along a road that challenged us daily in many different ways. The road between Brisbane and Cairns was not very scenic, but between Port Douglas and Cairns is one of the most scenic routes in Australia. With crystal clear ocean on one side and beautiful landscaping on the other side, it was a great experience. Being close to the ocean made this part of the walk quite scenic, but the grueling task of walking 2000 kilometers stretched ahead of us.

Our first and only night in Port Douglas was spent in a local caravan park close to the beach. I was glad to take time out and meander along the beach, thinking about being 2000 kilometers away from Zoë and Erika and wondering how they were getting on. This was our first time apart and Erika was alone in caring for Zoë, but I was convinced I was doing what I had to do: Undertake a challenge that would take me out of my comfort zone to raise money and awareness for a Children's Hospice in Queensland, which was sorely needed. For forty-three years I had lived in the shadow of self pity. It was time to find the real Nigel Reed. The sand felt good between my toes and the smell of the sea filled my nostrils. Twenty-one days from now I would have my daughter in my arms again.

On day one, we awoke just before sunrise. It was obvious that the tension was still there but all of us focused on the task at hand. There was very little conversation, just the odd glance thrown each other's way. We were supposed to start from the Sheraton Hotel reception area but were unable to find the hotel, never mind a reception area. Pete and I agreed to be dropped off at 5km intervals. At each finish point, we were to be met by a vehicle to have our condition checked and take on food and water. Mike doubted the sense of doing it this way and suggested we leapfrog, as he had done on a charity walk with the Parachute regiment. We listened to him but decided against his advice.

We finally got underway at 6 a.m. It was full light and we thought it would be safe to be on the road. Marty decided to be my back-up, dropping me off then going on ahead to keep me informed on how Pete was going. My first stretch of road took me right in front of the Sheraton Hotel where we were supposed to have started from. Pete was dropped off at the junction with the main road and he headed off along the first stretch of beachfront road. Whether it was the beauty of the surroundings or the terrific weather I don't know, but something influenced him to run. Running was not included in our plan. Wasn't this a Charity Walk? I was doing about 7km an hour. I was amazed when Marty informed me at my first break that Pete was running. It was here that I made my first mistake. I decided to try and keep up by walking faster. It was impossible. I had hoped that we would gradually work ourselves into the level of fitness required to complete our task. The plan was to do two twenty-kilometer sessions by midday, with a thirty minute break in the middle. Instead, I was walking at about 8.5 kilometers per hour. For Pete, this would barely be jogging. Thanks to Marty's help by standing in for me for the next 2 kilometers, I could rest. Without that rest, I would have had to quit and I'd not have made it to the first scheduled break.

This first break almost ruined the whole walk. The sea looked so inviting that we stripped down to our jocks and plunged into the surf. It was refreshing and invigorating to feel the surf break over our heads and, once refreshed, we agreed to take it easy from then on. What we had forgotten was to wipe all the sand off our feet. Over the next 20 kilometers, we gradually sandpapered the soles of our feet and by the time the first day ended I had two small blisters. Pete was in far worse shape because he continued to run after the break in spite of our agreement to take it easy.

Just as I reached the outskirts of Cairns, a young boy with Cystic Fibrosis named Cameron greeted me. Cameron was a friend of Zoë's whom she had met during her hospital visits. Although Cameron lived in Cairns, sooner or later all the Cystic Fibrosis children made their way to The Royal Brisbane Children's Hospital, as that was where the best treatment was. Cameron was a bit older than Zoë but he hadn't forgotten her. This bought on a burst of renewed energy and I raised my head and battled on as I knew Cameron would have to. Within about 400 meters of the shopping centre, Pete appeared on the horizon and he looked agitated and yelled that people were waiting for us at the mall and to hurry. At that point I was angry with him for running and getting the schedules out of kilter.

Once in the mall, I saw a group of families who had come to welcome us. It had the desired effect of lifting my spirits. I only hoped that I had enough puff left to talk with everyone and say thank you. It was my first attempt at public speaking. I was very nervous; the Mayor and press had turned out to greet us. Somehow I managed to draw a long breath and say the right words.

After the mall we found a Camping Ground on the sea front, showered and surveyed the damage to our bodies; mostly our feet to see if the flesh was still intact. I was fortunate to have only two blisters of medium size, but Pete had four. They did not look too good. The sand had done its job on us. I decided to apply methylated spirits to the affected area. This is an old army trick whereby you thread a needle, dip it in the methylated spirits and then carefully push the needle through the blister to drain it. Then you cut the cotton off the needle and leave the cotton on the blistered area. It will eventually dry the blister and harden the skin for the next day.

The local Cystic Fibrosis Association had organized a barbecue for the evening at a local resident's house. While at the barbecue I met a 40 year old woman who had Cystic Fibrosis. This was amazing because most people with Cystic Fibrosis die by the age of 25 years. What a will to live she must have had! After chatting with several other people, I very tiredly went back to the camp to get some much needed sleep. It was a good feeling to be welcomed and an equally good feeling to finish the first day. I just knew that when I woke the next day I would go the distance.

The next morning the alarm went off at 5.00am and I felt surprisingly good. My body was a little stiff but it soon loosened up whilst moving around getting ready for the day. In my heart I knew that I would finish this walk. I glanced at Pete as we both applied Vaseline to our damaged feet. He looked okay. I was hoping that he would take things easy because of his damaged feet. We were moving onto Babinda next and the road was not exactly the best. One thing that stuck in my mind was the amount of road kill that littered the highway. I suppose when the roads are built, little thought is given to the effects on the wildlife.

By this time, it was pretty obvious that in order to survive we had to reduce our mileage. Pete's blisters were difficult to treat as they seemed to be getting infected. Mine were manageable but now I started getting severe shin pain as a result of walking on one side of the road, the side that was facing oncoming traffic. That was the only way one could see the Mack truck that may hit one. The highway can be a scary place when one is walking on the side of it. The only thing I could do was apply a crepe bandage to my calves and ankles. Pete was convinced that this would see me reliant on them but all I needed was support until I was used to the daily mileage. With Pete up front, I counted on Marty for information about how Pete was doing physically, and how Mike and he were getting on up front. At camp at night, you could almost cut the air with a knife with Mike being insistent on the issue of food. Pete felt we were underfed but, to be honest, at the end of each day all I wanted was to get my feet up and let the blood flow in a different direction.

We were making good time, although painfully. By the end of day two we had reached Innisfail, having travelled about 170 km, most of it through cane country. On one occasion we took time out to watch a spectacular cane burn-off. As the flames climbed twenty to thirty feet in the air, it was amazing to watch how the cane farmers controlled the fire. In two days we were at the next stretch of roadway that ran alongside the beach. We entered Cardwell, which was a really attractive township on the beach. My feet were now quite manageable, although I kept getting small blisters. Pete was finding the going difficult. His blisters now had burst and the skin was peeled away so that his feet resembled raw hamburger. It was a lesson to all of us in courage and perseverance. In order to cope with his sore feet, he had to alter his walking gait, which created small sacks of fluid in his groin. Pete chose to wait until Townsville before seeing a doctor who prescribed antibiotics to heal his feet and groin. While I let Marty do the odd leg for me, which allowed me to keep on track, Pete refused Mike's offer of assistance even though his feet were a mess.

As we got close to Cardwell there was one very funny incident. Erika had given us some liquorice and I had convinced Pete that it would help him. After about two hours, when he'd consumed a fair amount of it, he dashed into the bush. By the time he had gone about

15 yards his pants were already down around his knees. The liquorish sure had worked! But none of us had noticed that the railway line also ran next to the roadway. Just as Pete squatted down, along came the train. I often wonder what the passengers thought. Pete had some great jokes about what he would say to Erika next time he saw her.

On the next day we passed the turn off for Halifax, which brought back memories of my marriage to Janet. We used to visit her grandmother in Halifax. I had admired that old lady greatly and always referred to her as Queenie. She was tough. Janet once told me of an incident where there was no doctor nearby and Queenie had a badly damaged finger. They decided to take it off with a knife with no anesthetic. Years later Queenie died and was buried in Halifax.

Halifax was a remarkable town that time had left behind. Most of the residents were of Italian heritage and spoke Italian when in the hotels and shops. Many of them had started out as cane cutters, living in barracks for accommodation. They saved all their hard-earned money, until they finally had enough to buy out the Australian farmers. During my time in Giru I discovered that many Australians were resentful of the Italians' success.

Our next major stop was Townsville. The road to Townsville was a pretty boring stretch. The only thing you could watch was the fresh water pipeline that ran alongside the road. Marty, who had remained very calm throughout this first leg, decided to walk along the top of the pipeline whenever he gave me a break. It was amusing to see him perched, umbrella in hand, balancing on the pipe top. Up front, though, was a different story. Pete was under considerable stress from his infected feet and the sacks of fluid in his groin, which had grown in size. One could sense the level of frustration whenever we stopped and talked. On our arrival in Townsville we had to get Pete to a doctor. It was disappointing for me that we had to bypass the city centre. Deep down inside I would have liked to have seen Janet (my first wife), as I still had some warm feelings for her.

We were to be met at the new McDonald's restaurant by a group of supporters made up of families who had children with Cystic Fibrosis. McDonald's hamburgers are not the best food when you're walking 2000 km, but by now we welcomed anything at all. It was always uplifting when people met us, especially when they were the people we were hoping to help, but I had begun to wonder whether we would in fact raise very much money towards the $1,000,000 needed for the Respite Centre. Eleven years later, while speaking to a Rotary Club, I discovered that at least one mother had felt that day that someone in the city cared about their situation. Many of the families we spoke to along the way felt isolated and there were very few members of the local medical profession who knew much about Cystic Fibrosis.

Once we had carried out the formalities, we were whisked away by one family to visit a sports medicine doctor. Pete was the first of us to climb gingerly upon the examination couch. The look in the doctor's eyes said it all. "When do you expect to be walking again"? He asked. "Tomorrow", Pete replied. "You will never make it", said the doctor. But the doctor did not know Pete. Courage & Perseverance were his middle names and still are to this day. This obviously was a crisis point for Pete, but I was confident he would continue. He had to make sure I did. He would not allow me to be the only one to finish.

There is a wonderful quote by Edgar Cayce. ***The soul is ever greater than its circumstances if it takes what it has and offers it freely to others. We only keep what we give away"***. Pete was offering what he had, not only to the families but to all of us sharing the road.

The doctor cut away the dead skin on Pete's infected feet, and then treated them. It was a mystery that he could still walk at all. My feet were nowhere near as bad and the doctor was convinced I would be able to finish. We convinced Peter to at least take one day off. It was then decided that Mike and Marty would leave us with the family and undertake a full day of walking. It does not sound too hard if you say it quick, but to do 80 km between the two of them in one day (without any training) was going to be tough. This day proved to be the turning point because from then on all four of us walked, leap-frogging as Mike had suggested in the very beginning. By leap-frog I mean each team of two would drop off the first walker at a 20 km interval to start walking. Then the driver carried on a further 10 km. He would then stop and park the vehicle, leaving the keys in some place safe that had already been agreed on and start walking. When the first walker reached the vehicle he would then drive the vehicle 10 km and have a rest.

"Each time a man stands up for an ideal, or acts to improve the lot of others, or strikes out against injustice, he sends forth a tiny ripple of hope, and crossing each other from a million different centers of energy and daring those ripples to build a current that can sweep down the mightiest walls of oppression and resistance. Robert Kennedy 1966.

For Pete and me, the rest was most welcome and we gained a little confidence from the doctor's treatments. Once again, we dared to hope that what we were doing would start a ripple that would become a tidal wave and sweep aside all resistance to providing a hospice for children in Queensland. Perhaps we really would see the families that struggled with terminally ill children finally receive the help they deserved. I became aware much later that one of the ladies who provided respite for us in Townsville went on to found a volunteer physiotherapy program for her local area. She, in her own way, became part of that tidal wave.

The road between Townsville and Rockhampton was really uninspiring. The competition between Pete and me is the one thing that kept us going. Physically, I felt a lot better after the doctor's treatment, and the one day of rest worked wonders. I was truly amazed at both Marty and Mike's fitness as they had not been able to train the way Pete and I had. But here they were, doing exactly the same mileage as we did, day after day. On the first day out of Townsville we could smell the sugar cane being processed at the mill in Giru. Once again, the smell that hung in the air conjured up memories of the hours I had spent cleaning the pipes in the sugar mill, earning a few extra dollars to buy my first Australian home. Every 20 minutes, a cane truck would fly past on its journey to the local mill carrying the harvested cane from every cane field along the road. My mind went back to my old friends at the Giru International Pub where I had first lived when I came to Australia.

We found a spot on the side of the highway and camped for the night, happy that the cane trucks had ceased to buzz past. Everybody seemed okay that night, too tired to say very much, but I think we all acknowledged the decision to leap-frog had made the walk more comfortable. As I lay there beside the road, my mind was focused on how I had enjoyed my time at the Giru hotel. I had secretly hoped that I would catch a glimpse of Janet, my first wife, but it wasn't to be. It had been sixteen years since I had last laid eyes on her, as we walked out of the solicitor's office in Townsville. I wondered if she was okay. I had never been able to speak to her once we had parted, to say I was sorry and thank her for keeping her promise to forward all my things and my share of proceeds of the house sale. I guess my separation from Janet was the hardest event for me to get over as it was completely out of the blue.

The next thing I remember is the noise of a cane truck as it flashed by. I looked over at the sleeping bags and everybody was stirring. It was 5:30am and time for our daily ritual of bathing the feet in salt water and applying "Second Skin" to sore spots as protection against further blisters and infection. We were introduced to this wonderful product by a chemist in Townsville. He had phoned the company that manufactured it and they had agreed to sponsor us. Thank goodness!

We headed off to Ayr, still being very careful to avoid being hit by one of the many trucks that passed us almost constantly. We spent the night in that busy little cane town that had more pubs than shops. At least that's how it appeared when you had consumed too much of the amber fluid. We managed to get some food into us, a Chinese meal if my memory serves me right. It was good to get a rest from our own cooking, for now we all took turns since Mike and Marty were walking the same mileage as Pete and I, we shared the tasks equally.

Everyone's attitude was still good. Mike would walk away from the campsite and undertake his Tai Chi exercises, standing for some time in one spot like a praying mantis. It worked for him, so who was I to laugh at it. It sure worked for David Carradine in the Kung Fu films. What worked for me was Marty's sense of humour. His antics on the water pipeline outside Townsville had kept me sane. He made me realize that we should not take ourselves too seriously, no matter what undertaking we were doing.

As we travelled south, it was hard to believe that off to our left, behind the sugar cane crops, was one of the world's most beautiful stretches of coastline, the Whitsunday Passage. In 1978 Jane (my second wife) and I had spent two weeks at Airlie Beach. On one memorable occasion we sailed out to the far reef on one of the many charter boats. Our boat was one of the few that had participated in the Americas cup yacht. While sailing along the beach at Brampton Island it wasn't hard to imagine how Captain Cook had felt when he discovered this wonderful country. I had wanted to return to Rochedale, sell all we owned and purchase a boat, any kind of boat that I could use as a charter boat.

But back here on the road, no such beauty, just more road kill and the sour smell of harvested cane. There would be the occasional sting as a small blister burst, as if God was still grabbing your attention to keep your mind on the job at hand. We passed the Airlie beach turn-off at Proserpine and headed for Mackay, two days away by our reckoning (190 km). We finished the day's walking in a small township called Yalboroo according to the plan. The following day we made for Mackay. My spirits were a little low, for by now it was obvious that we were not going to raise very much money. I wondered how the others felt, having given up 3 weeks of their life in a failed quest to help children and families who were battling Cystic Fibrosis. For days my mind had been drifting back to Erika and Zoë. This was my first time away from them, though I had kept in contact by mobile phone.

Both of them sounded in good spirits but I knew that it was tough on Erika, who had to do all the physio and treatments *plus* work. What kept me going was the memory of Terry Fox and his willingness to go the distance. The secret to making a difference was going the distance and not getting down when things were rough.

The work of the individual remains the spark that moves mankind forward. Igor Sikorsky.

The next leg, Mackay to Rockhampton, was to be the worst leg of our journey. It was 334 km with just one town to look forward to, Sarina. But no matter how beautiful Sarina was, it was only 38 km outside of Mackay. That left 296 km of very little cover, not much to look at, and nine small townships in which to refuel and take on rations. By now, all four of us had some form of injury and no matter how small these injuries were, they niggled away at our spirits. Even Marty's reliable humour was wearing thin and he seemed to find it hard to keep a smile on his weather-beaten face. He had injured his arm a month before we left Brisbane, slashing all his tendons in a fall through a glass window, and it was giving him considerable pain. He had not told any of us until now; he had just focused on helping us to achieve our goal. For the next four days, tempers frayed, blisters got bigger and not a lot was discussed. We just got up each day, covered our distance, went to sleep and did the same again the next day. No matter how focused and passionate we felt, one step at a time was boring. At times like that, all we could do was cling desperately to the big picture, the initial vision.

Little did we know that Rockhampton had a surprise in store, a surprise that would raise our spirits and give us the much needed boost we had to have to help us finish this adventure? When we walked into Rocky, there were families waiting to greet us and feed us. We were taken to one of the local pubs and made to feel very special. It was nice to be able to talk to people who felt we were doing something important, especially those who came because they knew Zoë, Erika and me. They had organized for the local press to interview us, which gave me an opportunity to talk about the need for families to receive some form of short or long-term respite from volunteers at a residential respite centre. The media took photographs of us and disappeared into the sunset to cover some other story. We never knew if our stories would go to print, but this time it did. It was good to see parents of sick children nodding their heads and agreeing with what we said about respite. It re-affirmed my belief and strengthened the team's commitment.

We made Gladstone the next day and met with more families. The common thread among them was their disillusionment with the Cystic Fibrosis Association, which was founded by a caring and disillusioned grandfather but the longer the organization existed, the more his initial vision became distorted. Committees often forgot they were there to serve Cystic Fibrosis Association members and instead started to tell members what they perceived was needed. This was the complaint of many members we met along the way and Erika and I felt the same way. Little did I know this would be a battle I would later become deeply embroiled in?

We received a call telling us we would be met by our friends and families at the Mobil service station in Burpengary. That was also the place where Mike would leave us. Things had gone well overall and it had been good to share the highway with someone who was very special to me. Mike had not only embraced the cause but inspired me by his commitment. The fuel station was still a fair way off and we still had not raised very much money. We had learned a hard lesson: If the charity you represent does not fully embrace your efforts, you have very little chance of success. If the charity does embrace the efforts, families in the townships along the way get involved. Linking up with community organizations such as Lions or Rotary would have also increased our chance of success.

Next stop Bundaberg. Here we saw strong community support for Cystic Fibrosis families. A second-hand shop was raising a lot of money for their sick kids, but sadly the cash went to head office in Brisbane and was not distributed in their community. A group of heroic elderly ladies in Bundaberg had toiled away day in and day out for years without any acknowledgment from the Brisbane office. As we crossed over the Bundaberg Bridge and watched the trickle of water that was the Bundaberg River, it was hard to believe that at some periods of the year it flowed like a torrent. I knew exactly two things about Bundaberg: 1) It was the home of Australia's legendary Bundaberg Rum, and (2) a polar bear resided somewhere nearby.

On to Childers, a place I had visited during my first trip to Townsville in 1993 when Janet and I set off from Townsville to have a holiday on the Gold Coast. The road was much different then, with many stretches of dirt. It was an interesting journey. We had purchased a Datsun 180B, a car not well suited for long distance driving. My inability to drive put a lot of stress on Janet, but she was a tough lady and we got there in one piece. I was able to help by map reading and doing first parade on the vehicle in the morning, checking the oil and water, kicking the tires, rocking the car to test the springs and making sure we had enough stubbies to complete the journey. Back then it seemed people measured distance by the number of stubbies that would be consumed. (Thank God that part has changed.)

The team was doing well now; we were all coping with our little physical injuries. But I was homesick and wanted to hold both Erika and Zoë in my arms. We still had another 3 days (300 km) to go before we would meet everybody in Burpengary. We passed through Maryborough, a timber industry town, and 89 kilometers later came to Gympie, a gold mining town. Gympie was the birthplace of my old friend from Giru, Duncan Melville. Gympie's hilly countryside reminded me of mining areas in Wales back in the United Kingdom. Unfortunately, the tendonitis in my ankles and shins began flaring up in Gympie and I had to use hot water and ice packs to relieve the pain.

Finally we were on the leg that would see us meet our friends and family at Burpengary. There was a very noticeable spring in our steps, something that had been missing for a few days. Pete did a little bit of running again, but no one cared at this point. Barbara and Jodie, Pete's wife and daughter, were going to be there. When we arrived,

Barbara was there but Erika was not. While we were standing talking Erika and Zoë flashed passed on the other side of the highway. They had missed the turn. It took another 15 minutes for them to return, and it seemed like a lifetime before they finally stepped out of the car. The smile on Zoë's face said it all. My heart was galloping and there were tears running down my face. Zoë looked terrific and well. I could see the look on her face change, as for a moment she was wondering why I was crying. Then there was the big hug and kiss! I turned to Erika and she smiled. I held her and tried to give her a kiss on the lips, but somehow that never happened. My kiss rested finally on her cheek. We obviously still had a long way to go if we were to save our relationship. Zoë made up for our awkwardness by being bubbly and full of cheek. We had some food, talked about Zoë's health and how Erika was coping, but all too soon the time came to say "see you soon". Those couple of hours had been special. I loved both of them and promised myself I would fight with all my life to rebuild our marriage. We said farewell to Mike as he headed home to Melbourne. Thanks to him, we had managed to get to Brisbane. The early difficulties were long behind us, left on some deserted roadside. I still thank God for Mike's help and hope our friendship will be rekindled someday.

Friend: One who knows all about you and loves you just the same. Elbert Hubbard.

We reached Brisbane the next day in fine style, thanks to our recharged batteries. As we entered the city limits we had to pass the Royal Brisbane Children's Hospital. Unbeknown to Pete, Marty and I, the kids that were in hospital, along with the nurses and physiotherapists, came out to see us. I was in tears as I waved to them. All the pain and struggles we'd encountered over all those hundreds of kilometers paled into insignificance when compared with their journeys.

Shortly after that we were joined by one of the Brisbane Lion footy club boys who ran alongside and collected donations. As we entered the George Street Mall area, we were met by a radio personality, a Courier Mail reporter and a photographer. We were then joined by Stefan (Steve Akerie), a well-known and successful hairdresser, who presented us with a cheque for $2000. It was the largest donation we acquired during that walk. Zoë was there again. My inspiration! I picked her up and put her on my shoulders, carrying her high above the crowd, proud to be her father. How I miss her today. Sometimes it is as if someone has ripped my heart out in one fell swoop. Other days I feel confident she is in a far better place and one day we will embrace as we did on that day. What stories we will have to share!

We got to spend that night in our own beds. I had clung to the hope that on this night absence would have made Erica's heart fonder, but alas it was not to be. We said our good nights turned off the light and turned away from each other. My heart ached and tears ran down my cheeks. But almost immediately I fell into my first deep sleep for two weeks and dreamt of happier days. Sometimes my dreams seemed better than my normal day-to-day life and I happily embraced the darkness of night, hoping for a future reality that could match my dreams.

It was hard to get started the next day, having spent some time at home, but the finish line was only one day's walk away at Southport Spit by Sea World. I wondered what would happen at the finish line. That day's walking passed uneventfully, apart from one family who came out to the roadside near Beenleigh and cheered us on. We decided to walk together into the car park at Sea World and as we approached the entrance we could see some families and representatives from the Cystic Fibrosis Association. They applauded as we arrived and many came over to thank us. Zoë gave me a kiss and a cuddle and I suddenly realized it was over. We had done it. 2140 km in 25 days. To this day I am not sure how much money was raised, but I do know we gave some people hope.

Without hope there is no desire. Without desire there is no growth. Nothing can survive without hope. Unknown

The journey we undertook for those sick children was worth it, even if we had only helped one family survive another day.

We cannot become what we need to be by remaining what we are. Max Dupree.

Nothing had changed between Erika and me. It was much like the first time I returned home on leave: business as usual with no intimacy. Not even a cuddle from Erika. Thankfully, my little angel Zoë came straight to the rescue. She never failed to tell us just how much she loved us. It wasn't much longer after that when she gave me a short note, that read, "Dad thank you for looking after me all of my life". She gave her Mum a similar note.

SYDNEY TO BRISBANE 1992

1992 was a good year for Zoë, even though the doctors were concerned about her decreasing lung function. In no way were we going to give up without a fight. We heard about a well-known naturopath, Henry Osiki, who had some success with sufferers of Cystic Fibrosis, so we paid him a visit. He convinced us that we should take Zoë off cow's milk and give her goat's milk. This, combined with regular visits to the beach and the Mirage Hotel swimming pool at Southport, really helped Zoë's lung function increase. She looked a million dollars.

During a visit to see Zoë's specialist, Dr Alan Isles, he mentioned to us that whatever it was we were doing we should continue to do it. We decided not to mention the goat's milk, for there was a strong belief amongst the people that cared for Zoë that she needed cow's milk for its high caloric value. With Cystic Fibrosis patients, the pancreas does not work. To overcome the problem of weight loss and poor absorption of nutrients, Zoë and her mates (even at age eleven) had to take as many as ten pancreatic enzymes with each meal to help digest the pint of milk they consumed along with their meals.

Soon I was getting itchy feet to walk again. I was disappointed at the monetary result of the Port Douglas walk, although I was sure that it had been a public relations success. Considering that we had done most of our marketing through the Cystic Fibrosis Association, it had been a great success. The branches had done a wonderful job in ensuring that everywhere we went we received a wonderful reception.

I decided that I would undertake a walk from Sydney to Brisbane. The respite centre project had been shelved for the time being, but Cystic Fibrosis families still needed help. I asked physiotherapists at both of the main Brisbane hospitals what we could do to offer some immediate help to these families and was told that some form of aerobic equipment would be of greatest value to the kids, perhaps step aerobics supplies or static cycle machines. We decided to attempt to raise sufficient funds to purchase three machines.

For the first walk, we had purchased and hired whatever equipment we could not get sponsored. I hoped that we could find a major sponsor for this new challenge and decided to look for a footwear sponsor before I put together a crew. The crew is always the most difficult challenge in identifying people who had time to spare and the skills it took to ensure that the walk went smoothly. While I was shopping one day in the Mount Gravatt Garden City shopping centre, I came across a shoe store called "Williams the Shoeman". The young manager, Chris Gallagher, was very receptive to the idea of the walk for children and he agreed on the spot to provide the initial shoes for the crew. Even better, he was prepared to get the whole company behind the walk, not just his store. Chris was to become a good friend and in the future would support me on many other occasions. Excited at the thought of our first major sponsor, I returned home to tell Erika and Zoë. Chris had mentioned he would like to meet Zoë, and although she had previously asked to be kept away from cameras, she seemed happy with it and agreed to meet him at the store.

Next, I called my good mate Rod Ihia, a crazy, one eyed Maori who could sing the first line of every song. Rod was looking for work and he was the perfect person to organize some of the logistical issues. When I asked him, he jumped at the opportunity. He then suggested we recruit Marty who had been such a wonderful source of support on the last walk. A further meeting with Chris Gallagher proved very beneficial as this time we had our team assembled. Chris had recruited his marketing team from Williams who provided our logos, shoes and a vehicle to meet us when we reached the Queensland border. The employees at Williams shops situated along our route would participate. Surely, all this help would ensure a far better level of success. Was I wrong?

It is amazing how interstate charitable organizations can be so parochial when it comes to fundraising. This walk would prove no different. With everything planned and myself having reached a level of fitness I had not achieved before the first walk, we set off for Sydney. It was hard to leave Zoë behind but I felt that in some way this time apart would help Erika and me to become a little closer. It was hard looking back as we headed away. There was a little apprehension with regards to our very last recruit. Michael, a young friend of Zoë's, had asked if he could fill the last position in the back-up crew. Against my better judgment, I agreed that he could join us. I felt he was a little too young at 17 to be able to focus on someone else's welfare, for during a walk of this nature every walker needed as much support as possible. My fears were justified. He often ran ahead of me, which made Rod angry because he was responsible for our safety and felt we should stick together. Michael eventually agreed, but it soured the relationship. Later on, we also realized that Michael's extensive mobile phone use cost us extra money we hadn't planned to spend.

We were starting the walk from the Westfield Shopping Centre in Hornsby NSW, and although we had not received much support from the New South Wales Cystic Fibrosis Association, we hoped that they would at least organize some media coverage. We had agreed to give all funds raised in New South Wales to that state's Cystic Fibrosis organization in the hope that they would participate in some way. No such luck! Their president attended, but there was no media and there were no families to say bon voyage. All of the lads were disappointed and now all we wanted to do was to get started. We were so excited that this walk would directly help Cystic Fibrosis children. Our major sponsor, Unilife (a manufacturer of fitness equipment) was going to provide three hospitals with tread mills and static exercise bicycles.

However, if the response in Sydney was anything to go by, raising funds was going to be difficult.

My standard of fitness was much better at this point and those first days went fairly well. The main problem was flies. It seemed as soon as I stepped out of the vehicle, flies arrived from all over the countryside with the early ones taking pride of place on my face. At every break I would find a blanket and cover myself to at least get some rest from the frenzied attack of flies. We had some success raising money by going into shopping centers and taking the hat around. Michael seemed to relish the opportunity to talk about his little mate Zoë, although he received no major donations. When it came to any major involvement, the rest of the crew did nothing. Of course this had a terrible effect on morale and tempers were short. As the one doing the walking, it was hard to keep things under control. Very often I would feel my emotions welling up. At the end of every second day I would contact Erika and Zoë. Just hearing their voices lifted my spirits.

One day a police car pulled up to chat. During our conversation I discovered that one of the constables had a friend whose son had Cystic Fibrosis. He was angry because as far as he knew, they had not been told about us and he was sure they would have wanted to participate. It was obvious that the New South Wales Cystic Fibrosis Association had done nothing to promote the event. Without both the business and general community's involvement, it was going to be hard to conduct a successful event. In recent years I've seen sports figures undertake such walks and it would leave me wondering: how would we have gone with the corporate backing they had? In those early years I was still trying to develop some credibility. Sporting personalities had already achieved that on the playing fields. And unlike them, we received no pay from the money raised. The policeman we met worked hard behind the scenes and we started to notice a growing support within the community. As welcome as the donations were, it was sad that it was coming from the families we wanted to help not the business community. We stayed in contact with Chris Gallagher at Williams Shoe Store and he assured us that by the time we reached

Queensland he would have been able to generate some support. His promises kept us going. I could see in Chris, even at the early age of 23 years, an understanding of corporate responsibility and the value of helping those in need in the general community.

What I learned most on this particular walk was the value of teamwork. Success comes when we have a team of people with different skills pulling together, or in this case, walking in the same direction. "No man is an island." We were not doing this and it was reflected in our attitude, both toward each other and toward the public. We had enjoyed a limited amount of support in NSW but we only had raised about $500 in cash. When the blisters felt sore, it was hard to keep going. Luckily, we received some much welcome support in Tweed Heads. A grandmother had raised quite a few hundred dollars. Immediately, I saw the spirits lift and the smiles came back on the guy's faces. Apart from two families who had walked with us, we felt that New South Wales had been a failure. All we could hope for was that someone had seen us or heard of us and had been inspired to do something after we passed through. All we thought about was getting to Queensland, where we would have some local support. By the time we reached the Queensland border we were truly down. However, true to his word, Chris Gallagher of Williams, the Shoeman, was there to meet us as we crossed the border into Queensland. There on the side of the highway was a black Lynx four-wheel drive and Chris's smiling face.

We were in for a shock on the last day when we finally walked into the Hyper Dome at Springwood. The Queensland public had responded for there were families and children to greet us. Chris was there, along with his boss from Williams the Shoeman. After each team member had spoken about the journey, the General Manager presented us with a cheque for $9000. It helped the team feel that the walk was in many ways worth doing. I was glad to see my little angel's smiling face at the finish line. She always looked terrific, and I had missed her so much. That night we all laughed and joked about the walk, although I sensed that things had not changed between Erika and me, I made the best of it just being with my sweet Zoë. She watched as I dressed my feet and explained that no matter how much Vaseline I applied and how good my socks were, I always had my fair share of blisters because of the shape of my feet as my big toes are about two inches longer than the rest of my feet.

AN ENGLISH HOLIDAY FOR ZOË

In October of 1992 Erika and I took Zoë to England to meet some of my family. On the way back, we were also going to Disneyland and Hawaii. As the time grew close, I was not sure who was more excited, Zoë or me. I was so proud of how she was growing up I could not wait to have friends and family meet her. Zoë was looking forward to a great adventure. The holiday also entailed many health issues and concerns. Because of the state of Zoë's lungs, we had to check with her specialist to see if she was well enough to travel. Fortunately, because we had been so careful with Zoë's nutrition, she was extremely well and her doctor was confident that she would travel well, as long as we made sure that there was oxygen available at all times.

The big day arrived and Zoë looked fine. Thankfully the flight went well and we arrived at Heathrow Airport to be met by her Godfather Ernie Arnold, my old mate from the army days. As we drove from Heathrow to Hullbridge in Essex, I could see the excitement in Zoë's eyes. She was on a high and Erica and I were so very proud of her. The next few days we were able to take her to a few places in the London area. I spoke to someone in charge at my old regiment (the Blues and Royals) and got permission for the three of us to visit Hyde Park Barracks to see the Horse Guards of my army days. Zoë was amazed at the size of the horses and enjoyed her tour of where Dad had worked. I kept her entertained with funny stories, like me bobbing up and down on my trusty mount, Troubadour as I rode behind the Queen on my first escort. I had lost both my stirrups and was bouncing around like a pea on a drum. I could just imagine the queen putting her head outside the carriage window and telling someone to lock me away in the tower for my unmilitary behaviour. But I escaped with some very painful saddle sores and a big case of embarrassment.

We planned to meet up with my birth mother, who was still living on the Isle of Guernsey. She kept her word and called us at Ernie's house to set a date to meet. Zoë was very excited to see her other Gran and as the day got closer, she asked me about her. Sadly, I could not tell her much for I had spent so little time with her over the years. The night before she was due to arrive, the phone rang and lo and behold it was my mother saying she was not going to come. I tried to understand, but deep down I felt hurt for Zoë's sake. Erika's response was understandable. "Why would she be any different towards Zoë? She was not willing to raise her own son". At the time I thought Erica was right, but now I believe in walking in people's shoes before you judge them. Zoë never said anything. She was enjoying everything else and we were able to hide our disappointment from her.

Ernie organized a barbecue and, to my amazement, another army mate showed up; Totty Flude, one of the regiment's characters. Totty and I had spent many hours at B Squadron Bar together. The funniest thing I ever saw him do was during our amalgamation weekend when he was asked to escort Ben Turp, one of the most respected Chelsea Pensioners. Ben had taken part in the very last cavalry charge for the British Army. Both Totty and Ben enjoyed a tipple or two and on that day they had partaken of the amber liquid. As we stood on Parade, the Sergeant Major's concern was written all over his face when these two cavaliers came tripping around the corner, each wearing the other's hat. What could anybody say? The look on the Sergeant Major's face was not one of a happy camper. Far from it! The barbecue went well. There was plenty of tale telling and I ended up in the pool. I'm not sure if I jumped or was thrown in. We had all consumed a great deal of beer.

Our next trip was to Long Eaton to visit my family. Many had not met Zoë and the rest had not seen her for about six years. Everyone was taken with how well she looked and that she was keeping so well. We took her from place to place, from Dovedale to Derbyshire to Nottingham Castle. She seemed to be enjoying herself, and I was enjoying showing her where I was raised. We managed to get her to pose for a photo beside good old Robin Hood. I don't think I convinced her that he was real. To be honest, it always bothered me that the last arrow he shot from his cell in the castle was supposed to have landed at the Royal Oak in Sherwood Forest, well over 10 miles away. The day before we were to leave Long Eaton, the family organized a party for Zoë. Not only was she blown away by the turnout of family members, but so were Erika and I. They had done a wonderful job with a cake and decorations, plus a few drinks for the adults in the back room. It made me feel very proud and a little sad that we had to leave. Little did anyone know that would be the last time they would see my little girl.

We arranged to drive back to London to see Erika's parents' house and do any tidying that needed doing, as it was on the market to be sold. It was like a jungle when we got there! We had only allowed a day for tidying, so I had to work like mad to get it finished. I was not exactly dressed for it, and eventually I was covered in dust and dirt. By the time we could see the fence at the end of the garden I was definitely looking forward to a cold beer to wet my whistle.

With everyone visited and a good time had by all, we were ready for a holiday at Disneyland in California and then on to Hawaii. The journey went well until we got to the airport at Los Angeles, when a customs officer asked if we would open our cases. As we turned Zoë's bag over, a voice from deep inside growled, "Move over, road hog." We had activated a doll inside Zoë's case. Thankfully, the customs officer grinned and said we could move along. By this time, Zoë was almost crying with laughter. Erica and I held ours until we were out of sight of the customs area, but Zoë didn't care. Disneyland was all that we had hoped for. One of the attractions was the ET ride. Before we got on the ride, we quietly gave Zoë's name to the ticket person. When the ride was finished ET's finger pointed to her and ET said, "Goodbye Zoë Reed". For the rest of her life, she never figured out how ET knew who she was.

After two days at Disneyland, we flew to Hawaii. We were looking forward to just relaxing, but that was not to be as the following morning I woke feeling very ill. I was having difficulty in breathing. Since the holiday had taken its toll financially, there was very little on our bankcard and cash in the wallet was also very low. As far as treatment was concerned, all we could afford was a chemist. I decided that I would be okay to walk as long as I didn't exert myself too much, but that afternoon it became more difficult to breathe. For the first time, I felt I really understood how our little girl felt with her ongoing battle with asthma and cystic fibrosis. I asked Erika to walk more slowly and tried to keep up, but when we reached a certain pedestrian crossing I had to stop. Erica and Zoë continued to cross the street, so I called out saying I was having difficulty breathing. Erika did not come back across the road to see how I was; only Zoë. I then knew for sure it was over. Our relationship was non-existent. When we finally reached the hotel I said, "You do not care, hey"? She replied, "What do you want me to do, dance around you"? I knew it was well and truly over. As it happened I consulted a doctor upon arriving back in Australia and was told I had an acute infection in my lungs.

MY LAST YEAR WITH ZOË

1992 and the first three months of 1993 was the last year I spent with my little girl and it was one of her best years health-wise. We found a swimming coach for her and took her swimming on a regular basis. The combination of swimming and good care from Erika and me kept her well enough to stay out of hospital, other than for "top-up" treatments to boost her immune system; intravenous antibiotics and night feeds to boost her caloric intake. Unfortunately, it was a terrible time for Zoë's parents. The final straw in our family breakdown came at a Tom Jones concert. Erika wanted to see him perform and a doctor friend and his wife offered to watch Zoë, so we had a rare opportunity for a date. Confident that Zoë was in good hands, we went off to the Gold Coast Casino. Not long after being seated with a group of young women Erika asked me to dance. As it was clear there wasn't a lot of room to do so, I declined, so she went off to dance with two of the young women. As soon as she left, the remaining women started taunting me saying I was scared to get up and dance and that I could not dance. My male ego eventually got the better of me and I agreed to have one dance. Within seconds Erika started to verbally attack me. "How dare you", she shouted. I said it was just one dance and tried to explain why, but she wouldn't hear any of it. Unbeknown to us while we were arguing we had somehow managed to end up back stage behind the performance and our performance was witnessed by all and sundry. What must Tom Jones have thought? Anyway we argued our way around until finally I said I had had enough and went back to my doctor friend's house, where I stayed for the night.

The next day when I awoke I realized that Erika had come back during the night, taken the car and driven home by herself. Things between us looked very bleak and I was concerned about Zoë and the effect it would have on her if we separated. We were finally becoming part of the statistics being around 75% of the parents who care for terminally ill children end up in divorce. Ironically, the hospital and Cystic Fibrosis Association often sent distraught parents to us for advice believing that Erika and I had a solid relationship. We were so good at hiding our misery that no one noticed our relationship had all but died. The only thing holding us together was caring for Zoë and loving her so deeply.

Around midyear Zoë took a turn for the worse and had to be admitted to hospital. Erika and I would voice our anger with each other but always tried to get on relatively well in front of Zoë. On one particular visit to see Zoë we both became aware of how she was battling and on leaving we decided to have a meal together. During this meal we agreed to try once again, but from Erika there was one proviso; she could not guarantee that she could return to any form of intimacy. I accepted the situation as we kissed each other on the cheek and ate our meal.

At the end of the evening we left together got into our cars and drove off. As I pulled onto the freeway my pager fell off the seat and slid under my right foot. As I bent to retrieve it, I looked up to see a multi-car crash right in front of me. I swerved but was unable to avoid catching the rear end of the car in front of me. I called Erika and she came to pick me up, but I could see by her expression that she was very angry with me. As we drove away from the crash scene, she said she wanted a separation. We agreed to talk about it the following day. We went to a psychologist for counseling and I remember the word "freedom" being tossed about without any thought being given to the impact on our little girl. "You seem to be panicking a little, Nigel" the counselor said. I told her that wherever freedom is fought for, there is a cost, and very often that cost is the loss of life. I was afraid that the cost in this case might be our little girl.

Shortly after awaking the following day, the silence was broken as the telephone rang. It was Aunt Joyce, my father's youngest sister. She had bad news about my father's sibling. Maurice was very ill with cancer and not expected to live too much longer, and Betty was seriously ill and in danger of losing her legs. Maurice (or Moggy, as we had called him) was my father's second eldest brother, a wonderful friendly gentleman. These uncles and aunts had all helped to raise me and had become more like my own brothers and sisters. My immediate feeling was, "What the hell is happening, what have I done to lose so many family members"? I was stunned. Not only was my marriage in tatters but now two family members were fighting for their lives!

I immediately thought that this could give Erika and me time to be apart and, possibly, see the error of our separating forever. So I suggested that I'd go home to see my ill family members and take twelve weeks to do it. Zoë was regaining fairly good health again after her top up in hospital and Erika's parents were due out for a visit so they would be there to help her. Erika agreed to this trial separation. While it was hard talking to Erika, I feared that breaking this news to my wonderful little Zoë would tear me apart. Here we were doing what previously had been unimaginable. She was our life. Although I was going to visit family before death took two of them, Erika and I were effectively entering a separation.

As we entered the ward her eyes lit up as they always did when we got together. As I approached her I could not hold back the tears, and as I pulled her into my arms with the other parents looking on, I told her that her Mum and I were separating. I was still hopeful that it would be temporary and that things may change once I got back. She held me tight and as I sobbed I told her about Maurice's cancer. Erika sat next to me. Zoë seemed okay with what we told her and she was very concerned for her uncle Mog. That was Zoë, the parent amongst us.

The flight took a while to organize. A friend gave me some work painting so I could get some money together. To be honest, that period in my life is almost a blank in my mind today. It seemed to go so fast. The next thing I remember is driving with Zoë and Erika to the airport. I was in tears, then holding Zoë in my arms and promising her I would be home in twelve weeks. For the first time in years I felt Erika's arms around my shoulders as she wished me well. Walking toward the passenger lounge, I turned and saw my beautiful daughter's face. Already I was looking forward to the next time I would hold her. The flight was lonely and sad, to say the least. It was hard to understand how I could be leaving the only person who accepted me for who I was, but here I was heading towards England. Since I had only sufficient funds to purchase a one-way ticket, I knew I'd have to get some temp work in England in order to buy a return fare.

Erika's parents met me at the airport. We had only spoken of the illness in the family but as they greeted me at Heathrow I could see in their eyes that they had guessed what had happened. Over the next day we talked about the separation and both of them were convinced it was not permanent. They thought we would get back together for Zoë's sake but in my heart I did not share their confidence. The following day I set off by train to Nottingham full of concern for both Betty and Maurice. I wondered how I would be received. I had always felt like the black sheep of the family, returning to the shelter of the pen when the wolves were close at my heels. My meeting with Maurice took place next door to where I was raised. He sat in his chair looking tired, but his first words where typical of the man I considered a brother, "How are you, my mate, and how is little Zoë"? I learned from his wonderful wife Betty that he had no idea that he had cancer. He still believed that he had asthma, which had been the initial diagnosis.

I initially stayed with family, but the search for work had to begin and I needed a more permanent place of my own. Without a job, I knew it would be hard to find a place to live. As I sat in a local Pub pondering my predicament, an old friend walked through the door, Byron Tully. Byron and I had had some good times together. He used to be quite the larrikin. As we talked, I mentioned my predicament and to my joy he told me he had a vacant furnished flat that I could use free of charge. Byron had his own share of bad luck being involved in a bad car smash and was living with his mother at the time. He had badly damaged his legs but through determination had mastered walking with only a walking stick. Sadly, he'd also become an alcoholic. Each day was started with a double stones ginger wine and a half pint of beer. But in spite of his struggles, he was a mate who was there for me when I needed him. I found work as a relief manager with a local brewery and soon was earning some money. With Byron taking me to the first Pub in Loughbro, I asked him to take a break and stay with me. I was pleased when he said yes, but sadly the first morning after moving in, having had his early morning drink, he set off for Long Eaton in his Ford supercharged Cosworth, one of two in the local area. The other belonged to the police. Byron would often skite about his car being the better of the two. During the journey home he was chased and caught by the police. When breath tested he was well over the limit, even though he had only had a couple of drinks. Obviously he was just topping his body up.

As for me, I spent some wonderful personal time with Maurice and grew ever fonder of him as we talked. Unlike Stanley, who lost so much weight that he looked like a returning prisoner of war, Maurice was bloated. I guess it was the steroids they were giving him. He was disappointed that although he had stopped smoking some years earlier, illness caught up with him. I never let on to him that he had cancer. Although I had lost many close family members by then, when Maurice died his death cut deep.

Sometime later I met up with my in-laws and they advised me I should only return to Australia when I had enough money to show Erika I could support myself. That was a long way off, but I was determined to go back with something. However, a few days later a fellow tenant complained about me living in Byron's flat. Evidently Byron was renting the flat and living mostly across the road with his mother to keep her company. Some sticky beck decided he should not be doing that and allowing someone else to live in the flat. Not wanting to cause Byron trouble, I moved out. The only option for me was a second hand car I had bought, so during the heavy winter and snowfalls I slept in any safe parking place.

Then, out of the blue, the earth collapsed. Erika's father, Richard, contacted me and told me to call home as Zoë was seriously ill in the Royal Brisbane Children's Hospital. As if struck by lightning, I was suddenly on my knees sobbing. Only two weeks ago I talked to Zoë and asked her to tell Erika that if she would have me, I would walk back. My mind was racing at two hundred miles an hour. Over the next few hours I was able to speak to Erika. She said that Zoë was fighting, but was still very ill. I told her I would get home as soon as possible. I contacted the company I worked for and they bent backwards to arrange my severance and holiday pay. Still in a haze, I drove home, picked up some of my belongings, organized a flight and dealt with all the details. I made good time driving to Heathrow; Zoë was in my mind's eye the whole time. As I approached the airport and thought about where I was going to park the car, I quickly decided to give it to Ernie Arnold, Zoë's godfather. I left it in the 24-hour car park. This seemed to me as good a plan as any but what a mistake it turned out to be. Many months later I discovered that there was a bomb threat at the airport soon after I left. Before Ernie had the opportunity to collect it, the car became another possible bomb threat. It also incurred a heavy parking penalty. Ernie was not very happy with me, but I think he made some profit.

The flight to Australia was terrible, an emotional roller coaster. I tried not to think of the worst outcome and I prayed that God did not need her this time and we would have her safe once again. I hoped that my comments to Erika and the physiologist about freedom and its cost would not become a reality. When the plane touched down for a stopover in Bangkok I could not wait to find a phone. I managed to reach Erika at the hospital. Her words were like a dagger piercing my heart. "Get home quick, Nigel. Zoë is not good". I dropped the phone and literally ran towards the plane only to be stopped by one of the stewards. He took hold of me and asked what was wrong. "My daughter Zoë is dying in the Royal Brisbane Children's Hospital" I sobbed. With that I was whisked away to first class. A hostess was chosen to sit with and care for me. It made a difference having someone to talk to. They were wonderful. All the cabin crew made me feel that it was okay to cry.

On arrival in Sydney they swiftly took me to the gold card lounge and provided me with food, drinks and a phone. This allowed me to talk to Erika once again. She sounded tired but a lot calmer. I had decided that whatever the outcome I should not look for blame, but be there for her. She just said "Get home quick, Nigel". The plane arrived in Brisbane around midday and as I left the aircraft a steward handed me a bottle of champagne to celebrate Zoë's survival. As we were led through customs I was pleased to see how much help I received until it came to the agriculture inspector. Although the steward was with me, the inspector was determined to search me. Both the steward and I looked on in disbelief as the minutes ticked away. I finally got to the arrival lounge and was met by a good friend and President of the Brisbane Cystic Fibrosis Association, Ross Metcalf, whose daughter Carley was afflicted with Cystic Fibrosis. As we drove to the hospital Ross said not to worry about anything as the association would be there for us.

I raced through the hospital and as I entered the ward I was greeted by Erika. She looked so tired, and she had reason to be. She had been awake almost all the time Zoë had been in the hospital, supported by her friend Pam who was also waiting next to Erika. Little was said between us as I was directed into Zoë's room. As I opened the door she was lying awake in her bed with a nurse attempting to make her cough by using what is described as a tickler, a long straw like implement. As the nurse pulled it out I said "I love you my angel". She replied "Love you too, Dad". Then once again the nurse tried to make Zoë cough so as to bring the phlegm up that was drowning her lungs. Sadly this was to no avail. At this, Zoë was heard to say sarcastically, "And wasn't that fun"?

I sat on the edge of the bed and held her hand. At this point neither of us was aware how close to death she was. I just could not believe that Zoë would lose this battle. She had always pulled through. We had worked so hard to keep her healthy. Since she was a baby we had focused all our energy on keeping her well. Apart from the last twelve months we had stood side-by-side believing we could beat this shocking illness. But now here we were again with nothing else to do but place our faith in the nurses and doctors who had helped us get her to the age of eleven.

As I sat and talked to her she seemed to drift in and out of sleep. We told each other how much we loved one and other. She asked me if I was going to walk from England to Australia as I had told her over the phone. I said "No I am home for good. I am not ever leaving you again". We talked about her school work and she seemed to be battling to stay awake. Erika was asleep in the parent's room and I held Zoë's hand until she was finally asleep. I felt some one next to me. It was the nurse. She said, "You had better fetch Erika". I replied, "Why"? "Zoë and she are both asleep. Let them catch some quiet time." The nurse replied, "Sorry Nigel, Zoë is close to dying. She is now unconscious". I heard my heart call out, "No No She is sleeping"! Before I left, I lowered my head to hers and whispered, "I will do that walk just for you, my angel". I was not sure if she heard me but that did not matter, I would somehow make something good come out of all this.

I quickly ran down the corridor and as I gently shook Erika, I was fighting to find the right words. How do you tell a mother her only child is dying? I myself was finding it hard to grasp. Both of us rushed to Zoë's bedside. With Erika taking her in her arms, I laid as close as I could on the other side of her and we both stroked her brow. At bedtime, Zoë would always say to her Mum, "Send Day in" (Day being her name for me). Was this to be the last time for Mum and Day to be able to sit beside her bed and tell her we loved her? I prayed that she would pull through but I soon found myself saying words I never imagined I would say. "You do not have to fight for us, my angel. If it is time to go then go. We will always love you." As we had been told, a short gasp, a rattle and she was gone. No longer was the earth blessed with the presence of a little angel, our Zoë had gone.

What Comes Next

The minutes, the hours, the days that followed are hidden so deep in my subconscious that I find them hard to recall except in bits and pieces. I remember Erika asking me if I wanted someone special to be with. "You are the only person that I want to be with" I told her. I knew in my heart there was someone else she wanted to be with. Thankfully, a good friend offered to take me home. I believe that Erika organized the funeral and everything else. The president of the Brisbane Cystic Fibrosis Association, Ross Metcalf, had the association pay for the funeral. Thank God for that, as I had very little money left after using most of what I had to get back to Zoë.

The day that I bought Erika a dress for the funeral, we met for lunch at the Britannia Inn Brisbane. It was then that she told me she was seeing someone else and that she wanted him to be at the funeral. Of course I didn't want him to be there, but she was obviously fond of him so that was that. I had the deepest sadness in my heart. I had just lost Zoë and now discovered Erika had formed a new relationship while we were separated. The days that followed continued to be a haze for me. It was like my mind had shut off to protect me from overloading on emotional pain. A few months before separating from Erika I had confirmed my belief in the Lord Jesus. Erika and I had attended the same church and we had no hesitation in asking Steve Parish our Pastor to conduct Zoë's funeral. An organization called the White Ladies handled everything and the funeral was held at The Garden City Crematorium in Brisbane. As Erika and I drove up the drive to the crematorium it became obvious that our daughter had touched many people's lives. The number of cars that were parked there was incredible. As we walked up the stairs and into the hall I was astounded by the number of people, many of whom I did not know. I could feel the emotion swelling from the tips of my toes right upwards swirling through my body. Tears ran down my face as I looked into the faces of the people who came to celebrate the life of my angel. She had reached into oh so many hearts: school teachers, parents, school mates, nurses, physiotherapists, our friends, and most of all fellow Cystic Fibrosis sufferers who were Zoë's hospital mates.

Until that day, I never fully grasped how Lindy Chamberlain stayed so calm when she lost her child. I realized that someone would have to be calm but I most certainly could not. At the start of every word I broke down. Erika and I were supposed to talk at the funeral but I was in no state to be able to carry that off. All I remember saying was, "I have shared the planet with an angel." Erika was the one who kept it together, at least externally. Today I look back and appreciate the depth of her fortitude and courage. She was able to get up in front of everyone and talk about our Zoë and to thank everyone for being with us to celebrate and mourn our little girl. One thing I'll never forget was Jeff (Erika's new partner) standing quietly with a single rose. I was furious. "How dare you stand there," I thought. However, as if my little daughter was leading me, I decided to walk over, shake his hand, and thank him for looking after Zoë. The look on his face said it all. I think he was surprised that I wasn't angry.

Of all the handshakes that day, there was one that meant more than any other and that was Zoë's physical education teacher. He had undergone his own massive problems yet here he was paying his respects to my daughter. I held his hand and said, "God bless you" as I recalled all he had done for my little girl. Another person I saw that day was Anna McMahon, a newsreader for one of the TV channels who had befriended Zoë. As she shook my hand she said, "I hear you are going to walk again." I asked who had told her that and she replied Michael. Michael was the friend of Zoë's who had been a part of the crew when I walked from Sydney to Brisbane. Anna then told me if I needed help, she would be there for me.

I left the funeral with the image of my little girl in a coffin. There was no doubt she was gone, hopefully to a better place. It seemed right to tell her, "You do not have to fight for us, go to a better place." But how the hell do we know if this little girl who had fought for every last breath of air, is in a better place? I envisaged her sitting bolt upright in that hospital bed and shouting, "Dad you told me to fight for life, that I can beat anything, now you are saying give in." I never got the chance to explain. She was gone in the flick of a butterfly's wing. I can only hope she was spirited up into the place where all her mates must surely have gone. A place much better than here on earth, a place where she no longer felt pain and no longer had to battle for each breath.

My good friend Rod had prepared the house for those friends who wanted to join us. It seemed strange holding a party even though it was to celebrate Zoë's life. After having just grieved for her passing, what do you say to people? I wandered into Zoë's room and memories came flooding back to me. All the times she had called out, "Send Day in". The tears found every crack in my face as they ran from my aching eyes. I just sat back on the bed and cried. I had lost my little angel. One of our friends Ginny came in and sat next to me. We talked of the need to do something. Should I join the ministry? Should I walk again? At this point I had no idea where I was going. She was kind to get me thinking about the future when I felt so strongly that there was no future. What I found strange was how friends even in death take sides. A very old friend phoned and asked if she could come over. I replied, "Of course." When she arrived, she asked me where Erika was and then walked straight by me, even though I had befriended her long before meeting Erika. Galena had been the wife of one of my best friends, Colin. Yet during the course of the whole evening not one word of support did she offer to me. Thanks mate. She obviously had taken Erika's side in our personal problems without ever hearing my side. There was another knock at the door. This time, to my amazement, it was Jeff. He said he had come as a representative of Hyne and Son, the company both he and Erika worked for. Thank God for the little voice in the back of my head saying, "Dad let it go, it's not worth it". It was hard to not call him a lying bastard, but I kept my cool and fetched Erika. She joined him outside as no way was he coming into the house.

In the following days I began to focus on another walk, but it was hard to concentrate on anything at this point. Sometimes I was so positive and full of plans I felt almost manic. Then I would wake the following day and feel that life was not worth living. Tears were my constant companions. As I look back it is hard to say where I was, whom I was with, or what I was doing.

About a week after the funeral Erika and I went to the crematorium for Zoë's ashes. We walked in and were greeted by a receptionist with a very matter-of-fact look upon her face. "May we have the ashes of Zoë Reed please"? I asked. I am not sure what I expected, but she looked under the reception desk, brought up a white plastic box and went to hand it to me. I lost it and started sobbing. All I could do was get out of the office as fast as possible. Once again the tears were falling fast and freely. Thankfully, Erika stepped in and collected them. The drive to Byron Bay was long and hard but that was where we had agreed to scatter Zoë's ashes. Was this all that was left of a once vibrant life? How could anyone find life after death? Where was the soul? What was the spirit and where did it reside? The night after Zoë had died I had woken from a dream in panic. I was distraught that I could not protect my daughter. It was a dream. She truly had gone now and I was going with Erika to scatter on the ocean what was left of our daughter.

We both stood at the water's edge on Watigo Beach. It was an overcast day and there was a cool breeze. Erika had said she did not want to go into the water so I stripped down to my bathers and swam about 100 metres out. I was still able to stand and cast the ashes above my head. At that point my daughter would have had a fit of laughter as had she been watching; she would have seen the wind pick up the ashes and blow them all over my face before they drifted onto the water. I had imagined that it was going to be a very beautiful experience. Instead all I could do was smile and wipe the ash from my face. As I swam the few metres back I could see Erika's pained face. I wanted so much to be there for her. I had promised Zoë that I would remain her Mum's friend whatever happened. Little did I know how challenging that would be?

That night Erika wanted to be alone although I wanted to be with her. She told me she was going to her friend Pam's house, so I decided to go to the cinema. Unfortunately, the movie I wanted to see had started. With very little money on me and no transport or house key, I decided to ask my friend Gary to give me a lift to Pam's house to pick up the house key. Gary was very hesitant to drive me to that house. He was convinced Jeff would be there. He was right. As Pam let me in, I saw a shadow out in the garden. I decided to confront him so I chased him and caught him but, fortunately for me, he broke away and scrambled over the fence. Once again I heard Zoë saying, "Not worth it, Dad". Thankfully Gary had waited for me and offered to take me home. It seemed I was sinking further and further into a dark pit of grief and anger, unable to see any light at the end, yet I had read somewhere that "from the bottom of the darkest pit very often the brightest night sky can be seen". Maybe another walk would help me resolve my grief, conquer my anger and move on. I was certainly hoping so. A short time later, the Cystic Fibrosis Association came to my aid. I had been staying with various friends, always aware that I did not want to wear out my welcome. Jenny, the president of the association, heard of my plight and offered me the use of their unit above the office. I was so pleased to have a place of my own even though I was not sure how the loneliness would affect me.

I managed to stay a few weeks there, but loneliness was a challenge. When you lose a child, no one checks on you. You go from being part of the Cystic Fibrosis community to being alone. One minute, parents were being directed to us for support and the next minute I was on my own. Friends got on with their lives. Some were unsure what to say, others were focused on their own family issues. Even though you know this to be true, it still does not help when the darkness comes. I took comfort in sleep because I found my dreams to be more comforting than my waking life. When the light came through the windows of the old house, I would battle to stay asleep, dreading to open my eyes. I would look around and see the bareness of the flat and my inner voice would say, "Look where you are at. No home, no family and no life". Everything that had been dear to me was gone.

I discovered how quickly parents who have cared for a sick child can find themselves lost when their child passes on. The medical staff had to stay focused on the living. Many of the associations are focused on raising funds for critical research into finding a cure. Since my daughter was beyond a cure and no longer among the living, I felt completely isolated, especially in the dark hours of the evening and on weekends. I prayed for the phone to ring. I wondered what happened to the 100-plus people at her funeral. Once long ago, at a Cystic Fibrosis Association meeting, a father who had lost his daughter to Cystic Fibrosis came in asking for help. After he left the room, one of the committee members said, "I don't want to listen to him, he represents the negative side of this illness". I felt stunned because it occurred to me that we all, at some time, would represent the negative. I was disappointed that we had no way to help these parents. Now it was my turn to be lonely.

I thought of the doctors and nurses who cared for our kids. What did they feel when time after time they lost children they had cared for? I decided to contact Erika to ask if she would come with me to visit the hospital ward and some of the staff. She agreed. We also had a framed sketch of Zoë we wanted to give to the ward. The day we went we caught up with a couple of the physiotherapists we knew. Thankfully, we also ran into Zoë's specialist, Dr Alan Isles. He said it was unusual for parents to visit him so soon after losing a child and how glad he was to see us. My good mate Colin Walker also turned up and we sat and discussed my desire to walk from England to Australia. He could not see what it would achieve and in honesty, neither could I. It was just something I still felt I had to do.

Shortly after that I met two people who inspired me: a young boy with Cystic Fibrosis named Ashley and a woman named Janet. Without these two people it would have been hard to have initially kept going. I met Ashley through his wonderful mum who, like many mothers, was caring for a sick child alone. She was a beautiful, intelligent lady caring for this terrific young man alone. We shared time together for months and it would have been nice if our relationship had blossomed into something deeper, but that never happened. I thank Ashley and his mum for the companionship that helped so very much in the early days after Zoë's passing. Knowing in my heart that the relationship with Ashley's Mum was not going to progress, I was open to meeting someone. The lady, who cut my hair, Janet, was very interested in who I was and what I did. I saw an opportunity to develop a friendship with her but my courage with the opposite sex was not my strongest point and I left the salon unable to ask for a date.

I walked straight over to a bookstore and bought a book by one of my favorite writers, Og Mandino, called *The Rag Picker*. I then proceeded to walk past the salon about five times until I gathered my nerve enough to walk in and ask Janet out for lunch. She agreed to have lunch at the garden restaurant in the botanical gardens. What I dreaded turned out to be relatively painless and she had said yes! Janet would prove to be my saviour. We spent time together off and on for the next year. While we had some good times, I was not really ready for a full-time relationship and Janet also had her own problems to deal with within her family. Like Ashley and his mum, Janet's friendship seemed to come into my life for a reason.

A few days after my first lunch with Janet, my mate Colin Walker called on me at the Cystic Fibrosis house. He wanted to talk about my promise to walk for Zoë and the kids but to be honest; I found it hard to focus on the walk. I had drunk a fair bit that day trying to "drown the pain." Colin kept asking the same questions: Why do you want to do it? What will it achieve? We talked about sponsors, costs and time frames. I wanted something of value to come out of Zoë's death, but I also felt guilty for not having been there for most of her last year. Had anyone told me that I would have left my little angel for a month, for a week, or even for a day I would have laughed in his face? Little do we know what life has to dish up? All we can do is deal with the issues as they arrive on our doorstep, praying that we have the courage to do what is called for. At one time or another we all have made decisions we wish we could change. But the bottom line of every decision is that they are made with the facts available at the time. Hindsight does not come until later. I think people need to consider that before making judgments about other people's decisions. While I was away from Zoë, we wrote to each other constantly and often talked on the phone. Every day I awake to the fact that I missed almost all of the last year of Zoë's life and that she missed most of her last year of being with me. That is something I cannot change and it is something that constantly haunts me.

PREPARING FOR THE WORLD WALK

Walking From England Though North America and Back to Australia

We gave ourselves 12 months to put the whole project together. Colin pointed out that it was important to involve an international group that had a presence in all three countries. Both of us felt that Lions International was the ideal organization. I was a little hesitant because when we had lost our home in 1987, both Colin and I were members of the Lions Club that we were now proposing to approach. They couldn't do much for us back then. It was a fellow AMP worker who actually provided food for my family. Even though that was in the back of my mind, I agreed to approach the Rochedale Springwood Lions Club and the Cystic Fibrosis Association for support.

I also phoned Zoë's wonderful friend Anna McMahon, the newsreader who had approached me at the funeral. Anna reassured me of her commitment to help. Then another wonderful friend offered help. Judy Stone, my mate Rod's partner, worked as an account executive at the Advertising Agency MOJO. She spoke to the CEO of Queensland, Andrew Delbridge, and they also agreed to help. Colin and I agreed to first approach the Lions Club. When I thought about the Lions I could not think of a group of people better suited to support our cause. Formed on June 7th 1917 in Chicago, Illinois, USA, the Club had grown to be the world's largest community service club with 1.35 million members in 45,000 clubs throughout 197 countries, worldwide. Our meeting at the Lions Club was emotionally charged for me. My memory of the time we lost our home was still painfully raw and it was hard for me to stay calm, but I managed. Fortunately, one of the founding members of the Club was someone who knew exactly what we had gone through. His name was Greg Nothlin. Greg was a founding member of the club who was very committed to his community. He had cared for a child with Cystic Fibrosis and he asked the other members if any of them could contemplate giving physiotherapy to a child for 30 minutes twice a day, every day. The club fell silent when he stood and demonstrated how it was done. Colin and I had their commitment from that moment on. We got a second leg up with another Lions member whose good friends in the USA proved to be wonderful ambassadors for the walk, contacting many lions clubs along the route in America.

Colin and I had another meeting organized by Judy Stone. She had spoken to people at MOJO advertising and they were prepared to help by preparing a fundraising submission. When we entered the building, we were joined by Anna McMahon. I felt a buzz in the air when we all sat in the boardroom discussing how we could make the walk successful. We tossed about a name, something that would capture people's imaginations, not just in Australia but the USA and the United Kingdom. We agreed that the Lions Club involvement was the key to the walk's success. Lions were present and very active in communities in all three countries. Before leaving the meeting we arranged for Colin to meet the person who would assist him in producing the submission. MOJO was going to offer the project to their junior staff to see who wanted to work on it. I was starting to feel like someone up there was most certainly on our side. I believed it was God.

That night I met my new friend Janet for dinner and we discussed the week's events. She was a beautiful, spiritual lady and to say I was falling in love with her was a very true statement. That night as we stood on her small balcony overlooking the river I felt happy. I watched as the small ferryboats shuttled like dragonflies across the water. I hoped that this was a new beginning. A few days later, Janet phoned and said that she was keen to have a permanent relationship with me. My response was extremely joyful, so joyful, in fact, that it apparently put her off the idea. We never became more than good friends.

About this time I received a call from the President of the Cystic Fibrosis Association asking me to vacate the flat, as a family needed to stay there that weekend. Although I had no place to go, I agreed. In some way this highlighted the need for a respite center, a place where the focus was shared between child and family. My needs as a separated grieving father had to take second place over the family with a sick child. There was no support system that cared for the whole family. Luckily, since I had a job as a cleaner with Pickwick Cleaners, I was able to afford to move into a house with Zoë's friend Michael, the same Michael who had walked with me. His parents also helped us get established.

Colin had another meeting with our friends at MOJO Advertising. He was introduced to a young lady who had jumped at the opportunity to help. During the course of the day he was amazed at how much this young girl knew about all aspects of the illness that had killed little Zoë. Finally his curiosity got the better of him and he asked her how she had become so familiar with the disease. When she told him she had Cystic Fibrosis, he was blown away like a feather caught in a gale.

What were the chances of a major advertising company taking on the project pro bono and then a young lady with the illness appearing out of their employee list? Again, I saw the hand of God at work. When he told me about it later that evening, the two of us just cried. I was sure at that moment that Zoë Reed was watching over us. How did I know? I just felt it in every cell of my body that my little girl was helping her dad.

They came up with a name for the project: **The Zoe Reed Memorial Bridge Project**. We saw the project as building the largest bridge in the world, a bridge that would link three great countries in a fight against the pain, suffering and hardship caused by illness. We saw Lions Clubs as the Construction Companies and their members as the Construction Workers that would assemble it. When asked how high it would be I replied, "High enough for little Zoë to reach out and touch it". How wide would the bridge be? The bridge would be wide enough to accommodate the thousands of people who would accompany me during and after the walk. It would also be strong enough to remain in the hearts of millions of people worldwide, made with bricks of love, spans of hope and understanding. We also decided that any funds raised in a community would stay in that community to help anyone who battled with a life-limiting illness.

Before the walk even started, the Lions Club got moving. District Governor Bill Whitestyles and Regional Chairman Ray Hogan presented The Royal Children's Hospital in Brisbane with a cheque for $25,000 towards the new ward where little Zoë lost her battle to stay alive. Even though positive things were happening, the voice in the back of my mind continued to fire negative remarks. The black dog of depression would not stop barking, "You have failed at most of the things you have attempted. You will walk away when the going gets tough". What was hard to comprehend was the following day the dog would stop barking and I would feel positive. This had been the pattern of my life. Each day was like a roller coaster, one day up the next day down. I honestly believed it was a wonder I had ever achieved anything. I began working again on my physical fitness. Although I had done many kilometers on foot, I wasn't a naturally fit person. It took many hours of walking in the hills at the back of Beenleigh to attain a level of fitness acceptable for the journey I was about to take. I had also been able to attract sponsorship from the Healthworks Gym in Beenleigh.

While I was busy getting fit I left the corporate side of the project to Colin. The submission from MOJO was very professional. Just looking at it I was able to see that the content was from the heart. The young lady with Cystic Fibrosis who had assisted on the project told Colin that her family stayed away from the Cystic Fibrosis community and basically allowed their own doctor to treat the illness. Many parents choose different treatments for their children. Once a parent confronted me in the lift at the Royal Brisbane Hospital saying I should not be discussing the negative aspects of Cystic Fibrosis in the media. All I wanted was to speak the truth and try to improve the lives of Cystic Fibrosis children and parents.

Colin had an idea to approach someone from his past. He had been a music roadie in his younger days and knew people like Glen Wheatly. He had also touched base on occasion with Paul Hogan and John Cornell of Strop. He knew that one of the groups owned a small shop in Byron Bay, so we decided to kill two birds with one stone. We'd visit Watigo Beach and drop a submission into the shop in the hope it would reach one of the guys. The Healthworks Gym agreed to put on a fundraiser. They would invite people to participate in an aerobic session for the walk. The day of the session I received a huge shock. I hadn't seen Erika for some time and when she arrived at the gym she looked ill. When she took her tracksuit off I was so stunned: there was no fat on her and she only weighed about five stone (70 lbs.). She looked like a concentration camp survivor. I told her I was being sponsored by a company that provided me with protein powder and that I would give her some to take daily to stave off this weight loss. This was the second time I was able to help her. She had wanted to do an Interior Decorators course, so I had agreed to help with her portfolio. I hoped that little Zoë was watching and that we were keeping her happy by remaining friends.

I did have one sponsorship concern and that was the corporate sector. Colin estimated that we needed approximately $150,000 to fund the project, which included air tickets for support people, fuel, back-up vehicles and accommodations. Colin planned to come along and be the advance man, setting up publicity and speaking engagements along the way. With only six months left before our projected start date, we had received no corporate funds whatsoever and Colin informed me he could not make the trip. I was beginning to feel pretty low and found it hard to train. I was relying on my relationship with Jesus to sustain me through my grief, never losing faith that this was His project and I was to be the conduit through which He could reach those in need.

I decided to approach my good friend Chris Gallagher at Williams the Shoeman to see if we could put something together that would result in funds. We decided that shoes would not be an issue and I suggested a 500km walk in 5 days. Something short and sweet that would attract donations. The venue would be Zoë's school at Slacks

Creek where I would walk around the oval. I felt that my fitness was coming on and around November I would be ready for the attempt. The school principal agreed to provide the oval for the 500km walk and wanted me to finish my walk from England at that same oval. Then we received a frantic phone call from John Cornell's manager saying they had been trying to contact us to donate $2000 and needed to know where to send the cheque. I felt that things were starting to happen and that the walk had a hope of succeeding. The Lions club was working very hard through people like Ken Bury, who contacted other clubs along route 10 and started to receive letters and phone calls of support from people prepared to provide food and accommodation. This support was crucial because apart from the gym fundraiser giving us a few hundred dollars and the cheque for $2000, we were nowhere near our required total.

Without the support of Janet, it would have been even harder to stay focused. We would have some wonderful hours talking about the challenges life would throw up and how we had both confronted them. One wonderful quote that has helped me was, "We have two ears and one mouth so we can listen more than we talk". It saddened me that it had become apparent that Janet and I would not become a couple but she often spoke of how people came into our lives for a reason and influenced us in many different ways. I felt that our time was drawing to a close and both of us were soon to continue on our own life's journeys.

The day of the 500 km walk was approaching and Chris Gallagher, as always, came through. There would be full involvement throughout the five-day period. Colin got the Broncos to send a couple of players down to the school grounds, along with Leroy Loggins. The school fitness instructor proved to be a wonderful support arranging generators, lighting and even a caravan. This enabled me to feel positive, even though I had come to the realization that I would be undertaking the long walk alone. With that realization came a few nights of worry. Did I have the courage to step out alone on a journey of such magnitude? Through Anna McMahon we were able to get some coverage from Channel 9 television. They came and interviewed me regarding what I intended to undertake and promised to help as much as possible.

The day that I started walking around the oval arrived. They say any journey starts with the first step. Little did I know what it would take to walk consistently for five days? I got some helpful advice from a wonderful runner named Ron Grant when I first started walking so I was prepared for most things, but the tiredness was a problem. One challenge was the young children who joined me during their breaks. They walked close, talking constantly, and they literally got under my feet, making it quite hard at times. I was usually relieved when their breaks were over. When the two players came from the Broncos, I got the opportunity to discuss the coming intercontinental walk in the hope that maybe the club would help me. I secured some advice on my training from the club's fitness coach, Kelvin Giles. We received some good news from Williams the Shoeman; they would be giving me a cheque at the end of the walk. That buoyed my spirits, but by the second day on the oval the blisters arrived. The only way to treat them was to once again perform my old army trick with cotton soaked in methylated spirits in order to dry the blistered areas. I also had some tins of second skin, which had to be applied on a few occasions, but I was able to treat myself and continue to walk with little pain.

At night the Lions Club lads turned out in support and I was often visited by good friends. This companionship kept my spirits high enough to continue. The early morning hours were the most difficult. The lighting would turn the trees around the oval into dancing figurines. My mind would occasionally play tricks and I would imagine Zoë was with me, and that she was watching me from within the shadows. Sometimes the tears flowed but then day would break and the rays of light, like Gods fingers, would cover the ground and I would be able to face another day. Young Ashley, my little mate with Cystic Fibrosis, came and walked with me, too. I could see how much he struggled to walk along side of me, and it was a great inspiration. He told me that Zoë would be proud of her dad and I cherished his words. Here was an example of someone again coming into my life at the right time so much wisdom in such a young man. On the fourth day I was joined by a sporting hero of mine, Leroy Loggins of the Brisbane Bullets.

We walked a few laps and he was full of kind words. It was not long though before he was spirited away by the kids to go one-on-one. He was a true gentleman. That night when I went to sleep I felt exhausted and my nerve ends were jumping all over. It seemed like I had only been asleep a short while when I was awakened by voices I did not recognize. It was the fathers of a couple of the school children. They had come to help and did I need it!!! I could not move a limb. Every bone in my body ached.

The final day arrived and the end was in sight. I was due to finish at midday. By now it was obvious I would not complete the 500 km, but about 420kms. As the final laps arrived I was joined by Ashley once again. Then with one lap to go, we both decided to jog. To cross the line was a highlight of my life and I am sure, had Zoë been alive, we would have finished together just like Ashley and I did. God Bless you Ashley. The pain disappeared and I felt a sense of achievement. We had raised enough money to fly to England and America.

It was now Christmas 1994 and I really didn't have anywhere to go. Erika asked me if I wanted to go to Melbourne and visit my friend Mike Whelton. I think her relationship with Jeff had hit a snag as well. I jumped at the opportunity to spend some time with her although I was sure that it would only be as friends, but I guess somewhere in the deepest part of my heart I hoped for a second chance. The drive there was difficult. Erika had to do all the driving because she had a manual car and I had never mastered the art of driving anything other than an automatic vehicle. Her need to go fast cost her two tickets in the two days! We spent most of the time visiting friends of Mike's. It was hard for me; I seemed to be the only one who owned nothing and I felt out of my depth in conversations. All my marriage break-ups had left me penniless. I missed my friend Janet.

This was my first Christmas without Zoë and I could not shake the feeling that she would arrive at any moment. I was battling with the grief. I needed to stay focused on her inspirational life and remember all our wonderful days together. Mike gave me a book to read called **Even Eagles Need A Push** by David McNally. Here was someone else who had been inspired by Terry Fox. The book helped me realize that I could use Terry's story as an inspiration as well. On the way back Erika and I had planned to visit Byron Bay. We headed straight for Watigo Bay and both stood there staring at the sea. Overhead were the darkest clouds, but in no way did they match the clouds that surrounded my heart. The reality was that Zoë was gone and my marriage was well and truly over. I risked being pushed away when I held Erika in my arms. I could feel her whole body shaking but I felt helpless. I could do nothing to help other than be there. It was like two unhappy souls that could no longer connect. There was much too much of a gulf between us.

On getting back home to Brisbane I discovered that the United States of America had turned down my application for a visa. I needed that like a hole in the head. I hoped that the Lions Clubs would accept crossing Canada instead as part of the route. I resigned myself to the change in route. I then met up with Janet only to discover she also viewed our relationship as a friendship. I decided to place everything at this point into God's hands. I kept thinking of my friend Pete Why and how he continued on with the walk in spite of adversity and it helped keep me semi-focused. It was like a point of reference to return to when things happened, which caused me to lose focus.

On 10 January, 1995, I attended a meeting at the Lions Club. It was good news. They had reapplied for the American visa. The lads were enthusiastic at what could be achieved. With only a few days left before my scheduled departure for the UK, they had worked wonders. Ken had put together my itinerary assuring me that Lions in all three countries were ready to support me. They had been holding sausage sizzles to raise support funds and had done a wonderful job. I then met with Colin and some other friends and assured them that all was OK and that I would be home in less than 12 months. I thanked them for all their help and prepared to leave.

I had one person to catch up with and that was Erika. We had coffee together and she did not look or sound too good. There had been a lot happening that at that time I was not aware of. Erika and I had had dinner the previous night and she told me where I had gone wrong in the relationship. I should have been more caring and shown more responsibility. I pointed out that there had been a period when I had worked three jobs: the production line at Ford, a small marketing consultancy at the Jindalee Hotel, and AMP (where the sales, were credited to her). I thought I had done my best. It was a difficult dinner, to say the least.

After we said our farewell I drove down beside the Logan River and prayed for her safe keeping. Erika, like her father, was an atheist and had chosen not to come to church with Zoë and me. But I knew Jesus would be there for her. What happened the next day was nothing short of a miracle. She called early in the morning and said "Nige, I do not know why but you have to take me to church on Sunday". I heard my inner voice say WOW and agreed but I had one problem: I was scheduled to fly out on Sunday. Thankfully I was able to change my flight date. That Sunday was best described as awesome in spiritual terms. Erika shook all over and I could not stop crying. I knew that Jesus had answered my call for help and she was amongst friends. The night before I left I was able to see Ashley and his mum. When I was talking alone with Ashley he gave me a note and told me not to read it until I was on the plane. When I left them both, I wondered if it would be the last time we would meet.

That night I also said my farewell to Janet. I knew in my heart that we would never be anything other than good mates, but she had in her own way been my strength through that year. She gave me a small book to carry by the name of *God Calling* and written inside were the words, "With love and appreciation of your friendship and support. Love, Janet". I carried that book everywhere on the journey. So much had taken place since I flew back into Australia nearly 12 months earlier. I had lost my only daughter, made many new friends and survived.

THE WORLD WALK BECAME A REALITY

As the plane took off, I realized I was headed to an adventure into the unknown. I knew of the beginning but had no idea what the middle or end would be. I relaxed for the first time in a long time and settled down to read Ashley's letter and poem to me. I could feel the goose bumps already forming as I started to read it:

Here is a poem if you ever feel sad it may not cheer you up but it will give you something to think about on your walk.

> If you are ever feeling blue,
> And you don't know what to do
> Just look in the mirror and know that you are you.
> Then say to yourself I am Nigel Reed
> And I am the best that I can be.
> We all know that's true.
> So now you shouldn't feel blue anymore.
> But if you do still feel blue.
> Here is something else to do
> Just think of all the happy times you had
> And block out all the sad.

NOW!!!!! Nigel if the poem did not work this passage should.

> "You are Nigel Reed and there is no one like you!
> And there is always someone loving you".

I'll write to you soon your Pal Ashley.

He was concerned for my welfare and he understood the challenges that were ahead. He had taken time to give something that

I could always reflect on, something to lift the soul. All that from a 13 year old! How amazing is that.

During the flight I had a stopover in Los Angeles. While sitting in the transit lane a remarkable thing happened. An elderly American of Japanese heritage came over to talk to me. He had seen Zoë's soft toy (Garfield) hanging on the back of my pack. He asked me what the significance of it was so I shared my story with him. As I came to the end of my story he dropped to his knees beside me. He then asked what advice I could give to him about life. All I could say was, "You have lived far longer than me and know more than I and just place your trust in God." He then left for a short while and returned with his daughter and introduced her to me. I was amazed! Already so far from home, yet my daughter continued to inspire people. When I arrived in the United Kingdom, once again my wonderful friends Ernie and Sandy met me and I stayed with them for a few days. That evening I had dinner with some friends. During conversation I discovered that Erika and Jeff had worked things out and were planning a trip to Europe. I guess that was what was wrong with Erika before I left.

I soon received some good news, the American consulate had agreed to a visa. Terrific! That lifted my spirits even though I had many reservations as to how the walk would pan out. I had some money left but needed it to last so that I had funds during the walk. The Lions Club was going to be putting the proceeds of the "sausage sizzles" into an account for me on a regular basis, but I needed to budget carefully. I was concerned about my homecoming in Long Eaton, so much so that I was struggling with my ulcers. I did not know how the family would respond to my plans to walk the world. I was struggling with self-doubt and worried what people would think. It was late afternoon when I arrived in town. I headed toward my stepsister Joyce's house. When she answered the door I could see the surprise on her face. When she asked me where I was staying, I was unable to find the words, "Would you help me?" for fear of rejection. I told her I was staying at a hotel not too far away. I had enough money for about four days, but I had four weeks before I was to set out on my journey. Had I explained everything to Joyce, she would have had me stay with them.

But the way I felt I am sure goes back to my childhood. Although I have no doubt that I was loved, and I was bought up in a good family, I always felt that I was not equal to other family members. I needed Joyce to offer to have me stay rather than me to ask her. I didn't want to be rejected.

The next four days went fairly quickly, visiting mates and arranging to speak at the local Lions Club. Confronted with no place to stay, my only option was to find a place to camp. I chose a place along the canal bank where I had played as a child. Luckily, I had all my camping gear but it was winter and the nights were really cold. Those days were by far the hardest. Here I was in my hometown, my place of birth, and I had hoped someone, mates or family, would offer me accommodation but no one had. What was crazy was at 50 years of age I did not have the confidence to ask. I took the time to visit the Oasis Church on Derby Road. I had been there once before and discovered that the young pastor had a sister with Cystic Fibrosis. It helped a lot to talk to someone who knew the pressure that families face when caring for a sick child.

The first night it threw it down with rain and as I lay in my tent I could hear the locomotives shunting about 300 yards away. The camp I had chosen was between the canal and Toton sidings. As a child I had gone over there with my grandfather when he was collecting his pay for driving steam trains. I'd also spent many happy days with my mates Mick Severn, Dave Gregg and Norman Smith doing all types of things in the place, we called our adventure play ground. We made boats out of blades of grass and watched them disappear down the weir alongside the locks, then reappear out the other side. We searched for newts and used our catapults. On the odd occasion we would release Mike's dog and he would dig up the nearest field chasing the scent of a rabbit. I remember once how I tried to impress Mike's girl friend by hanging from a tree upside down, but they just kept on walking. As I attempted to get down my leg became jammed and I ended up the laughing stock of all in attendance. Now 35 years later I was back here again. It seemed like ages before sleep finally came. In my dreams I was miles away in Australia.

The next morning I was concerned about a couple of things, one being the security of my personal effects. I did not want to be seen walking around town with my kit so I used my knowledge of camouflage to carefully hide it. If I could conceal a 52-ton Centurion tank, surely I could hide a rucksack. My other concern was personal hygiene. I would have to find public toilets where I could wash myself. The Lion member I was told to contact owned a clothes shop in the town centre. After tidying myself, I set out to make my first contact. Everything went well. They had organized a meeting to outline the upcoming walk. The problem was, I walked away feeling that they had left it too late to put much fundraising together. That night I felt completely down. I had hoped that the Lions Club would have responded better and it looked like I would have to start organizing things without some sponsorship here in the United Kingdom.

I needed some publicity but didn't know who to contact, the Cystic Fibrosis Association, the newspaper, the radio or television stations or a gym? It would have been difficult in a normal situation, but living in a tent alongside the canal was not the ideal environment. But that was all I had so I decided to approach a gym situated in town. The premises had been many things: a dance hall, a room for political meetings and, on Armistice Day, a place to honor those like my father who had not returned from wars. I had seen my late grandfather address those in attendance when he was the local president of The British Legion. Now it was a gym! It was early February and still very cold. I was so grateful to find a warm place as I made my way up the stairs to the club. I met with the owner, a dynamic guy by the name of Shaun Davis. He was so receptive from the beginning and so were the patrons and staff of the Clarence Court Club. It would not hurt to have a former Mr Universe on my side. One lady who immediately offered her help was Suki Achar. She was three times British Power Lifting Champion. She proved to be a good trainer.

If I could get some coverage from the media maybe other people would step forward and help in some way, so we approached both the Long Eaton Advertiser and the Nottingham Evening Post.

I also decided to call my former employer at the Greenhill's Brewery in Nottingham. The first thing they said was how pleased they were that I contacted them and how sorry they were to hear about Zoë. I began to feel a little better. In addition, some money had arrived into my account from the lads at the Lions Club so I was able to get a bit of decent food. I had been in my tent on the canal bank for a few days when I had to go to my first Lions Club meeting. My major concern was my general cleanliness, having had to use local toilets for a bathroom and having few clothes other than those I was going to carry on the walk and wear during the next 10 months. Nevertheless, I managed to present myself in a reasonable state.

On my arrival, the president asked me what school I attended and who was my science teacher. I replied, "Wilsthorpe School and Ken Hyde was my Science Teacher". As luck would have it, Ken was the Club Treasurer. The president asked me not to say anything and that he would introduce me. Ken entered the room and said nothing to indicate he had remembered the chubby kid that I had been. When the meeting commenced the president said, "Mr. Treasurer, one of your students has travelled from Australia to give you the home work he forgot to hand in on his last day of school 35 years ago, Mr Nigel Reed". Ken replied, "Nigel Reed was never late with his home work". Wow, the fact that he remembered who I was made it a special moment as we shock hands. Sadly though, my concerns were proven right; the club had not organized much in the line of sponsors or fundraising. I think they wanted me to do it and saw it as a means of publicity for them. However, it was a nice evening and I was invited to attend one of their fundraiser Amateur Boxing nights to be held in Ilkeston in the Co-Op centre.

The following day I decided to call on my old mate Byron Tully. I walked along Bennett's Street looking forward to seeing him again and having a drink with him. As I reached the house I noticed that the car he was so proud of was not there so I thought he had already gone to the local. But when his mum answered the knock on the door, she broke into tears. She told me he had died only 3 days after I left England the last time. That meant that he had died only three days after Zoë. He had just walked down the stairs in the morning, sat in the chair and died. Another young life gone! No matter what people said about Byron, he had been a loyal mate to me and I would miss him greatly. I hoped he had finally found peace. Grief was with me once again.

By this time I had become concerned people may be aware of my presence on the canal bank so I decided to move alongside the river Trent near Old Sawley where my best mate Mike lived. The walk there was full of memories, like the old shed where we used to go and listen to skiffle, the rage in the late 1950's. Singers like Lonnie Donnegan inspired a few of my mates to become musicians. There was a small stretch of sand we had named Trent Shallows where we would often swim. Guys and their girlfriends used to disappear into the small sand hills while we sat and thought about what it was like to have a girl friend. We had also lost a mate there, Shiner Bryant. He drowned trying to cross the river Trent at night. All types of rumors surfaced after the fact, but to this day I do not know what truly happened.

Being there also brought back memories of Barbara, a girl I had been in love with from afar. I wondered where she was now and if I could contact her. The last I had seen of her was shortly after my marriage to Jane. She had not attended the wedding, because she was angry I had not sent her and her friend Jenny a formal invite. Having pitched my tent, I decided to go into town to see if I was entitled to some assistance for being homeless. I made my way through the town centre to the unemployment office and was very quickly told that I would have an appointment the following week. I turned to go, a little dejected, when a voice said, "Is that you Nigel?" I looked up and it was Barbara's old friend Margaret. She asked me to wait while she dealt with some business, then we would have coffee together. She had helped once before when I was on leave from the army by providing me with accommodation. It proved very valuable as I went down with Asian flu that year and she nursed me through it. As Margaret and I made our way into town she asked me how long I was intending to stay and where I was living. It was easy to answer the first question, but I struggled to tell her I was living in a tent. We managed to find a coffee shop and we sat and discussed my pending walk. She continued to probe about my living accommodation until finally I told her. She immediately offered to put me up at her home, which just happened to be around the corner from the home of Fred, my Gran's second eldest son.

I suddenly thought of Barbara and asked how she was. Margaret's face changed and she replied very quietly, "Barb's dead". She died some years before from cancer of the cervix. I felt numb and was unable to respond, and then slowly the tears started to run down my face. It was hard to believe that in a period of two days I had learned that I'd lost two good friends. "What about her family"? I asked. She said that they were all there with her when she finally passed away. Then, like a miracle, Margaret told me to look across the street where a beautiful young woman was walking past. Margaret told me it was Barbara's eldest daughter. I got up from my seat and walked across the road to her and introduced myself. "Hi, I am Nigel Reed, you may not remember me but I was a friend of your mum's and I loved her very much". She looked at me and said, "You gave my mum a golden fish necklace". I told her how sorry I was for her loss and asked her to give my love to her brother and sister, and then I bid her farewell. It was unbelievable that Barbara had shared the origin of the necklace with her children.

I left Margaret at the marketplace and headed off to collect my belongings. It was about five miles to walk and during that time I could not stop from thinking that even if I had married my childhood sweetheart, today I would still be on my own. It was as if no matter which direction I had gone in, I would have had to aid people dealing with death. The following weeks passed quickly. I was so thankful for Margaret's hospitality. I had gone down with a lung infection and once again she nursed me to good health. It helped also because I was more relaxed. I had continued with my training but still felt weak, but I knew with the start date not far off I had to get much fitter.

I had meetings with the brewery and agreed to start from one of their pubs. I caught the interest of the mayor when attending the charity boxing match and he promised to come to the start. I also attracted some support from an Australian-style bar and restaurant called *Ned Kelly's* in Nottingham and we had organized a small function to be held at the end of the first leg from Long Eaton to Lands End. It was plain to see that the planned format had to be changed, with me reliant on the Lions Clubs along the route to provide accommodation and food where possible. There were no escort vehicles and no advance party. If ever there was a leap of faith this was it. For about the hundredth time I felt like not going through with the walk. I knew I needed to take the first step or, as my mates back in Australia always said, "Just put one foot in front of the other". I needed to set the dream in motion.

My health was not very good, mainly the ulcer was playing up, and I had not been able to train very much. I realized I needed to get back into the gym and called on Sean. He also contacted a clothing company in America for sponsorship. I spoke to the Loughborough Lions Club. They had held a sportsman night and raised £250.00. They also had organized for me to visit the local university for a fitness test.

I received a letter from Erika. She was excited because someone had supposedly gotten her a ticket from Qantas and maybe $10,000. I hoped that it worked out for her as everyone wanted to hear the mother's story as well. I heard later that it was all a sham. It was some mongrel winding up a grief stricken Mum. I had not received any letters from Janet for a while and I hoped she was well. The mail from Australia kept my spirits high.

I decided to leave my journal alone for a few days. Margaret was getting a little stressed over something and I was feeling stressed also. I was hoping that once on the road the walking would bring me together both physically and mentally. My cousin, Mike Reed, agreed to organize a family gathering at Ned Kelly's. March 6, 1995, I resumed my journal. I asked myself why the tears continued to flow. It was as if with every tear I emptied my soul. Every dream I held for Zoë had gone. I remember desperately trying to keep her well so as to take advantage of any cure, and had held onto my English nationality to take advantage of any cure in the United Kingdom as well as Australia.

I received some good news the next day. The clothing sponsor Sean had procured wanted to meet me in Washington. The Glastonbury Club also got me a shoe sponsorship from Clarke's. Sean also arranged for me to meet the food sponsor in Coventry. Greenhalls raised a small collection from the staff, gave me a shirt and informed me that two pubs were going to participate, one in Market, Harburough and the other in Kettering. Although I received no contact from the BBC, a Sky Television program called *Boots and All* said they would cover it. Sadly, the Cystic Fibrosis Association would not participate. I felt a little like Terry Fox and hoped maybe people would pick up the baton along the way. My meeting with one of the owners, Martin, at the Flap Jack Company went well in Coventry. Sean drove me to meet them and they just could not do enough. With all this support, I just wanted to get on the way.

That night I phoned Colin in Australia and he informed me that he had met someone wonderful and was getting married. I sensed he still felt bad about how things had worked out regarding his participation in the walk, but that was behind me now. I was about to start the journey of my life. I received confirmation of two cheques: one at Loughborough and the other at Leicester. Margaret told me I had missed a phone call from Janet. I prayed she would call back. That afternoon I visited the cemetery and sat opposite my Gran's grave and talked to Zoë and her. I still felt unsure. Should I walk, or should I settle down? As I walked away I spotted the grave of another late schoolmate, John Windfield. Again I counted the many people in my life that had died in the last couple of years and felt grateful that at least I was still able to do something.

THE WALK BEGINS IN ENGLAND

March 12 1995.

We all assembled outside the Barge Inn on Tamworth Road. It was good to see my old area manager Spencer and some of the staff and members from the club. It was truly nice to see Mike and Ray Reed, Fred's sons. I felt very nervous about the whole project but the time had arrived to place the first foot firmly down. The Mayor offered his best wishes but Channel 9 never arrived so I set off with a group of about forty supporters. They were very enthusiastic and were setting a brisk pace. I was concerned about over doing it on the first day and possibly finding myself with blisters from the very beginning. We had approximately 16 miles to cover. Our first stop was to be at my Scottish mate's friend's pub the Cremorne, in the Meadows, an old suburb in Nottingham. Most of the supporters completed this leg of the trip. I escaped getting blisters, but my back and shoulder were aching and I was ready for a rest. The supporters kept my spirits high and I felt more positive about the project. I also received a letter from Erika saying she would join me somewhere along the route, which gave me something to look forward to.

After I had a drink and some food with my friends, everyone dispersed and I was able to relax and have a bath. That night I had a few drinks with my friends who owned the pub. When I finally made it to the bedroom I simply crashed on the bed. I was asleep in seconds. The next thing I knew was my alarm going off. It was time to leave and this time on my own. We raised £1000.00 that first day. Day two was a challenge for me. I was walking along the river Trent through an area I had often taken when calling on Barbara. Trent Bridge, where she had lived, was a nice spot with large trees along the riverbank and playing fields on the other side of the road. Apart from my thoughts of times long gone, it was a pleasant walk, although my chest was still infected and I was coughing a fair amount. Also, the orthotics I was using, were starting to rub.

After I had crossed the Trent Bridge, home of cricket in Nottinghamshire, I was soon opposite the flats where I had spent many happy hours with Barbara. I said a little prayer as I stood outside for one last moment, then continued on my way to Loughborough. In the village of Bunny I spotted a house along the way dated 1726. That day's walk was fairly tough as the blisters arrived and, try as I may; I found it difficult to carry the heavy pack. A health food company had provided me with muesli bars to eat along the way but I had not considered the added weight they would bring to my pack, which was already filled with my clothes. Around midday I started to jettison both clothes and bars of muesli but the pack did not feel much lighter and it continued to chafe my shoulders. It had been a lifetime since I had visited Loughborough as a young fifteen year old, on the back of my friend Mike Severn's Triumph Speed Twin Motor Bike. It was the place where he had met his lovely wife of many years, June. Life was simpler back then when all that mattered was having a good time. I envied Mike his long marriage. I had not been so lucky. Either I had destroyed all my relationships or I was attracted to the wrong women.

That afternoon I was to meet Phil Edmonson, the president of the Lions Club and I must admit to being worried. This was the first test of the Lions' commitment to the project. I should not have been worried. A tall gentleman greeted me with a firm handshake and told me they had found me a home to stay in and had organized for the local Cystic Fibrosis Chairman, Mark Jennings, to attend the meeting that night. The club had raised £500.00 and presented a cheque to Mark. Mark had a son of his own with Cystic Fibrosis and was as full of hope as Erika and I had been when we first discovered the defective gene that caused the disease. Things were also a little more promising now with heart and lung transplants. I hoped his son would survive. Everything was finally coming together and the first charity was gaining from my deeds. What a wonderful feeling! That evening I stayed with Mike (a Lions member) and his wife. We had something in common as he had also been an army officer. After a lot of reminiscing, the clock chimed midnight and we finally gave in and retired to bed.

I was two days into the first leg. The English section of the project would see me walk approximately 450 miles down to Lands End at the south end of England. I had estimated it would take 28 days. The route would involve passing through places like Leicester, Northampton, Oxford, Swindon, and into Trowbridge, where I was joined by a couple of fellow Lions, Clive Brooks and Bill Cooke. There were other wonderful people along the way, all Lions Club members, committed to helping those less fortunate. People like John and David in Leicester and Bob in Market Harbour all opened their doors to help a father carrying out a promise.

The 14th and 15th of March 1995 were very difficult walking days due to high winds. I had developed some minor blisters and shin splints, but history had shown me that they would be easily managed. I saw written on a church notice board, "Judge not the outside appearance but by what's in the heart". Oh, if only the world would adopt that principle. The following day something drove me to take out Zoë's school dress which I was carrying along with her Garfield toy. I smelled it, hoping for one last lingering aroma that I would identify as her, but it had long gone. The night of 17th March I stayed at the Brackly House, a guest house, sponsored by the owners. I needed to have some time alone. It was hard to keep talking about the pain and suffering of families challenged by caring for a sick child. I needed time for myself to recharge my emotional batteries.

Oxford and Farrington were great. My knee was sore and Bill and Ron met me in Oxford. We spent a wonderful evening together and it took my mind away from the pain. Then I moved on to Farringdon, where I was met by Mike, an optometrist, at a little restaurant just outside of town. That night I stayed at his wonderful house where we (along with a friend of his) played Snooker on the same table that Jimmy White had played Steve Hendry for the world championship. Mike had bought it at a charity auction. He agreed to take the Cystic Fibrosis story to the next district Lions meeting to see if they would adopt it as a district project. Next I passed through Shepton Malet, which had been a garrison and military prison town. When I arrived after walking 41 miles, the local press turned out and I talked to the president of the club, who told me how they had successfully attracted young Lions called Leo's into their group. Unlike many clubs who were struggling with membership, they were in a good shape when it came to future members. The aging Lions membership was a general topic at most clubs. They all seemed to be looking for ways to attract young people.

The next night, after covering another 42 miles, I stayed with a really nice family in Glastonbury. That night over dinner we discussed the origin of the legend of the local privet bush. It was rumored that Jesus had traveled overseas as a youngster with his uncle and had landed on this particular stretch of beach. He had left his staff made of a privet branch and from it, a bush grew. I understand each year at Christmas a sprig is taken from this bush for the Queens table. The following morning I was at the Clarke Shoe Store by 9.30am. They had chosen a new type of sports sandal and were prepared to ship new ones anywhere I needed them. They mentioned that they might have funded the walk had I contacted them. Too late now, but maybe next time, I thought. Apart from one large blister I was physically okay, but my emotions were a little tattered and torn. I stayed with a nice Lion member, Gordon. That night I read the book Janet had given me, *God Calling*, and on page 25 I found the following passage:

You cannot escape the discipline. It is the hallmark of discipleship. My children, trust me. Me always. Never rebel. The trust given to me today takes away the ache of rejection of my love. That I suffered on earth, and have suffered through the ages. I died for you my children and could you treat me so.

The following day was again made difficult with strong winds but it proved to be an inspiring day. I was once again greeted by a fellow Lion member, Lester, and taken to his home. He apologized for not being able to call a meeting but he had organized dinner that night with a good friend of his. During dinner I discovered that Lester had lost his wife not long before, yet here he was listening to my sad story. That night on our return to his home we sat well into the early hours discussing our grief. He was a very motivating man. I was so pleased to have met him. That night as I lay in my bed I thought of another fellow Lion I had met earlier in the walk. He had lost his son to Cystic Fibrosis and had left the Lions club in his bid to move on. Though only recently introduced to one another, we stood together holding hands with tears flowing freely down our cheeks. His last words to me were, "There will come a day when you will have to move on yourself Nigel. I pray you find the life you deserve".

I remembered the Buddhist story of the mother who asks Buddha, "Why me? Why have I lost my only son"? Buddha, looking kindly towards her, replies, "Mother, go into the village and bring back to me an acorn from every family that has not been touched by death". Seven days later she returns without one acorn. All families have felt the pain of death but it would be many years before I would be able to move away from the loss and emotional pain which haunted me. That morning I said farewell to my friend of 24 hours and headed for Barnstable. Little did I know how this day would affect me? Initially, all I could think about was dealing with the high winds that attempted to blow me over and, if that was not enough, the slip stream from passing trucks that almost pulled me under them.

In the afternoon I was met by Ray, president of the Barnstable Lions Club. As we sat in his home talking about the family's need for respite care he became excited and said, "Nigel I know just what you are talking about. We are involved in a project here to build a children's hospice called "The Little Bridge House". It was the dream of a mother named Jill Farwell with two sick children. He described what a Children's Hospice was. It was not, as I imagined, a place where children went to die, but a place where a terminally sick child could go when the family needed help. The research figures he mentioned showed that as many as 70% of families who cared for those children would end in divorce, either before or after the child passed away. That was the same figures as I had heard of back in Australia. Ray made some calls that night and although Jill was away, they agreed to allow me to visit the building. It was very impressive and almost completed. Jill apparently was a very motivated person and, like me, she had rallied the Lions Clubs in her area. She had embarked upon her fundraising campaign by speaking at the Barnstable Lions Club. Over the following months she saw that one club's support grow into a district club project. Once this happened, people started to take notice.

I knew there was nothing like the Little Bridge House in Queensland, so on my return I committed myself to building the first one. I had the strength of Lions already behind the project so we had a head start. If nothing else, this walk had led me to what would be the best project I could imagine in honour of my daughter's life. Zoë would be honored to think that a hospice could be built and that it could help so many families. Now I had a direction. The rest of this walk was to bring about awareness of terminally ill children and how hard it is for families to cope without support systems. A children's hospice would fill a vital need in any community.

Over the next two days I passed through Bidiford and Bude. As before, I shared the company of many wonderful people and their hospitality was remarkable. The Lions Clubs that participated had clearly taken on the project and the foundation for a successful walk was laid. I was able to stride out with a sense of achievement, and pride in being a Lion nearly overtook me. The aching back, sore knees and blisters were easy to deal with in the knowledge that the first leg would be soon over. The only disappointment was that the Bude Club had not responded. Lion's administration sometimes means that correspondence is late being read.

Between the 30th and 31st of March 1995, I covered about 56 kilometers. I made Wadebridge and felt positive that on my return to Queensland we could build a children's hospice. The walk into Redruth made me realise what is meant by a Cornish mile; long and hard and it was many hard miles until I met my hosts Steve and Joyce. They owned two wonderful retrievers just like Timmy, the dog Erika and I had. Both Steve and Joyce came from Raleigh in Essex and they reminded me of GT, Erika's Grandmother. We talked of a fundraising event they have in Wadebridge called a Sand Castle Race, where you have to build it before the tide comes in. Good idea, I thought.

The following day, April 1 1995, I needed to reach Penzance, which was 30 kilometers away. I wished myself happy birthday and went on my way. By now my left foot felt like it was on fire and my hip was sore. While I was feeling sorry for myself, God sent me another wake up call. As I walked along in the mist a person suddenly appeared on the other side of the road. He was walking alone and looked to be in his mid-fifties. He beckoned me to talk so I crossed over and we chatted. He had lost his wife to cancer and was walking from Lands End to John a Groats. I asked where his back up was he replied, "I have none". Here he was alone on the road with his grief. How lucky was I? In Penzance I was joined by members of the Lions Club and taken to the house of Dennis and his wife, where I was to stay. They were lovely people who made me feel very much at home. That night was very special. They presented me with a birthday cake and we had drinks and a good time.

On 2 April I completed the final few miles and arrived at the cliff edge about midday. Other members of the Lions Club were there but, sadly, the one person I hoped would be there could not make it. That was Ernie, my old army mate and Zoë's God father. Apparently, something had come up and he could not make the journey to Lands End. I looked down into the sea and saw what looked like dolphins. In my heart I knew Zoë was close by. That afternoon we all met at the local pub, played French Bowls on the lawn and consumed a few beers. My final night was early to bed at Steve and Joyce's. I was able to make it back to Long Eaton to attend the party being held at Ned Kelly's Australia Style Restaurant. Graham and Janice, a couple of friends, drove up from London for the party. They were able to drive me back to London to prepare for the next step of the journey in the USA. During the drive through London suburbs, we spotted something remarkable; a fox in the city. As I flew away from England toward the United States I couldn't help but wonder what the next few months were going to be like and what level of success the walk would achieve.

TRAVERSING NORTH AMERICA

I touched down on American soil on April 11 1995 at Dulles International Airport in Washington DC. I had no idea what to expect and I was full of apprehension about the next day or two. There had been some good contacts made and if the United Kingdom was an indication of how Lions would respond, I was in for one great journey. But I was still scared. Taking the first step on any journey into the unknown is hard, and knowing my financial support was in the hands of the Rochedale and Springwood Lions Clubs seemed like a huge gamble.

The first challenge to overcome was the customs official. She had difficulty understanding how I was being cared for by so many Lions Clubs. It took a lot of convincing on my part as I had very little cash on me, and I had to make her believe that I would be able to care for myself whilst in the United States. Finally I convinced her it was charity and that I was staying with a fellow Lion's member here in Washington. As I walked through the baggage terminal I wasn't sure who I was looking for but assumed there would be some Lions insignia. The guy that Shaun had arranged to meet me was difficult to spot. I knew nothing about him other than his company name, so as I came out of the baggage area I scanned the crowd. My attention was caught by two gentlemen, one in a blazer with what seemed to be a Lions insignia, and a grey-haired gentleman beside him. They turned out to be District Governor Pete and a member of the Fairfax Lions Club Elden Wright. I began to feel more secure almost immediately. Governor Pete greeted me with a firm handshake and introduced Elden as the person who would be hosting me during my stay in Washington. Pete said that we would be touching base later at a club meeting, and then he left. I followed Elden to his car. Elden was quick to make me feel welcome. On arrival at Elden's home in Fairfax, I met his lovely wife Mary Lou. She was truly a terrific lady and made me feel so very welcome.

That afternoon Elden and I stood on his patio and I was absolutely amazed at the squirrels as they scurried up and down the oak tree branches. I judged from the artifacts around Elden's home that he had a military background, which made it easy to feel more at ease. We talked about Vietnam, of which he was very knowledgeable. He was there with the US Special Forces. My only experience of combat was as a corporal with the United Nations in Cyprus. In spite of our military differences, we had a long talk. In the evening we went to Governor Pete's club, where I gave my first talk on American soil. I have never been confident when speaking but I did feel that this talk went well. After my talk, I participated in the 50/50 raffle. Like all Lions meetings, a certain portion is strictly for fun. In some clubs it is riki-tiki, in this club it was 50/50. At the end of the evening I was presented with a cheque for $100.00. As I lay down to sleep that night I had a feeling of being welcome and accepted.

The following day Elden took me for a tour of the wonderful city of Washington. I could almost feel the buildings emitting power, with the stories of politicians past and present. I was reminded of John F. Kennedy. Where was I the day he was shot? I was on a bus going home on leave. He took me past the White House. It was a shock to see the homeless sleeping so close to the Lincoln Memorial. Elden explained that there were some no-go areas in the city, even for him. We had a very interesting day. Elden strengthened my confidence by mentioning that should I need help I was to just phone and he would fly straight out to help. I was amazed at such commitment to someone he had only met two days earlier. I then met PJ, a wonderful lady who was a member of Elden's club. She offered a place to stay should I want to re-visit Washington. That night I almost got run out of town winning another raffle. Elden could not believe my luck.

On Thursday of that week I was joined by Elden and some other Lions for a 17 mile walk. It was very inspirational walking alongside a 72-year old Lion who had overcome pneumonia not long before he joined us. We started outside the Capitol building and walked past the Lincoln Memorial heading towards our destination of Fairfax. I was so impressed with the city, amazed at the number of squirrels everywhere and the beauty of the Capitol and the bridges. Elden decided to take us through the Old Guard Barracks where, along with the squirrels, there were also many homeless people. We then proceeded to Arlington Cemetery, where we were joined at the gate by two members of the Arlington Lions Club. Over the years I had heard so much about Arlington Cemetery and when I actually got to see it I was stunned by its beauty but heartbroken at what it represented. I had had a similar reaction at Runnymede Air Force Memorial, where airmen who had no known burial site were remembered. So many young men lost in battle. I remembered standing with Zoë and Erika next to my own father's grave and wondered whether much had changed since then, if we were still losing so many young men and women. That night PJ informed us that there were still letters and emails of commitment coming in from other clubs across America. We also received 13 faxes, including one from Zoë's old school. It was hard to stop the tears from flowing, but that night I went to sleep feeling proud to be Nigel Reed.

I arose the next day at 5.30am, very excited and not sure what to expect. On reaching Denny's restaurant in Fairfax, I was absolutely blown away. There were so many people. A former United States Ambassador to Papua New Guinea, a State Senator, the Mayor, six Lion Presidents, local council officials and, of course, the press. Elden was the first person to speak. His comments brought tears to my eyes and I could see many of the people sitting around the tables in tears as I stood up and said thank you. There was no doubt that The Lions Clubs of America were behind me. Here I was in the United States of America, the birthplace of Lionism. How could I not succeed? That day saw me walk about 16 miles accompanied by a group of Fairfax Lions. The countryside was beautiful, so green and neat, for this was Middleburg, which I was told was the wealthiest area per square mile in America. We reached the State line and were met by Lou Gringo, the president of the Middleburg Lions Club. My hosts that evening were Lou and his family. I realized before falling asleep that I had already passed through Washington DC into the state of Virginia. It seemed surreal that I was moving so fast.

The following day was Saturday. Since it was a planned day off, I was able to see much of the beautiful town and to accompany Lou on some of his charity work. The first stop was a food delivery to an old black man who lived close to the Mellon family farm. Lou told me that the stables on the farm had piped music and chandeliers, yet here was an elderly man still with dirt floors. He needed food delivery because he was too old and frail to walk to the nearest store and there was no public transport. Here was an indication of the value of Lions worldwide, the commitment to help those less fortunate. After we delivered the food we went to the Red Fox Inn where I met one of the managers, a wonderful young lady. That grand old farmhouse was steeped in history and full of historical artifacts. A young surveyor named George Washington had stayed there. Much later, Confederate generals had stayed there, as well.

The horizon of the Blue Ridge Mountain was full of challenges, but by now I was very confident that Lions here in the USA were willing to support me. Their hospitality was tremendous. As we left the Inn I was introduced to the local sheriff. He said that when I reached the mountains I should be wary of any ugly guys wearing John Deere hats (I guess he was referring to the movie *Deliverance*) and offered help if I needed it. Later that day I met an interesting man, an ex-Red Beret soldier named John Miller who had built his own fortified castle called the Bull Run Castle in Aldie. I took two hours looking around this remarkable building with John, who was a very opinionated person highly committed to his project. On Easter Sunday I had a meal with another family with a wonderful little girl named Becky. She had been adopted by the family and was so beautiful that she reminded me of Zoë. I told her that I was adopted as well and her face lit up when she realized that there were others like her. I attended a beautiful sunrise service at the local church. Nature was at its best, sunlight was highlighting the browns, greens and yellows of the trees and foliage. What must this country look like in the fall? As I watched the sun rise I wondered where my little girl was. It seemed God was weaving his magic to bring all the people that I needed into my life when I needed them. In the evening I attended a Lions meeting, and as I entered the door Becky saw me and ran the whole length of the hall to give me a cuddle. It was so hard to hold back the tears. I was surprised to see about thirty people, including Governor Pete. It was a successful meeting and some funds were raised.

The following morning I was to set off for Winchester. I had arranged for my host to wake me early. The night had been a tearful one as I lay in bed remembering past events. No sooner had I fallen asleep than I heard the knock at my door. I carefully dressed and packed and went downstairs to find the house in darkness. Not having a watch, I located a clock and discovered that it was only 1:30am. With that I chuckled and returned to my bed. Obviously I had been dreaming.

Over 60 people were in attendance at the lunch meeting that day. They informed me of my contact in Winchester and I set off with a full stomach and a positive attitude. I arrived in Winchester after passing through some wonderful apple orchards and found another town filled with history. I saw George Washington's office and also the headquarters of General Stonewall Jackson during the Civil War. Although I'm not a Country and Western music fan, I was interested to learn that the late great Patsy Cline was born in Winchester and was buried at the Shenandoah Cemetery. The start of the walk was just outside of town and sadly my starting point had some terrible history. A murdered child had been dumped there. I felt goose bumps when I stepped out of the car. How could anyone murder a child? What fear would that child have gone through? The Club had done a wonderful job of organizing radio and press interviews. I left Middleburg having learned a lesson: no matter what challenges we face, there are others less fortunate who we can help and by doing so we see our own problems in a clearer perspective. I covered 12 miles that day on a hilly road with only little blisters that were easily manageable. I found it hard to push myself up those hills when negative thoughts crept in.

The family I stayed with that night was wonderful. Over an evening meal at an English style pub we laughed and joked. It was good to find I could relax with people who were virtual strangers. The next morning several of us walked as a group to the radio station. The six fellow Lions who accompanied me ensured that I received a good greeting from the media. The interviews were great and fellow travelers on what is called the loneliest highway in America were encouraged to blow their horns in recognition of what I was doing. That was Wednesday 19 April 1995. I heard that the FBI building in Oklahoma had been bombed and I felt it very deeply. Here was a nation that had responded to a father's cry for help by opening its doors to a total stranger and someone had deliberately set out to kill everyday people like those that had shown me such friendship, support and care. Like everyone, I felt violated.

The route was now reasonably hilly and my blisters were playing up. It was not long before the first car horn sounded and that had an immediate impact in lifting my spirits. I had not been on the road long before a gentleman in a car stopped on the other side of the road, beckoned to me and I ran over. He very quickly asked me how many pairs of shoes I had gone through. I replied three. He then said thanks and disappeared. As quickly as he had arrived he was gone again in a cloud of dust. Not long after that another man stopped, just got out of his car and shook my hand. By this time I was very emotional with the responses of the people and I had tears running down my cheeks. I suppose it was hard to believe that people saw so much good in what I was doing. The kid who never felt worthy was doing something of value. I could not help but think of my father cut short during the war. In some way I hoped he was proud of me.

I was making for a small place called Caden's Bridge where I would meet John and Rosa, the couple I had stayed with the previous night. We estimated that I would get there by 4:30pm, but I made good time and was there by 1:30pm. This allowed me to look around the town and take in more local history; a battle between the Indians and the French had occurred nearby. As promised, John and Rosa arrived at 4:30pm and they took me to stay the night at their holiday home beside a river. It was absolutely beautiful. In the evening I attended the Romany Lions Club meeting. This club endorsed my cause straightaway and said they would refer the project to the Lions District, which could ensure funds from Lions in America. It was becoming evident that the Lions were interested in my walk. Part of my speech to the group was about how Erika had coped over the years and how she was coping now. I answered their questions the best I could but it meant discussing things that were painful.

The walk to Romney was wonderful. It followed a river that was absolutely full of fish. I wished I had brought a camera with me. On the night of April 21, while staying in Romney, I was able to phone Janet and Erika. On a spiritual level, Janet was always able to buoy me upward. It was great being able to talk of my experiences to both Janet and Erika. I had mentioned in my letters to Erika that people were interested in Cystic Fibrosis from the mother's point of view and she expressed interest in possibly joining me somewhere along the route. It was nice to know that even though the love relationships with these two women were gone, we were still friendly. I also spoke to a reporter that evening who, like me, considered himself a Christian. A former pastor, he had heard me talk at a Lions Club and just wanted to pray for me. I was moved by his words and felt confident that this walk was God's project, not mine or Lions', for we were all doing his work. That night was spent in the company of some local Lions. Just before I bedded down, I phoned Greg Carey on Brisbane Radio 4BC. It made me feel good to be in touch with the people I missed and sleep came easily that night.

The next morning I headed for Tollgate, where I was to meet the president of the Mount Storm Lions Club. I had to cover about 25 miles. I felt good and focused on the abundant wildlife all around me until I was met by a mountain of a man named Gary. Seated next to him in the cab of his utility (pickup truck) was an awesome looking dog named Bandit who, he assured me, was under control. It had been arranged that he would drive me to the top of Mount Storm to spend the night and then I would walk down the next day.

On arrival in Mt Storm I met Gary's Uncle Vernon, a wonderful guy who was a war veteran. He took me to his home in the woods.

Hanging from the roof of his verandah was a huge dead bear. Vern explained that it had been hit by a car and he had shot it to end its pain. I became a little concerned. If animals this size were hitchhiking along Highway 50, no wonder it was called the loneliest highway! I judged by the number of animal trophies on Uncle Vernon's lounge wall that either there had been a stampede where all the animals had charged his house leaving their heads jammed in his wall, or he was a very accomplished hunter. It turned out to be the latter. He was a great guy and a wonderful host. We got along well because, like me, he was proud of his military background.

It was a strange feeling to meet so many good and interesting people and then leave them. I have never been good at saying goodbye and my goodbyes were becoming even more difficult because everyone was so concerned with my wellbeing. Though it was a great feeling to know they cared, it often brought me to tears. That evening I stayed at the only motel I saw in Mt Storm. My hosts for two nights were Jack and his wife. They invited Vernon and his wife to join us for dinner and the five of us had a wonderful time. I was pleased to be staying in a motel room as it gave me time to myself. As a guest in a private home it was difficult to go to bed early or have any real privacy.

April 23 1995 was the hardest trek so far, but I made it a little easier by not carrying my pack. Gary offered to give me a lift. The old Nigel may have taken it, but not now. I did, however, allow Gary to take my pack to the next stop, as there was a very steep climb rising to 2896 ft. in five and a half miles. It was a real test of my cardiovascular function. I just hoped Kelvin Giles at the Brisbane Broncos had gotten me in the right shape with his advice. I made good time with Gary checking on me every now and then. About half way up I stopped and thanked God for giving me the opportunity to take in the special beauty of the Allegheny Mountains. I wished I had more time to explore the countryside. That evening was very special: Fifty people, two newspapers and a feeling of support that was hard to quantify. They gave me a donation of $100 and I asked that it go to a young girl whom they knew who had Cystic Fibrosis. I left the meeting place feeling good and as I looked to the skies I saw a wonderful sight;

snowflakes were falling. Although this held some challenges for me, I was inspired by the wonder and beauty of the moment.

Knowing I was leaving this community the following day, I reflected on a discussion I had had with Gary about how this little community was caught up in a difficult, no-win situation. There were two classes of people. Those who had no work because of the lack of industry and those who used the town as a weekend retreat from Washington. Gary was so pleased to see the press attend our meeting because his club needed to attract positive media support. We both hoped it would have a positive effect on the town. Here he was, having broken his back, still helping others less fortunate. I continued to see this selfless spirit as I traveled across America. Lying in bed that night, I asked the Lord about my life choices. Had I lost 12 months with Zoë in real life terms but gained an eternity with her by doing charity work? My last thoughts before I fell asleep were, "God bless you, Zoë Reed, and your Dad loves you".

The following morning there was about a foot of snow on the ground, so for the first time I had to dig out some warm clothes. The Grafton Lions Club felt that the mountain road was unsafe to walk with all the timber trucks that frequented it. I always listened to local people's advice on road conditions because I felt they knew best. I didn't see the walk as an attempt to beat the non-stop walking record; I was on a journey to help others.

I headed for a general store in Aura (which was easy enough even though it was snowing) but I noticed something strange as I walked along the road. People were coming out of the undergrowth wearing camouflage clothing and carrying guns. The proprietor of the general store informed me that it was his busiest day of the year: the start of the hunting season. I was picked up that afternoon and taken to Grafton, where the Lions Club had a great day planned for me. If ever I doubted why I was doing this walk, I would always have this day to remember to strengthen my resolve.

First I met Benita, a 33-year old woman with Cystic Fibrosis. The fact that she survived to the age of 33 was incredible. She maintained a positive outlook, even though I am sure she must have believed she was on borrowed time. I then met Danny, an 18-year old lad with Cystic Fibrosis. Sadly, the second meeting was much different. Danny was not well at all and he was very negative. I would have loved to have spent more time with him to listen to how he felt, and why. I remembered talking with Zoë the day her friend David died. I asked what she felt about it and she replied, "He should have continued taking his tablets Dad". In the last year of his life David had chosen to stop all medication and the physiotherapy regime that Cystic Fibrosis Sufferers have to follow. I guess Danny had reached the same point as David but at a much younger age. Seeing Danny was almost too much for me. I had always tried to get Zoë to use her condition as a reason to do things and not as a reason for NOT doing things. As I left the hospital I felt really sad that I would never see Danny again but he was to leave a mark on me. I wondered how much suffering one could endure. That evening I did not want any company. All I wanted to do was to have a few drinks by myself. Once again the darkness came over me and all the old questions came to mind. Why me? Why Zoë? What would have happened if I had not gotten home in time to see her before she died? I almost felt like screaming. The drinks went down all too easily and I fell asleep in my clothes.

On Wednesday the 26th I was due to walk from Grafton to Clarksburg, approximately 21 miles. It proved to be a hard walk even though I was accompanied by some great Lions Club members. All I wanted was to be alone. I could not get Zoë and Danny out of my mind. As I reached the city boundary I was met by a group of Lions and a father whose 13-year old daughter was being tested for Cystic Fibrosis. I tried to be positive saying all the right things about a cure not being far off, and heart and lung transplants were good now, but deep down I knew if the test was positive the family was in for the struggle of their lives. That day I received the Key to Clarksburg, which meant I was given the freedom of the city, a proud moment in a day of sadness. The American people I'd met really knew how to honour someone and make one feel special.

The next town was Salem. This was the first time I had to carry my pack for the whole day. There was no interest shown by their Lions club but, to be fair, two clubs in this area had closed. Although at times I drew a lot of encouragement from the interest of people, I also needed time alone. Unfortunately, very often being alone shifted into loneliness and I would begin to feel down. The news was full of the Oklahoma bombing. Even though this terrible, senseless crime had been committed against the American people, I was grateful that they still continued to welcome me with open doors and arms. God bless America!

My shoulders were aching but still I made good time. I was met by a lady name Maria Franceata who invited me to share lunch with her. Both the meal and hospitality were great but unfortunately the president of the local Lions Club did not want to meet with me. Maria explained that there was no motel in Salem and that they had organized for me to stay in a local house, the owner of which was living in a nursing home. To my absolute surprise, this home belonged to Senator Jennings Rudolf. The home was full of photographs of the senator meeting every important person you could imagine. As I walked through the house I could not help but feel that I almost knew him.

During the evening I had one of those moments when suddenly everything becomes clear. Jennings Rudolph had written an acknowledgement in a book I had read more than two years before called *Think and Grow Rich* by Napoleon Hill. What were the chances of staying in the home of someone who had endorsed a book one has read? I am a firm believer that along the route we choose in life, God will place indicators along the way. I felt that this was one of those times. Maybe this meant I was to return to the book because I had something special to learn from it so I decided to find the book and read it again.

That night I contacted Rob, the president of the West Union Lions Club. He expressed some concern that two clubs had closed between Salem and Clarkesville and that my route followed an expressway. In order to ensure that I was safe and kept to my timetable, they said they would drive me to the next stop. Before I went to sleep I thought about how a single life can change the world and how perseverance always paid off. The owner of this home, Jennings Rudolf, introduced the constitutional amendment bill that gave eighteen-year-olds the right to vote. He had to introduce it eleven times before it was passed. He was born and educated in this small town and tonight I was sleeping in his bed surrounded by a million memories. Thank you Lord, I wrote in my journal.

I woke early and felt great after a good night's sleep. It was April 28 1995 and I had to cover 13 miles to make West Union. My feet, although blistered, were holding up. The walk was through some very nice country but the hills were long and steep. I became aware that a car was following me. Every time he passed me he looked directly at me and smiled, then turned around and came by me again. He was obviously intent on something. I was not worried about defending myself but hoped I would not need to. When I stopped at the point where I had agreed to meet the Lions members, he pulled up and he asked if I needed a lift. I replied I was meeting someone and at that he drove off so I avoided any confrontation.

The two Lions, Bob and Sam, arrived right on time. We decided to go and eat. Although very often the host club generously provided or paid for my meals, I was always concerned that I would abuse my welcome. Sometimes the club in Australia that was raising funds to support me was unavoidably late with funds and I was left without money for food. Thankfully, this had not happened very often and it didn't happen that day. Bob and Sam and I had a very nice meal, after which the lads drove me to Clarkesville and helped me find a motel. This enabled me to have a rest day where I could patch up my bleeding feet. I also used the time to contact three Lions Clubs, but only one was able to help.

On April 30 1995 I had already been on the road 50 days. I was holding up physically but mentally it was tough; my emotions were all over the place. But I guess that was to be expected when attempting to help people understand the pressures placed on families who love and care for terminally ill children. I was continually baring my soul and talking about the most painful part of my life. The journey between West Union and Athens was the worst day so far, as it poured with rain. Thankfully, my waterproof held up well. I was more concerned as to where I was going to stay. I had not heard anything from the small township that was between the two bigger towns. I thought of Pete back in Brisbane who had said, "Nige, just put one foot in front of the other and you will make it".

I have a habit of turning things over and over in my mind and this often stops me from living in the moment. This time it was the possibility of some interaction with the Denver Broncos and Erika's sponsorship with QANTAS. So many people had asked how she was holding up. In the back of my mind was the resistance from certain members of the Rochedale Lions Club as to her joining me at some stage during the walk. Here I was, many thousands of miles away from Zoë's mother, and I could not present the case for her to be here. Rod, a mate of mine and a member of the Club, was making the case for me. He told me in a telephone conversation that Erika had reassured the club she would pay her own fare if the QANTAS sponsorship did not happen, and that she would provide for her own accommodations. Ken Bury, the organizer for Lions, was still adamant she should not go. In my mind, it had become an ownership issue. The Lions Club saw the walk as a Lions Club project instead of as them sponsoring us. Very often people are full of the best intentions and energy in the early stages, but when time goes by and the project eats into their day-to-day living, they become agitated. I understood from Colin that this was likely the case.

I arrived in the small town mid-afternoon and found a store. I asked about the Lions Club but the shop people were unable to help me. As I sat and enjoyed a soft drink, a utility pulled up and to my surprise it displayed a Lions Club emblem. I walked up and asked if he could help me. The driver displayed no interest and drove away. I consoled myself with the fact that in over 50 days on the road this was one of only the very odd refusals I'd had to date. I set about looking for a place to pitch my little tent and found a strip of bush and trees along the side of the highway. Thankfully, since this was called the loneliest highway in America, I knew I would not have any noise to contend with. That night was well and truly wet, cold and painful with the rain exacerbating blisters and a very painful little toe, but I finally fell off to sleep unaware of anything that took place outside my little cocoon.

May 2 1995 and I arose about 7.30am very stiff but secure in the knowledge that I was to be met by the local Lions Club president at a restaurant called "The Main Made Good Time". Although the countryside was beautiful, after about 10 kilometers my feet were not feeling the best so I removed my orthotics to see if it would help the pain. I reached the destination and while I waited I once again thought of Zoë and how quickly her short life had passed by. Once again, tears welled in my eyes and I felt the need for a close adult relationship as well. While I was waiting a truckie backed up to see if I wanted a ride. How nice was that?

True to his word, Marty arrived on time and we set off for the meeting that had been organized. This particular meeting was held at midday and there were many members in attendance. I was beginning to feel more comfortable talking and the people genuinely seemed interested (as well as shocked) when I spoke of the pressure placed upon the extended family and how grief could extend out into the community. The second speaker talked about the scout movement and the number of scouts who had gone on to be highly successful people, which I had not realized. I found this to be truly amazing. I supposed it was similar to service in the army, where young men are taught many values that serve them well into later life.

One of the Lions members had organized for me to meet Mike Brooks, the president of a local company called Rocky. Rocky was a wilderness equipment company that was well placed to assist me with my boots. Without any hesitation, Mike escorted me around the store and helped me choose some boots that fit me well. He then told me that when they wore out all I needed to do was phone and he would send them ahead. As I left, he offered the same deal for Erika, should she be joining me. Once again I was astounded and humbled at the generosity of a stranger. I spent the rest of the day with Tim Rose, a proud 71 year old farmer. He introduced me to the president of a local beer importer who offered assistance, but by this time I was about to move on so I just thanked him for the offer. My host had organized a full day for me. First, I sold roses to raise money. Then I visited a primary school, where I enjoyed talking to children who were very interested and asked many questions. Finally, I visited a special school for disabled kids where I met a 9-year old girl named Amanda who had severe autism and was locked away inside her own mind. Watching her father with her was heartbreaking. She was so beautiful, yet totally unreachable. I suddenly realized how lucky Erika and I had been with Zoë having been so full of life.

That night I stayed in Albany with Everett, a retired farmer. I was truly impressed with the town and the university. I received two donations as a result of my talk on radio. It was always good to see some response as it made the feeling of making a difference very real. Maybe I had sowed a seed here in Albany. I revisited Slade School the next day and was able to address the whole school in the gym. Everett mentioned that three children had told their families about my talk the previous day and people wanted to hear more. He felt as I did that maybe the best way to reach families was to talk to children in schools. I shared the story of how the late Terry Fox had inspired me and how we can all make a difference. When I met a 70 year old teacher who still rode to school on her BMW motorbike, I realized that inspiration is truly all around us.

Having spent two days in Albany, it was time to move on. On May 6 1995 I planned to reach Macarthur, about 28 miles away. It was a beautiful day. True to their words, I was met by lads from the local Lions Club, where I was scheduled to speak that evening. I told them that Erika planned to join me and they were very pleased and excited for me. It's a pity my club was against it because it gave me something to focus on when the spirits were low. I was low on funds and nothing had arrived in the account, so the club gave me $80 for food. The generosity was overwhelming and seemed to be a common trait in America. The next morning I was able to talk with Erika. Initially she sounded well, but it was not long before she was crying. I immediately followed suit. Our emotions were still raw and I felt helpless at being unable to put my arms around her and comfort her. There was no doubt in my mind that parents who had lost a child needed support. During the walk that day to Chillicothe I was immersed in my thoughts, convinced that I was being helped along the way. I called it God. I knew in my mind that it was God and felt I was doing his work. That evening at the Chillicothe Lions Club I was given another donation for food and the club was impressed that Erika was going to join me. That night in my prayers I asked that God give Erika a sign that Zoë was safe.

I awoke early the next day because I had to cover 20 kilometers to get to the next town, Bainbridge. The president of the Lebanon Lions Club dropped me off at the start point. I was amazed at how green the countryside was. Before long I came across an old battleground dated 1759 that was the site of a fight between the Shawnee Indians and the local settlers. I made reasonable time and the blisters seemed to have settled down by the time I pitched my tent and settled in. As always, I prayed for all the people who helped me. The Bainbridge countryside was so relaxing that I soon dropped off to sleep.

Hillboro was the next town on my route. I felt good after a good night's sleep so I was able to be on the road for a 7:30am start. By midday I felt tired and decided to take a nap on the side of the road. There had been a warning about ticks so I was not able to fully relax. When I decided I was rested enough I started back on my way to Hillboro. After only about half a mile, a police car pulled up. The Sheriff apparently had received a 911 call saying there was a dead body in the grass. I explained that I had lain down a little way back and he accepted that it had more than likely been a mistake. He asked what I was doing and was happy with my reply so he wished me well and drove away. I reached Hillboro in reasonable shape. Euripides once said, ***"There is in the worst of fortune the best of chances for a happy change"***. With that in mind, I was sure that the buzzards that had followed me during the day represented my past and, should I stumble and go back; the past would indeed devour me. It started raining that night. I had to make Fayetteville, which was 18 miles from Hillboro, the following day. As I walked along, the rainwater filled my pockets. What money I had was wet and my boots were soaking so much that my blisters were hurting. That night I stayed with Steve and Rita in their beautiful holiday home beside a river. We also met a family who had lost a friend with Cystic Fibrosis at the age of 26. Steve and Rita were good people and made me as welcome as all the other people on the route had. They told me how they had helped a young family in distress buy a home. They offered to let me have a holiday in their cabin should I get the time to return to America. Although filled with grief, the year was proving to be so inspirational. The next morning I sat and watched the squirrels as they danced along the overhanging branches. Rita joined me and we discussed Erika and Zoë and the problems associated with Cystic Fibrosis. Steve joined us and we drove to the town to have breakfast in the local drugstore. It was hard to leave Steve and Rita as they had been such wonderful hosts.

The next day, May 10 1995 was time to move on and I headed for Milford feeling good after a very restful night. I was somehow determined that Erika would join me. She needed to share her story. I decided I would write to Elden in Washington to see what he could do. By midday it was raining again and my clothes were wet all over again, so when a café appeared in the distance I took the opportunity to shelter and put some hot food in my stomach. Sitting just across from me was a middle-aged man and resting across his knees was a wonderful carved walking stick. He offered to give it to me, but I felt it was too nice for him to part with it. As I was getting ready to leave I was joined by eight motorcyclists who were interested in talking and we had a wonderful conversation about Australia. I left and met Ed, my host for the night. I learned that night that he had lost his own son at age 18. It's sad that so few of us have not been touched in some way by crippling grief. As I lay in my bed that night I felt a dark cloud of depression sweep over me. Even with all the goodwill surrounding me, self-doubt was eating away at my mind. Would I be able to achieve my goal of building a Children's Hospice? Ed was an inspiration; like many Lions I had met, he was committed to helping those in need. His spare time was spent working at a rest home.

The next stop was one of the highlights of my journey across the USA. The Erlanger Lions Club was just one of several Lions Clubs in the Cincinnati area and what a club it was, with 120 members. The couple I spent time with proved to be great people, wonderful examples of what Lionism was all about. Smithy and Sarah made me feel so welcome. They organized for me to speak on the John Tolelke Radio Show. The newspapers were also interested. It was imperative for me to get the message across about Children's Hospices in America, for I understood at this point there were none. With the high cost of medical care in the USA, there was a great need for free care for both families and sick children.

The Erlanger Lions Club had a unique way of solving their fundraising needs. They had been given a block of land and had decided to invest their time and efforts in helping young children play baseball at all levels. What that did was give young people an understanding of the desire of Lion's Club Members to help the community. By doing this they hoped that some of the young children would want to join Lion's Clubs when they were older. Many service clubs have trouble attracting young people to the ranks. The Erlanger club chose to invest in the young and as far as I could see it was working. On top of that, they held a very successful fish and chip night once a week to raise funds for their charitable projects. That evening I spoke at the club and received a wonderful reception. A pledge was made to have the young players donate a dollar per person and collect cans to help the local families that struggled with terminally ill children. The Erlanger Lions Club also made a donation of $500 to me for food and expenses and once again I felt humbled by such generosity. I slept well that night with a feeling of satisfaction that the Erlanger Club would genuinely undertake fundraising for families with terminally ill children. Just before going to sleep, I phoned Greg Carey on 4BC radio to let him know how the walk was progressing. To date, everything was going very well.

The first night at Smithy's was a restless one. I was busy asking God for answers to all kinds of questions. Was this the purpose of my life, to share my family's challenges in a bid to bring care to families in a similar need? As always, I reserved the last prayer for Erika, asking that God continue to guide her. Slowly, I was beginning to understand what it meant to take life one day at a time, to live in the moment and cherish the small things in life. If I needed an example of living life one day at a time, my own daughter displayed an understanding far greater than I could imagine by seeing so many of her mates die after suffering with Cystic Fibrosis.

May 12 1995 was a rest day and I spent it with Smithy and Sarah. I could see in their club what Lionism was all about. No matter what position people held in the work force or how wealthy they were, Lions were committed to not only their local community but the wider world community as well. That night I discussed Erika's problems and how she had dealt with them. I guess the fact that it was Mothers Day the following day brought my emotions closer to the surface, so I shed quite a few tears. The old familiar "why us" surfaced. We had tried so hard to keep Zoë alive yet in the end we succumbed to the pressures of caring for a sick child. We were just a couple that wanted to lead a normal life but every year of care seemed like we were adding a straw that in time would break the camel's back and the family would split asunder. After such a soulful discussion, it was hard to say goodbye to both of my hosts, although I understood I would see them at the state conference I was going to attend further along the route.

The walk from Cincinnati to Warsaw was a hot one. Heavy thunderstorms the night before made it very humid. The roadway was covered with every form of insect and my clothing was very quickly soaked with sweat. I had become chaffed under my arms so the more I sweated the more it stung, especially where the straps from my pack dug in. That night I spoke to Erika and I sensed that she was not in good shape. She was having all types of problems with Ken Burry (Roachdale Lions). The fact that he did not want Erika to participate was troublesome. He still had not grasped the fact that I wanted to try to save my marriage and that people in America genuinely wanted to meet Zoë's mum. It was an ownership issue with him; since his Lions Club back in Brisbane had undertaken the accommodations aspect of the walk, they should control it.

I left Warsaw the next morning and after a pleasant walk I stopped in for breakfast at a café. The managers of the cafe had heard me talk on the radio and gave me my meal free of charge. After a good day's walk, I booked into the Blue Gables Motel at about 2.30pm, closed my eyes and rested so I'd be ready for the meeting that night. I was to meet with two Lions from Carroltown. We dined in a beautiful restaurant and after the meal my host drove me to a lookout where we could see down the Ohio River. It was truly beautiful and my host told me that all he wanted to do while in Vietnam was to be able to see this river once again. One of the first things he had done on his return was to stand in this same place and thank God he came home.

The rain continued for two days and was still coming down as I made my way into La Grange. I covered about 13 miles and the final part of the day's walk was up a very steep hill. I continued on to Bedford and made my way to the sheriff's office. Like many of the people I met along the way, the sheriff was a very godly person with strong beliefs. I spent a comfortable night in Bedford in a Best Western Motel. It was nice just relaxing in front of the television; sharing my story was emotionally draining and I needed some time alone.

I awoke the next morning a little achy and stiff-jointed. After breakfast, feeling much better, I was picked up by another sheriff whose life had also been touched by Cystic Fibrosis. His brother had lost two children to Cystic Fibrosis, one at the age of seven and one at the age of ten. How does a parent cope with those losses? After having watched one child die, they had to go through it all again. In this case, the father had almost been destroyed mentally. He turned to God after a spell in the hospital but the stress was too much and he died at age 60 of a heart attack. It was emotional saying goodbye to the sheriff. I had to make good time to get to Goshumd store, where I was met by a newsman from the local television station.

On May 18 1995 I reached Louisville, Kentucky. Physically, I was in good shape. My blisters were in check and my shin splint had eased. I discovered that the Cystic Fibrosis Foundation in Louisville had refused to participate, which was a disappointment, but all in all things were going tremendously well. I was picked up by Martha Wheeler, a wonderful lady who, along with her husband Ches, had taken on the task of spreading the word across America. They had done such a great job. Martha's home was a wonderful place on seven acres. Unfortunately, the weather began to change for the worse. We had tornado warnings and the skies looked awfully dark. Ches and Martha were friends with Ken Burry and as Ken had told me before I left Australia, they were wonderful people. They had organized a visit to the International Lions Eye Clinic, the Mohammed Ali Museum where, sadly, we just missed meeting Mohammed Ali. The curator said that Ali would be on the West Coast around the time I arrived and he would try to arrange something. The museum was a big thrill for me as I am a boxing fan and I was pleased to be able to write something in the visitor's book. The Lions Club members along the way were a great inspiration. There were many times where my spirits would begin to flag and then one of these wonderful people would be there with a meal, or a ride, or a meeting, or some other new arrangement. Such unselfishness is hard to find these days!

That evening we joined some fellow Lions members in the local Lone Star Restaurant. Midway into the meal we were informed that there was a tornado getting very close so we moved into a room with three solid brick walls. I could see the fear in most of the people's faces. At that point it seemed very surreal and I was hoping that everything would be okay and that I would never have to experience anything like it again. When the danger passed, the club presented me with a cheque for $1,000.00 for the Cystic Fibrosis Foundation. It was hard to calculate how much had been donated to date but I was sure we were making a difference.

That weekend Ches had arranged for me to attend the Lions State Conference at a Radison Hotel. It was a good opportunity to speak to present and past District Governors and National Governors.

Little did I know that on the first day I was to speak to the conference at breakfast time? Although I wanted this opportunity I was very nervous, having never spoken to so many people. I just hoped my passion for the project would carry me through. Here was my chance as there were about 125 people at breakfast. As I stood up I could feel the sweat running down my back. Initially I managed to string a view words together and then as I had hoped the passion took over and I completed a good talk. At the end I received a standing ovation. As I sat down I felt sure that something good was going to happen. People were listening and if I could harness their interest and support I stood a chance of getting home to Australia in a positive frame of mind. The coverage was a huge success and many wonderful people expressed interested in my dream. But it was a constant battle to stay focused, especially when I was alone. It was a catch-22. I looked forward to the time alone away from telling our story, but in those alone times depression crept over me like a blanket of grief. I constantly thought about the battle back in Brisbane where people in my Lions Club were preventing Erika from joining me along the route.

Next I walked 16 miles from Paoli to Shoals, where I met with the owner of the local newspaper. It was a good day for walking as the day before I had well and truly rested. The route was pleasant but in the latter part of the day the road started to climb. On reaching Shoals I made contact with Steve, the editor. He had organized for me to sleep at his daughter's flat. Apparently she was working with kids in need and Steve's wife was helping sick people obtain respite. I found that all across the land there were people who tirelessly helped others in all types of adversity. It also became obvious that there was not enough government assistance; communities and individuals had economic troubles and it was left to charitable and philanthropic people in each community to fill the support gaps. The club at Shoals promised to support me and explained that the next two towns were battling for members. Washington had no members and Vincence only three. The next day when Steve and I said our goodbyes he said, "If I had the money to spare I would give you a million dollars right now". I could see in his eyes that he meant it.

Another God incidence (not coincidence) happened when I spoke at the breakfast meeting in Loogootee. It was a beautiful morning when the local Sheriff picked me up and drove me to the meeting. I discovered that they supported a little girl named Sarah who had Cystic Fibrosis and had paid $9,000 for a vest that provided her with physio when she wore it. I had not heard of the vests until then and thought that it was a wonderful idea. What an innovation for children with Cystic Fibrosis! I believed that God was working His wonderful magic by bringing me into contact with ideas I could spread to others.

The next leg of the walk to Vincennes, was more difficult because I managed to get two blisters. I only had 15 miles to walk that day but every mile was a painful one. The heat made it worse and I began to feel faint and drained. The appearance of three wooden crosses outside a local church shook me into reality. It was time to grieve; time to cry and most of all time to ask Jesus why do so many children die? If I expected some deafening response from the heavens, it did not arrive. Just more tears for my family. That night as I sat alone, I remembered a passage from a book I had read that said, "We cannot become what we need to be by remaining who we are." I needed to focus on the suffering of others and not the matters of the heart that keep freezing me in time and allowing the same old negative companion to walk along with me.

I slogged along with floods on either side of the road. Speaking to a fellow Lion, I discovered that nothing was organized for me in Vincennes. Although disappointed that I would not be able to share my story, I felt happy to have a two-day break. As I approached a bend in the road I saw for myself another side of America. There was a sign outside a bar that read, "No Guns, No Blacks". Here I was, well into my walk across this wonderful country not having had one bad incident, and suddenly I was confronted with so much hatred in so few words. Just as it was starting to rain, I reached my motel. I had a wonderful shower and settled down to repair my feet; both of my large toenails had come off and there were a couple of good-sized blisters. Sleep came easily that night. I awoke to the sound of rain on the morning of May 25 1995 and realized I had been over two months on the road; Most of the day I kept drifting in and out of sleep. As was often when I was awake my thoughts were about my little angel Zoë and how much I missed her.

The next day my belief in Lions was strengthened when two more clubs contacted me. By taking the extra day of rest, I was running a little late on my timetable so when a couple stopped and offered a lift, I took it. I needed to be in Olney by a certain time. The couple seemed a little strange. They apparently drove along the highways giving lifts to young people in a bid to help them; they believed it was their ministry. It could have been more sinister than that I thought, but they drove me to the edge of the city, prayed for me, and set me on my way. It was sad to think that I suspected people of ulterior motives when all they wanted was to do good deeds, but there has always been evil in the world and I, like others, was suspicious of my fellow human.

The Olney Lions Club allowed me to speak at their breakfast meeting. Their cause was "Radio for the Blind". By now the thunderstorms were well and truly dropping rain in every direction and a club member agreed to drive me to the next town, Clay City. All along the roadside were oil rigs. I had been led to believe that most of the oil from this area was gone, but they seemed to be still pumping it out. It reminded me of a film I saw as a child staring Rock Hudson and James Dean called *Giant*. That night, according to the news, there was a lot of flooding. I hoped that it would not affect me too much as I was on a tight timetable with my visa.

After another rest day I headed for Salem on May 29 1995. As I started out my energy levels were low. They gradually improved, but as time passed it was obvious I was not going to make Salem on time. Storms were gathering, so I started to look for a place to camp. I came across a wheatbarn that had a sheltered area alongside it where three cars were parked. I plucked up enough courage to knock on the door. After a few moments a young lady opened the door and I started to tell my story in the hope they would let me camp there. To my surprise she invited me in and to my amazement it was a church. There in a barn was a church! They said that I was to stay at the pastor's house that night and we would all eat somewhere together. Before we left, we knelt and thanked God for bringing us together. We drove to the pastor's house, which was built into the side of a hill for protection from tornados. During our conversation at dinner I discovered he was the youngest pastor ever, having been ordained at age 19 years. It was another of those God-Incidences. I wrote, "Thank you, God" in my journal and fell into a deep sleep.

I was awakened by a wonderful sunrise shining through my bedroom window. It was May 31 1995 and I had to reach Salem that day. The one thing that concerned me was that I had no cash and I could not find any place to use my Visa card. I spent time that day with a wonderful family. We shared strawberries and cream for lunch and then they drove me to a Lion's meeting where I met a fellow Queensland Lion from Toowoomba. Don had secured the support of two clubs by the time I was ready to leave. Along the road, I was surprised when a lady gave me a cold drink of lemonade. She said she had heard me on the radio. She worked with children who had lung problems and wanted to help in some way. Her cold drink well and truly helped me. With so much generosity and well wishes, how could I fail? I knew this day that I was doing God's work. Was it my ministry to help families in need?

The walk between Carlisle and Breeze was one of the most memorable I'd had to date. A wonderful young lady, Krista Koch, joined me. Krista had Cystic Fibrosis and was the recipient of a new heart and lungs. Her story, like the tales of many others who battle such illnesses, was one of financial hardship and emotional turmoil. This terrible illness had also claimed her sister. She walked with me as a sign of support. It was more walking than she had ever done before in all of her life and it caused her considerable pain. It made me feel very humble indeed. I believe that even with the transplant Krista died about three years later. Breeze was a beautiful town where my home for the day was a beautiful bed and breakfast. I spent that evening at the Outback restaurant, which was styled on an Australian theme. The steaks were big but it was the size of their special dish, the Blooming

Onion, which got my attention. It was huge!!! I had to admit that I had seen nothing like this in good old Aussie.

On June 5 1995, I was walking along and all I could think of was the news that the head of the Irish Republican Army, Gerry Adams, was in America to do fundraising. The memory of my mates who had died in Ireland just would not go away. I reached the outskirts of St Louis where I was met by a group of Lions. As always, I was a little nervous but they immediately made me feel welcome. I believe that day taught me a lesson. My host for the next two days turned out to be a big lovable and generous Irish-American named Pat Hogan. Although not a Lion himself, he was a close friend of the club's president. The next three days were wonderful. Pat ensured that I had everything that I needed and he drove me around the city and took me to places of interest, like the Cahokia Indian Mounds.

On the second night, Pat asked me if I would like to go to the Lions International conference the following year in Montreal, Canada. Both of us felt that it was an ideal place to talk about the plight of families that cared for children with a terminal illness. I explained that I had taken all of my savings and superannuation to undertake this venture and, although it would be a wonderful opportunity, I just could not afford the trip. The lesson God had in store for me quickly surfaced, for Pat's next words were, "Don't worry about the cost, you just finish the walk. I will pay for both Erika and yourself to come over, all costs covered". I now understood why one should never judge a book by its cover; only 48 hours earlier I was convinced that the Irish Republican Army represented all the Irish people. Pat proved how wrong I was. On the last morning Pat and I went for breakfast at his favorite diner and it was a tearful moment as we promised each other we would go to the Conference in Montreal. For the rest of my journey, Pat Hogan banked $200.00 a month into my bank account. Sometimes the money coming from Australia was a little late, so now I could budget a little easier. Pat had to drive me some of the distance that morning to meet my next host, Mike. Mike took me to see the Jefferson War Memorial, which was immaculately kept. As we walked around, something caught my eye: two graves for Australians. It brought back memories of my father and how we never knew his last resting place.

My next stop was to be the township of Union. It was a hot and humid day and sweat was dripping off my hat. As I approached the turnoff for Union, Terry (my host for the night) pulled up with some friends and asked me to get in their car, pointing out the swirling storm clouds that were forming behind me. They told me that there were tornado warnings for the area and it looked as if one was forming nearby. We immediately found shelter in a school building. Once again I came face to face with the fear that these monster tornados generated. Thankfully, Terry had remembered I was out on the highway that day. The next day I saw for myself a small indication of what a tornado could do. About two miles along the highway, trees were uprooted and there was severe damage to houses. Thanks to Terry, I was driven past all the damage to a clear starting point. As on the previous day, it was hot and humid and once again storm clouds started to build. I was glad to reach Gerald, a town that is known as the longest town along one highway.

Due to bad weather and being driven I was ahead of my timetable by three days, so on June 8 1995, with the help of Pat's stipend I booked into a motel, dried my clothes and got some well-earned rest. In Jefferson, the Lion who hosted me was Mike Oldehar, an accountant. The family was wonderful and his daughter reminded me so much of Zoë. She was inquisitive, but in a very nice way. The general manager of the Ramada Inn was kind enough to give me a free breakfast. Another act of generosity! My host for the next two days was a wonderful ex-district governor named Art. We visited the State government building and the Churchill Memorial, where Mohammed Ali gave the shortest speech ever. All he said was, "Me We". I also spoke to the Linn Lions Club, where the president, Lee, committed his club to the Zoë Project.

After plenty of rest I was able to undertake the next 12 miles to Centretown, where I was introduced to former Lions International director B. W. Robinson. The walking that day was hard. It was hot and humid, my shoulder was very sore and I developed a very painful instep in my left foot. That night the owner of the Longfellow's Nursery allowed me to camp at the bottom of their block. As I pitched my tent, I became aware of tiny bright lights buzzing me like fighter planes. Once I finished getting myself organized, I took time out to enjoy the fireflies swooping down and all around me. They put on quite a pleasing show. I rose early the next day and the owners of the nursery gave me some orange juice and wished me well. By now, both my back and my foot were sore. The heat and humidity meant that I was also soon soaked with perspiration. A little dog joined me; every time I stopped, he would do the same. Although he occasionally crossed the road, he always came back. I was concerned that he might get hit by a car but that never happened. He did about 12 miles with me and only left when I went into a service station. That afternoon I spoke at a club where 75% of the members were women. They were very successful, which made it hard for some older members who felt Lions should be a man's domain. After speaking to two radio stations, I booked into a bed and breakfast motel. The Lions Club gave me $150 towards my expenses, which took some of the burden off my hard-working Lions Club back in Australia.

The trip between Centretown and Tipton went reasonably well, although the pain in my shoulder still lingered. The heat of the day left me feeling so tired I was forced to lie down under a tree for shelter. I awoke feeling lost, not sure of where I was. When I finally got my bearings I started to panic; my heart raced and I started sweating profusely. I was reminded of how I felt when I woke up the day after Zoë died. I made good time once I calmed down a bit. As I rested against a wall in Tipton, a young man came over and spoke to me. He was an Assistant District Attorney who was heading, as I was, to Colorado. Of course, he would get there long before me since he was driving a car. The object of his trip was to cycle in the Rockies, mine to walk over them. He wished me luck and I accepted it, glad that I had shared some time with him. Later, I met up with my host for the day, Don. He took me to his home, where I was able to rest before meeting about 16 fellow Lions in a nearby restaurant. Like many before, they agreed to help. After the meal, I went to another Lion's house where I met Doc, the local dentist, a terrific guy who talked about his trip down the Amazon with his sons and proudly showed me his impressive stamp collection. The next day he insisted on buying me breakfast. We were joined by Don, who agreed to transport my pack to Otterville. I never resisted an offer of help with my pack because by now the pack was more an implement of torture than anything else.

Walking along the old highway was very much a journey of wonderment with so much wildlife on the roads. I saved a turtle from sure death just by picking him up and placing him safely on the grass verge. The way I saw it, all life was important, part of the grand plan. I made my way to a café where a lady took me to the local Baptist Church. I understood I was to stay there for the night and was very surprised when the pastor asked me to address the congregation on Sunday, June 18 1995-Fathers Day.

It was disturbing how many towns along the railway had become almost ghost towns. I thought of the super highways that traversed the continent, leaving entire communities almost stripped of passerby traffic and income. Sedalia was one of those towns. We were able to stand in the middle of the main street and discuss the town's history without having to move for any traffic. I don't remember much about that history, but I do remember that Sedalia was the birthplace of Scott Choplin, a well-known songwriter. On the day before Fathers Day I gave my testimony in a small community church. I was constantly amazed at how, once I had committed to the walk, everything I needed had been provided for me one way or another. Every day I had opportunities to speak about my dream, funds to allow me to eat, and accommodations to rest my tired feet.

The following day not long after breakfast, while being interviewed by a woman reporter, tears rolled down my face as I discussed Zoë and how she had motivated Erika and me. Grief is such a strange thing. When parents experience a loss such as ours, they often find it hard to understand each other's reactions, which can lead to drifting apart. People deal with grief in so many different ways. This was very much on my mind as I talked of our loss. What was Erika going through at this point of time? Why couldn't some members of my local Lion's Club understand my need to have her with me? When we returned to Don's home, his wife refunded the money I had paid for my food in their café and gave me approximately $60 from the church collection. They also gave me a Walkman, which made my walk so much easier. Later that day, a lady from the church pulled up alongside me and introduced me to all her children. It humbled me that she wanted to introduce me to her family. A passage from the Bible was on my mind that whole day: *"**Jesus is not security from storms but a perfect shelter during the storms**".* How true that was proving to be.

The next day I was met by a lovely lady named Susan who had lost her husband at age 39. We talked about how we had both coped. She organized for me to talk to some of her friends and to speak to the administrator of a local hospital. Later that day, Susan gave me a copy of *Chicken Soup for the Soul*. Reading that book made me realize I wanted to write about my journey and share the stories of those I met along the way. Another day passes and another new face to meet. Jim Schrivers, a fellow Lion and local businessman who, in his spare time, dressed as a clown and visited sick children in hospitals. He brought laughter and joy into the lives of others far less fortunate. One of Jim's fellow Lions committed his spare time to teaching children with Cerebral Palsy. Along my route I'd met so many people were also helping their communities in other ways through Lions International. Where would the governments of the world be if the everyday people that make up service organizations stopped doing their charitable deeds? In a lot of financial trouble, I would suggest.

Later, something happened that completely made my day. While resting in my motel, I saw in the information brochure that the headquarters of the School of Unity was located in Lee Summit. Back in 1987, when my world had collapsed, a friend had referred me to a small Unity church in Woolloongabba, Brisbane. I had confided to Midge, the minister, about my disappointment at never being able to hear my parents say "Well done"! Now I was going to visit the headquarters of a church that had helped me in Australia. The Headquarters Estate was peaceful and calm, a place to retreat to in times of stress. It impressed me that they took people from all religions and asked you to love people of all denominations, colors and nationalities. They saw (as I now see) that love is the center pin and that everything is possible for a heart filled with love and a soul driven by grace. For the first time in a while, I awoke from a good sleep in tears. I dreamt that Zoë had visited me and said she was well. Each and every day, before I retreated to the warmth of my bed, I prayed to Jesus asking that both Zoë and her Mum be kept well. Maybe God had spared Zoë from whatever role she now played in the universe, just to come and visit me to reassure me. Over the next few days I covered a fair distance. Apart from very sore heals and aching shoulders, I felt positive and encouraged by a couple of families that I had visited.

The first was in Lenexa. After being rained out while helping at a mobile barbecue gathering that was the largest I had ever seen, I went home with my host, Jack. I shared my dreams and goals with him and his family. He offered me some sound advice: develop a vision statement. I talked of my turning point and how Terry Fox had inspired me. His son worked at a video store so we went and got the video of Terry Fox to watch that night. I was greatly impressed with his family. His children were so polite and very interested in what I was doing. The next day Jack tracked me down and presented me with some business cards that he had designed for me. It was once again a display of support that I would never have dreamt of before I started out.

The next day in Ottawa I met a wonderful elderly Lion named Charles. He was a full-blooded Indian with a full head of thick grey hair. Apparently, he also had an admirable military record. I stayed at his home by the lake and in the evening played cards with him and his caregiver, Joanne. All night I felt him kicking me under the table, winking at me and trying his hand, I thought, at matchmaking. Charles told me he had visited Australia during World War II at Townsville and Brisbane. He mentioned he had taken the train from Townsville to Brisbane and how he had enjoyed it.

Next I crossed into Kansas. With its long, flat roads it was a far cry from West Virginia's hills. I was feeling reasonably well and was still being welcomed at every home. I had not had one bad experience so far. I met an inspirational person named Don near Ottawa. I did my walking each day and at night we sat and talked about his experiences in Korea, the forgotten war. It made me think of my Uncle Fred and how he had to return home and pursue a normal life having seen so much death. Don and I said farewell and as we shook hands I could feel the calluses on his hands and I could see his tears as they rolled down his face. The emotion in me swelled and I uttered some muted sobs that I tried to hide. Here we only knew each other for two days but already felt a bond that was painful to separate. God bless you, Don.

The next person who entered my life would also leave a lasting impression upon me. Owen's commitment to his family was so great with his children having their own challenges in life, but he still spent time supporting me. That afternoon he organized a barbecue and asked if I would speak. Although I had a lot of speaking engagements during the walk, it was always difficult because of my emotional state. It was a roller coaster of emotions. At the barbecue Owen read a passage from *The Prophet* by Kahlil Gibran. His words about giving made me cry. An elderly lady came over and said, "Have you spoken of your dream all across America as you have today"? When I said that I did, she said "Do not fear failure, just think of the many prayer lists you are on". I had never thought of it that way.

Owen told me of his involvement in the space program. In order to ensure that his family had a better life, he moved from Los Angeles to Lebo, Kansas. What a leap of faith and what a change, from a huge city to the smallest of towns. But even though Lebo was small, the level of support was huge. Owen had organized a meeting at the local hospital to talk about the challenges faced by families caring for children who had a terminal illness. Owen was shocked by the high divorce rate among such families but the senior nurse I spoke to wasn't. At this point, no one had spoken about anything like a hospice in America. The major concern was fear of litigation through personal liability, something that was a hot topic almost everywhere.

Even the Lions Clubs I visited feared liability issues. Apparently a club in America had come under legal scrutiny after an accident with an inflated bouncy-house for children. In some ways Owen was a visionary in realizing the dangers to both human beings and the environment by pollution. He had helped a mother prove bad environmental policies in a power station which had led to her children's health problems. He had also been asked to investigate possible pollution problems with an Alaskan pipeline.

Both Owen and his wife impressed me so much with their words, actions and hospitality that it gave me a renewed strength to keep going. The story that left a mark on my soul was that of a single mother who had three children with Cystic Fibrosis. The two eldest boys were in jail and, because of the huge cost of caring for them at home, she was in some way happy they were incarcerated. At least they received decent medical care while they were serving time in a jail. How sad was that! The only chance these young people had was to be in jail. I felt lucky that we had been able to go to Australia, where medical care was so accessible.

July 1 1995 was a bad day for me. I wrote in my journal about how I had not provided Erika or Zoë with the basic stability, security or leadership they needed. Erika lost respect for me even though I saw myself as helping others. I should not have gone to see Maurice before he died. I should have focused on my own daughter. Round and round the negative thoughts churned. Once again, uplifting people appeared in my life when my spirits were low. I spoke at a breakfast in Newton and set out on my journey. At about the 8-mile mark a wonderful gentleman and his wife stopped and invited me to lunch with them. Larry had been a Mennonite minister who turned his hand very successfully to university fundraising. In 21 years he raised approximately $40,000,000. He advised me to find a Chairman, someone who could lead by example who had both influence and affluence. He said that once I had a Chairman with the credibility to ask his peers for amounts of money that are equal to his own pledge, funding would cease to be a problem. This piece of advice served me well in the future.

Although I felt positive on one level, I was still battling the voice that continually told me that I had no right to expect success. The next day was physically challenging. I had to cover approximately 20 miles and it was long and hard. Fortunately, I met a grandmother who had heard me talk about the need to help the families of terminally ill children. She wanted to shake my hand; her daughter had a 5-year old son who was battling Cystic Fibrosis, complicated by having a rectum that was turned inside out and a father who walked out on him. It made me feel that I was truly doing something worthwhile and that a children's hospice would help take the pressure off families and maybe, just maybe, more families would stay together. By the end of the day I had developed blisters again and my shoulder was aching. Even so it was a pleasing day and I lay down to sleep. Before I turned out the light I did what I had done every night and asked God to look after my daughter and her mum. I just hoped in some way God could hear me. With all the struggles taking place all over the planet, I wondered how He or She would find time to deal with my call for help.

July 4 1995 was a very hard day again, around 20 miles to cover. The shoulder was killing me but the blisters seemed a lot better. I was in a reflective mood, stopping three times to just stare up at the sky. The road gradually and almost unnoticeably climbed toward the Colorado Rockies. I made the mistake of not carrying water. Meanwhile, my little radio kept issuing tornado warnings and I made sure this time to look behind me. The meeting that day was a mixture of sadness and reflection. The president of the Lions Club had lost her husband after 53 years and the last words he spoke were, "I love you". It made me think of how much I had loved Erika. I spent part of that day riding on a harvester. I was met by a lady named Donna whose husband wanted to talk to me but couldn't because he was harvesting. She asked me if I would join him on the harvester and I was only too pleased to. It turned into a very inspiring day. Gerry and I talked for hours about a new movement called "Promise Keepers" formed by the coach of the Denver Broncos. Its premise was that Christian men needed to reclaim the leadership of their families by cherishing their wives and showing leadership to their children. I had also heard about this from other men, including Owen. Gerry told me thousands of grandfathers,

fathers and sons had pledged their commitment to God and their families at Bronco Stadium. A sea of candle flames flickered in the breeze, sons, fathers and grandfathers side-by-side on their knees.

July 5th and I had reached the halfway point, Kingsley. It was hot and windy and I only had half a liter of water. There was no cover and all I could see was the horizon. My back by now was truly very sore. Thankfully, Pete, my host, turned up, gave me water and took me to an alpha farm and factory. They cooled me down to normal, but I was badly dehydrated. Pete drove me to the township and I booked into a motel for two days. Then I went to the doctor about my shoulders and feet. The doctor said I had a bone spur and possibly arthritis. The next day was a rest day so I spent most of my time catching up with my journal. That day's page read, "My darling Zoë, the days are still hard, the sun continues to burn my face but I know that my little girl sits on the right hand side of Jesus and along with him watches over me. I asked Zoë for forgiveness and that you tell Jesus that we laughed a lot and cried sometimes, but most of all we loved each other". As on many other nights I went to sleep with tears running down my face.

On July 8 1995 I made it to Dodge City. Walking towards Dodge City was horrible: besides being assaulted with the terrible smell of cattle dung, I was eaten alive by flies. A local church pastor met me with water and offered directions. That night I spoke at a local restaurant and a fellow Lion gave me a room at his motel. It was obvious to me that I owed any success that this walk achieved to the fellowship of Lions Club members. After the dinner a member gave me a small copy of the New Testament to carry. Over the next three days I shared some good times with my host Alan and his family. They were wonderful to me. Unfortunately, their Mexican food played havoc in my system and I got 'Montezuma's Revenge', which is plenty of flatulence and a backside that felt like a furnace. I did not stop running all night.

I was keen to reach Colorado, having viewed the Rockies for many days. I was also concerned about the climb over the mountain range. As I walked along I thought some more about the Promise

Keepers. The belief that fathers had in some way lost control of their families was very strong, especially here in the mid-west. I thought it was sad that the women's movement protested against the ideas of the Promise Keepers, thinking it would lead to more violence for the families. There is a passage in the Bible that says, "Men should love their wives as they love Jesus himself". Maybe family values started to change when fathers took jobs in mills and factories and left their sons to be raised not in the fields alongside their fathers, but in the care of their mothers. I reached the Colorado border and decided to take 24 hours off to ensure that my blisters dried off and I was well rested and ready for the climb to Monarch Pass. While my blisters were healing, my shoulder was getting no better. The only pain-free days I had were when Lions were able to transport my pack to the next town.

In La Mar I was met by John, the local Sheriff. Later that afternoon we went for a bike ride and were joined by his son, Byron. Byron was a courageous and inspiring young man who, in spite of a badly deformed leg, cycled for his university team. I never had to look far to see people less fortunate who used personal challenges to transform their lives. What is it that drives them to make a difference? For me it was the feeling that life had done its worst to me in taking Zoë so now I could take on the world, for failure was just a speed bump along my journey. Yet I could not shake the inner voice, the one that said, "Don't kid yourself mate, the knock at the door or the ringing phone will bring news that will rob you of success".

That night I stayed at the Bent Fort Inn in Los Aminos where I spoke to the local Lions Club. That evening I decided to write to Joe Woblenski, a supposedly powerful and influential Lion, and ask if I could address the International Lions Conference in Canada. I hoped that my desire to keep a promise to my dying daughter would make him believe I was someone worth listening to. Little did I know that Owen from Lebo Kansas had already written to both a district governor and the international president proposing that the needs of families of terminally ill children, combined with my efforts, demonstrated a subject worthy of being heard at the conference? That night I was able to speak to Tony at 4BC radio in Brisbane and also Erika. Erika told me that a couple in San Francisco had offered to organize the finish. He was a baker and he and his wife both had committed their lives to caring for babies affected by drug-taking mothers. How they had come to volunteer their help was a wonderful story: while flying to America for a visit, a friend of theirs from Australia saw a story in a women's magazine about Zoë's illness and my walk. When the friend told them about it, the couple immediately wanted to help.

After walking through Kansas, so flat and hot, I was now in the heart of the state that John Denver sang about. Nothing was better for lifting my spirits than the sight of water rolling through the countryside. Along the river's edge and high on the mountainside were brilliant mountain flowers. I was even blessed to see deer and elks grazing along the distant horizon. I marveled at the beauty of God's handiwork and found myself singing as I walked along the riverside. If the walk was inspiring, what the Canyon City Club had in store for me that day was absolutely mind-blowing. They paid for me to go down the Royal Gorge in a rubber dingy. A man had recently died on the flooded river but the water had subsided enough to allow us to make the trip. The sight of rapids sent a shudder down my spine but, as I had young children sitting opposite, I held it together. I soon discovered our guide was a devout Christian who would scream at the top of his voice, "Thank you Jesus" every time we navigated a difficult stretch of water. Sheer rock faces in the narrow gorge made me feel almost claustrophobic and it didn't help my nerves when we were told that, with the water still being high, we could not be sure where the submerged rocks were. As we surged out of the gorge into the calmer waters of the river all of us called out, "Thank you Lord, thank you for this day." The only word to describe the trip was ***awesome***.

If I thought Tuesday the 25 July 1995 was great, the following day was truly heavenly. I had to cover twenty miles and a lot of the walking was through a beautiful valley with a river accompanying me most of the way. The sun shone and the waves had a special sparkle caused by the rays of the sun. I felt physically and mentally on top of the world, so much so that I knelt down and thanked God. I knew on this day that Zoë was in a beautiful place for if God could create such a place on earth, what was Heaven like? On my left far into the distance was the beautiful Sangre de Cristo mountain range. In Spanish, that meant Blood of Christ. It was called that because at sunset the mountain tops were colored red by the sun. This mountain range was the most southerly of the Rocky Range and had a number of peaks over 14,000 feet. I was already at about 7000 foot and although reasonably fit, the height was having a noticeable effect on my breathing.

My host was Wally Mauck, a salt-of-the-earth type of guy. I called him my mountain man. He lived in a charming house up in the mountains and really knew how to make me feel special. Together we went to a local Lions meeting that night and I saw another example of what Lions did for their communities. The focus of this club was helping people who were blind. During the conversation they talked of how to get people to donate. Wally's idea was to wear dark glasses and use a white stick to draw attention to the plight of the blind. He said it in a jovial manner, which surprised me. Later, I learned why the club members seemed unshaken by his humour. Wally's late son had been blind and Wally fully understood the challenges facing the blind. Later that night he told me stories about his son and read me some poetry that his son had written. I also spoke to John, a father of a young boy who had Cystic Fibrosis who would be my host further down the road.

Thank goodness another rest day and Wally took me into town where we had a cold beer and pizza. That night Wally and I sat on the porch of his cabin looking up at the sunset, listening to the humming birds watching Wally's two Australian sheep dogs beg for their evening meal. My time with Wally enabled me to charge my emotional batteries and rest and I felt ready for the climb over Monarch Pass later in the week. One thing that always amazed me was the number of people in America who owned more than one gun. Wally was also a gun owner. He explained to me about the wildlife that frequented his land. Bears rummaged through his dustbins and when they found nothing to eat they threw the bins sky high. If that was not enough to convince me of the need for a rifle, his story of a six-foot bull snake did. My last night with Wally was difficult for me. He had been a wonderful host and I knew I would miss my newfound friend. It seemed like the grieving process started all over again with my spirit going into the dark area of my subconscious. There were tears in my eyes as I realized I would more than likely never see Wally again.

On 29 July 1995 I had to walk 15 miles into Salida where I met a couple who were Promise Keepers. We had a wonderful discussion that reinforced my belief in the concept of fathers once again becoming leaders in their homes. The next day I was met by Rhonda and taken to a multi-denominational service at the show grounds. It was something special to be with people praying to the Lord out in the open with the backdrop of the beautiful Rocky Mountains. Later that day I met John and Jonathon, an 11-year old boy with Cystic Fibrosis who reminded me of Ashley, the lad who had wanted me to marry his mum. If ever I needed proof of the value of a children's hospice, I found it in this wonderful family. Jonathon had more than his share of challenges. He had a very bad hearing problem as well, but in spite of his physical limitations he was a delightful, inspirational and brave young man. Jonathon had a doctor's appointment in Aspen on the following Monday so John and Joanne decided to drive there on Sunday and stay in a hotel. They felt it would be a nice way to show me some wonderful countryside and talk about the challenges facing families in America. The biggest challenge they faced was the health insurance system and the costs associated with the care of sick children. Again, I congratulated myself on choosing Australia as the place to bring Zoë to live.

We took time out along the route to visit Leadville. As we stood together on the pavement you could almost smell and feel the people who had made this old mining town such a remarkable part of American history. Sometimes this place was referred to as the Two Mile High City or the Cloud City because, at 10,430 feet, it was the highest incorporated city in America. The legendary Doc Holliday spent a lot of his life living there for his health. He suffered with tuberculosis and the high altitude helped him breathe. Who would have imagined when I left Australia with only my return ticket that so many people would have responded to my call for help and I would have been privileged to visit so many wonderful places? Although I regretted that I was unable to share them with Zoë, I was sure that she was playing a role in guiding me through each day. Maybe she watched me from afar during those early years and saw me as her project, someone who often looked at life through the eyes of a child and had so many questions he was too scared to ask.

That night we stayed in a hotel in Aspen. No wonder so many celebrities stay there. Very impressive! After a good night's sleep, we found ourselves locked out of the car; Jonathon had left the keys in the car. His wife had not slept well and she was not too happy with him, but before long we had the door open and were able to get Jonathan to his doctor's appointment. When he came out I could see that they were concerned. It turned out that his hearing in his left ear was 20% down since his last visit. As we drove away I wondered about Garry, a friend in Australia whose little baby had both Cystic Fibrosis and very bad sinus problems. Was Jonathon's hearing loss a result of Cystic Fibrosis? We headed off driving toward Independence Pass, another glorious spot in countryside that was like one of God's oil paintings. Aspen was situated at the head of the Roaring Fork River, which lead to the base of Independence Pass. Although the views in the Maroon Bells wilderness area were spectacular (it is one of the most photographed places in Colorado) it was necessary to drive this section because 12,000 ft. was too high for me to walk without risking my health.

August 11 1995 started out well. I got a letter from Rod informing me that Erika would be joining me at Pollok Pines in California, which was very good news. I thought it a pity that she had not been able to tell her side of the story at all the places I had already been but was glad she would at least have the chance in California. I had not heard much from the club and that concerned me, knowing how some of them felt towards her visit. All I knew was that I was very happy. I had become a little concerned at my own grief and began to think that I should take some time out from talking about the loss of a child, even if just for a short time, in order to deal with my grief.

When I mentioned this to a friend, she said she felt that God would show me the way.

My next Lions Club presentation went down well. Like many other clubs, they donated a hundred dollars to help me with expenses. Although I was fortunate to have money from Australia, these clubs regularly provided me with what little extra cash was necessary. The next day, Wally turned up as promised and we said our goodbyes before he set off (with my pack in his truck) for the next summit at Monarch Pass. I started the slow climb from 8,000 to 11,800 feet. It wasn't as difficult for me as Mt. Storm in the Appalachian Mountains had been. After about eight miles of incline, I still felt good. My breathing was a little difficult due to the altitude but I was sure glad to have the pack off my back. At the restaurant at the top of the pass I found my pack where Wally left it and had a coffee.

Going down into Gunnison Valley proved far more challenging than the climb had been. I developed a couple of fair-sized blisters that made me limp. The pack also made it difficult to stay balanced as I walked. I had no clubs to contact on this leg of the trip and the nearest resting place was Monarch Ranch. My calves were aching and the blisters felt like they had burst but I had to make it to the motel as there was not much shelter and I didn't feel like camping out. Even though the painful day seemed endless, I actually made reasonable time. The last five miles before reaching the Ranch were pretty awful. The pack bit into my shoulders and my feet stung. Monarch Ranch was fairly expensive, but I really needed to rest and do some running repairs.

The next day I awoke feeling very stiff. The owner kindly treated me to a hearty breakfast and, with some good food in my stomach, I regained my strength and felt better. With 16 miles ahead of me to Gunnison I set off fairly early. It wasn't long though before the previous day's climb came back to haunt me. The climb at altitude had left me shot and time was getting away from me so I decided to try and get a lift for the last 10 miles so I could have a rest day. Thank goodness an elderly guy pulled up and drove me to a motel. That night I soaked in the bath to release my cramps and, when they finally subsided, I fell into a deep sleep. The morning after I was very sore and my legs ached so I took another hot bath. I had not felt like this before. Whether it was the altitude or not, I was well and truly exhausted! I was only able to do five miles. I took the pack off, pitched camp beside the road and slept for 2 hours. I still felt terrible. Once I was rested I introduced myself to two Dutch campers nearby. They were physiotherapists who had a good understanding of the needs of children with Cystic Fibrosis.

After sleeping again I was awakened by the sound of birds taking flight from the water, daylight illuminating my small tent. As I got into my clothes I thought again about how I had not provided any stability or leadership for my family, which made it hard for the relationship to grow. I began to get excited about meeting up with Erika; I had so many positive things to tell her. The Dutch couple invited me to a superb breakfast of refreshing herbal tea and fresh fruit. Since I had to keep my food stores to a minimum because of the weight factor, I didn't get many fruits and veggies in my diet.

As I set off the wind picked up and the going was hard. About an hour later the Blue Mesa came into view. What a sight as the wind blew across the surface of the water! It was if someone had scattered thousands of diamonds on the lake. Blue Mesa was a man-made lake created in 1965. The surrounding tundra looked like it had been raped by the gold-rush miners. All that remained was sagebrush and Rocky Mountain juniper. I had read on an information poster that humans had first occupied the Gunnison Basin 10,000 years earlier. The size of this lake almost took my breath away. It was the largest body of water in America created to help with agriculture, flood control, electrical and recreational purposes. The heat was almost unbearable. It must have been in the 100s and I was so tired that I sat alongside the creek and soaked my feet with a wet towel draped over my head. Although I was exhausted, I was intrigued with the moonscape scenery around me and enjoyed taking it in while I rested. I camped in a nice spot but soon became aware there were chipmunks everywhere. The chipmunks were playful, but they had a dark side. A sign in the campground stated that the prairie dogs, gophers and chipmunks might be carrying plague and that if you were bitten it was critical to get treatment straightaway. Wow, I thought, the plague! At least kangaroos just kicked you.

7 August 1995 was the worst day during the crossing of America. I was in a motel room and my spirits were so very low. My mood had been dipping lower and lower and I awoke in tears, worried about money. When I last spoke to Erika I discovered she had not gotten any money for me from the Brisbane Lions Club and I was missing Australia and my family. I looked through the telephone directory until I came across a church close by and made a phone call. It was obvious by my voice that I was shot to pieces. I explained how I was feeling and what I was doing and the message said a pastor would call back. I waited and waited with no response. It had been hard having been on the road since January and constantly talking about the loss of Zoë and I found myself craving time alone but, when I was alone I became emotional and lonely. The only answer was to sleep; at least my dreams might turn out to be positive. I booked into a campground in a very nice town called Montrose where I was to meet Gary Sumner, my host for a couple of days. I made my way through town to Harvey's Coffee Shop where I introduced myself. Harvey had been at school with Gary and I was able to talk to Gary on the phone. Harvey was a very nice guy. He gave me a local wrestling team T shirt as a memento.

Gary picked me up and took me to his home, where I was to stay. That night I spoke at the local Lions Club where I met many nice people including Gary's father. Gary and Melody, his wonderful wife were a terrific Christian couple. They were one of the families along the way who left their special mark on me. These Lions organized a meeting for me with the local television station that went well. All in all this leg of the trip had lacked media coverage because the highway was much quieter than the superhighways and the communities were much smaller, though very friendly and supportive.

August 10 1995 was a special day. Gary and I drove to Yankee Boy Basin where I was stunned to see a valley filled with mountain flowers and deer surrounded by majestic peaks that were blanketed by white silken snow. With my heart still fighting for oxygen, Gary and

I set out for a ledge. The basin was situated between 11,500 feet and 12,000 feet and my lungs were feeling every foot as we climbed. I tried to remain calm and in control but shale underfoot made climbing a bit dodgy. When we finally got to a safe spot, all I could do was look in awe of the sheer beauty of our planet earth. We sat there and watched two deer tangle antlers below us. They were either unaware or not concerned at our presence. It was hard to imagine anyone wanting to end their lives violently. Again, I was concerned about how many people owned guns and how strong the hunting and gun lobbies were. I had had my share of guns and shooting in the armed forces. 7.62mm, 38mm, 30 calibers, even 120 pounders. Once I left the service I never once craved to own a gun. The taking of any form of life is not a pretty sight. Looking down this valley all I could see was beauty. Gary and I talked about God and beauty as we ate lunch in full view of mountain peaks over 13,500 feet high. The air we breathed felt cool and clear. I still carry a clear memory of that day and I hope it stays with me always.

That night at dinner we talked about the challenges that faced me and how it was possible to rebuild broken relationships. Later that night Gary drove me to another fellow Lions house. Carl also had a very friendly family. The next day I was taken to see the town of Telluride. Oprah had just had a house built there not long before I was there. Once again I was awed by the beauty of Colorado. We had a wonderful time and it was a most welcome day off. In the evening I had dinner with Gary, Melody and some of their friends who had gone through separation and divorce and were now remarried and I was hopeful that maybe Erika and I could do the same thing. I found out that Gary and Melody were going to Montreal for the international Lions Conference so I knew I would get an opportunity to meet these wonderful people again. The next morning both Gary and Melody walked with me and as we discussed the possibility of young Lions members adopting Children's Hospice as an international project. We all felt that the younger Lions needed something that they could lay claim too. The older generation seemed reluctant to allow that to happen. I decided to surround myself with bright focused young people to establish Zoë's hospice. I wanted to embrace and channel their energy, vision and drive.

On August 14 1995, Lions District Governors took me on a trip of a lifetime: National Monument and Grand Mesa. We took a 63 mile drive along the Grand Mesa Byway, a wilderness playground blanketed in wild flowers surrounded by Aspen forests. National Monument covered 20,454 acres of magnificent wilderness. Many years earlier, the Ute Indians had made a home here and called it Thunder Mountain. The next day I spoke at the Junction City Lions Club about a children's hospice. Like many before them, the challenge was to keep the momentum going long after I had passed through. That night I received a phone call from Jim Bury, my American coordinator. He had nothing organized in California and there was only $200 left in the kitty. Only one thing had changed and that was Erika arriving in California. What amazed me was the lack of understanding or compassion for Zoë's mother. As much as the club had done for me; I could not help but feel angry. I wrote to Bill Wonder the International President of Lions to see if the organization would consider adopting Children's Hospice as an international project.

Grand Junction to Fruita was approximately 12 miles. I booked into a motel and the club organized a picnic at a local park named (strangely enough) Reed Park. That night I was picked up at 5.30pm. I was still concerned about money and a lack of interest being shown in California. What made it even stranger was how well I had been received elsewhere. It was not consistent with other Clubs. Not one person. I just could not believe it. On August 19 1995 I received $200 and some phone cards from Pat Hogan but nothing else came from my own club. I called Janet, my wonderful friend back in Brisbane. She was moving and I might not see her again, but she had been a great friend teaching me much about how people come in and out of our lives at exactly the right time. Two new Lions friends agreed to form a committee to look at helping families in trouble. That made me feel we were reaching some hearts; maybe things in America would change regarding Children's Hospice. If a hospice ever develops, it will have to offer counseling. Although I had spent lots of time talking about our loss as parents, I had not had time to discuss my grief. I was not sure where I should be in my own journey with grieving, all I knew was that most nights I would cry and ask for forgiveness. Almost every time I spoke to Erika I broke down in tears. I was told that fathers proved the most difficult to counsel and it seemed to be true in my case.

The club felt that the next stretch was too dangerous to travel unescorted so they decided to drive me 120 miles. I must admit that I did not fight to walk. It would be nice to be a tourist for a day. Nevada was a very different landscape. The terrain was very rugged and in many places isolated and the Lions Club would not take the responsibility for me being out on the highway alone. Water was by far the main issue. On August 30 1995 I set out for Lake Tahoe. The landscape changed again from desert to beautiful pines. As I climbed up to the crest of the mountain range the most beautiful sight came into view, Lake Tahoe. I was getting close to meeting Erika and that meant that I had crossed America. It was becoming obvious that this leg of the journey may not be supported. Thankfully because of Pat Hogan's $200 I was able to book into a cheap hotel ($20) in Reno Nevada. The following day I was going to make for Strawberry and this entailed a fair bit of climbing but I was walking on clouds in the knowledge that I would be seeing Erika soon. There had still been no contact from my Lions club in Rochedale and this did create some concern. How was I to get from San Francisco to Los Angeles?

September 1 1995 I awoke early and was on the road by 7.30am. The walk into Pollock Pines was a truly beautiful experience as the road followed a river. I traveled about 10 miles before coming upon a nice restaurant where I was able to take a short rest. As usual, when I took a rest from the walk afterward it seemed even harder but with the knowledge that Erika was in America and just one day away I felt happy. Before catching up with my next Lion contact, Mike, I managed to soak my feet in an ice cold stream, which felt absolutely marvelous. That night I stayed with Mike and spent some time talking to his son, a terrific young man. Later I spoke to Erika and both of us were excited at meeting up. Erika had received her boots from the

Rocky Boot Company, which had been great about supplying both Erika and me with boots.

The next day I reached my next stop, the home of Adel. She was a wonderful lady who had lost her husband late in life and had taken up painting. She had blossomed into quite an artist. No other Lions contacted us, which truly worried me. We still had a long way to go and Erika was now going to be walking with me. The following morning Adel drove me to the T Bar restaurant to meet Erika. I felt so nervous my stomach was churning. Erika was being driven to the restaurant by Linda, the lady from San Leandro, California, and Linda's mum. The time seemed to drag. Every time the door opened I would lean over to see if it was Erika. Finally she walked in, looking great as usual. As I held her, the tears flowed and I found it hard to talk, choking on my words. It felt like a lifetime since I had left Australia to start this pilgrimage. After a short time talking we set off all together for Adel's house, where she had organized a barbeque. A great group of people made the day wonderful. Linda guaranteed us that we would have a wonderful finish in San Leandro and set off for her home.

That night we just sat and talked. I had so much to tell Erika. We both shared the same dream now for Erika had visited The Little Bridge House and met Jill Farwell the founder. The main piece of advice Jill gave Erika was that we should keep control of our dream. That was so true but in the future we discovered how difficult it was to do. The next day we set out on our walk for San Francisco. After about 12 miles Erika was feeling the heat and her feet hurt. We knew no one to contact in Lions and there seemed to be very few places to stay so there was a decision to make. We decided to keep walking but attempt to get a lift to Sacramento where we had a contact with Lions. Apparently they had been contacted by Australia but there had not been any follow up. After another four miles we got a lift into Sacramento. We found the cheapest motel we could and booked in, then spent a good hour making phone calls in a bid to make contact with some Lions Club members. I just could not believe that after the wonderful reception across America, the last few days would not be in the company of fellow Lions, who had been my main support.

Since we couldn't make contact with anyone, Erika and I decided to share the cost and get a bus up to Tahoe and spend a couple of days together. There was a risk with the money but, thankfully, Pat Hogan helped me once again. It would have been impossible had he not come to our rescue. Although elated at seeing and spending time with Erika, I could not help but feel a huge disappointment in this section of the walk. We had to be in San Leandro California by 10 September, 1995 and I knew we could not do it alone.

Luckily we made our destination of San Leandro on time and as we walked toward our finish point we saw police cars and fire engines. We did not think that it had anything to do with us until we turned the corner onto the park and saw the banner welcoming us to a wonderful reception. Along with Mayor Helen Corbett and the fire and police chiefs, plus many other everyday people turned out to greet us. I was given a letter that proclaimed the 10 September 1995 as Nigel Reed Day in San Leandro. To say I was proud and elated was an understatement. The celebration put us in touch with the spirits of all those who had helped along the way throughout the USA. We were able to spend a few days with Linda and her husband. Both of them were very special people; they cared for twin babies who were born drug-addicted and sickly.

We continued to try and identify a Lions Club, to no avail. We never received any instructions on how we would travel from San Francisco to Los Angeles. With that in mind we decided to hire a car and drive Pacific Highway 1 down the coast. I felt I had earned the right to a little time to grieve with the mother of the little girl who had inspired this journey. I hoped maybe, just maybe, that Erika and I could resolve some of our issues and get back together. It proved to be a very special time. We talked not only about our loss, but also our dreams for other parents and their children. It was respite time, our first genuine holiday since Zoë was born. We could smell the roses and feel the cool ocean breeze on our faces. I had to make another decision and that was to cancel my departure time by one day to fly the same day as Erika. I was not going to leave her alone in Los Angeles. Like me she was still very tender. We had not been able to have Erika share her story to Lions Clubs, but we had been able to rebuild a friendship, something we both felt Zoë would want.

On 17 September, as I sat on board the flight home to Australia, I felt totally focused and committed on building a children's hospice in Queensland. I had been privileged to meet so many positive people who, in their own way, were changing their world and in so doing, changing the planet. Although Erika and I had a nice time together it was just as friends and nothing more. America had been a place of beauty, diversity, hope and support. On the other hand, it was also the place I had seen a sign saying No Blacks or Guns, a place where the FBI building was blown up by an American, a place where poverty still existed right outside the White House. I remembered that mother who felt that her sons were better off in jail because she could not afford the healthcare required to treat their Cystic Fibrosis. Even so, knowing all this those people who had been there for me had given me the strength to pursue my dream. God bless you, America.

THE AUSTRALIAN LEG
OF THE WORLD WALK

We were three hours late flying into Sydney. Erica flew back to Brisbane straight away and as there was nobody scheduled to pick me up I thought I would take a taxi to the hotel. Suddenly I heard a familiar voice. My mate Greg Nothling had come with both of his daughters, his wife and fellow Lion Charlie, a wonderful guy. After making myself comfortable at the hotel, I was told I was speaking at the Parramatta Returned Service League Club. According to the lads, the talk went well. All those present understood the concept of children's hospice. Dr Stephens, a physician who was in charge of the proposed New South Wales children's hospice, Bear Cottage, had previously addressed the club. After the meeting, all of us felt good about the progress being made.

The following day Greg organized a trip to the caves in the Blue Mountains, although his daughter and I did not really want to go. He was so insistent we both agreed to go. It proved to be a very nice trip, even though I was very tired after the long flight and a fitful sleep that was disrupted by Charlie's snoring. At home after the outing we sat and had a few drinks. I have learnt over the years that alcohol will free people to talk openly, and this night was such an occasion for Greg. He talked freely about his lack of confidence in my leadership ability and how he felt he might be better suited to take the project further. I saw for the first time the challenge that many visionaries face. My good friend Colin Walker calls it, "The Cuckoo Syndrome". As you may know, a cuckoo very rarely builds its own nest; it waits until some other bird has built theirs then swoops in and evicts the other bird to claim the nest as its own. This behavior is very prevalent in the human race. Very often a person will develop a vision, do all the hard work, then out of the blue others will turn up to claim the idea as their own. Greg was the first of many cuckoos along the way. I was a day late arriving in Australia and it was plain to see that the guys from my Lions Club were not happy about the fact that I had waited and flown back the same day as Erika. The Lions Club District Governor asked, "how did those loud Americans treat you" to which I responded, "if the Australian Lions do half as much as their American brothers, we will do very well". I guess the reception back in Australia was a letdown. There had been far too much politics involved with Australia, unlike both England and the United States where Lion members responded with great support.

Not long after I took to the road it became noticeable that drivers here in Australia were less careful than those in the other two countries. Within 30 minutes the occupants of two cars yelled abusive comments as they drove close enough by me too make me jump aside. I began to feel a sense of concern: how would I go about settling in here again, never mind achieving this enormous goal of building a children's hospice?

I was also looking forward to meeting up with Erika again at the Lions Convention in Dalby, Queensland. Erika, Rod and Colin, who represented me in my absence, had encountered some difficulties in dealing with some of the Lions members. On arriving in Dalby we soon discovered accommodations were at a premium but fortunately we were able to get rooms in an old bush hotel. The march into Dalby was an uplifting event. I hadn't felt such a sense of pride since walking into San Leandro. It is hard to describe the effect it had with the pent-up emotions I had carried for seven months. To say I shed some tears was an understatement. I just wished inside that I had my daughter walking along side of me. I was informed that I would be able to address the conference. Although I had by now spoken on many occasions, I was very nervous this time. Then I stood up on the stage, looked out into the group and felt a sense of achievement. I was almost home! I knew this was an important speech. If I could secure the support of a Lions District Governor, I had a chance of getting the project off the ground sooner than without his support. When I finished I felt that maybe, just maybe, I had said all the right things. As the District Governor stood up to say thank you to me I was left in no doubt of his support. Every word of support was engulfed in tears that flowed freely down his cheeks. The hospice was supported by the District and the Rochedale Springwood Club adopted it as a project.

A few days later I met up with Erika on the road and we spent some time together at the dam where I had previously gone with Zoë at her school camp. It was the place where she climbed to the top of a mountain. Although she was the last to the top, she made it where others failed. Erika told me that the Rochedale Lions Club, along with my friends, had organized for us all to march into Zoë's school. Our greeting was the greeting to beat all greetings. There was a band, many school children and friends, the press and of course Lions Club members. If I had felt proud in Dalby, what I felt here in Daisy Hill was spine-tingling. If only all of the people whose pride I had chased since childhood were looking down on me. More than anything I hoped that Zoë was in their company. I had kept my promise and out of that I had found some much needed self-respect. As I walked up the drive between the rows of people escorted by my friend's daughter Lauren, I saw ahead a beautiful garden with a large sign that read "In memory of Zoë Reed." Some of her school mates stood beside the sign. Every blister, every tear had been worth it. I thought of the numerous hands of support, and the well-wishers across the world as I stood with Erika alongside the garden. If not for the Lions, I could not have done it. I saw my friend Janet in the crowd, but was unable to speak to her that day. What must she have thought? I thought of my father, who had never seen his Son or Granddaughter. I hoped he was proud of all of us.

THE BIRTH OF A DREAM

"It's better to create than to be learned: Creating is the essence of Life." Reinhold Nelbuhr.

The first couple of weeks back in Australia after the walk were hard to adjust to and every moment was such an anti climax. Even now I cannot remember where I stayed during those early weeks. It was all a haze. My emotions were all over the place. Then things started moving again. One of the Lions contacted me to say that a Dr. Ian Waugh had seen me on television as I approached Brisbane and wanted to talk to me. Then Colin, my mate who had helped during the walk, offered his wealth of experience with associations. I had no money or work but the Lions once again came to my rescue. They knew someone who had an empty house that I could live in and they could also help with furnishings. The hardest thing of all was the isolation from extended family and friends. I did not want to pester those people who had already given so much of themselves.

I sat down one evening and wrote down some thoughts about how I should go about selling my dream to build a children's hospice. I realized that I knew little of the technical data required to build a team. At the same time, I remembered something Henry Ford had said when asked about his knowledge about building a car. He had replied, "I do not need to know it all, I just need a phone and to surround myself with people who do know". I needed to form a steering committee and secure some seeding funds. I had a little money in Zoë's bank account so I went to the local Commonwealth Bank and spoke to the manager. I asked if she would be interested in helping and, to my surprise, she offered to give us advice for free. So we had $200.00 and free advice to kick us off. One of the people who had been a source of support came to mind, Rod's partner Judy Stone. Judy was an account director at MOJO Advertising, the company that had produced the brochure for the walk.

One of the members of my Lions Club called and told me I was to receive the Richardson Award, the highest award in Lionism in Australia, at District Governors Presentation Night. It was an honour but I felt sad. I had not been able to maintain a regular appearance at the club because I was so short of money. I was able to catch up with Janet, who had taken care of my car while I was away. It needed some work but I would get that done later. We had a couple of meals together but it was obvious that Janet and I were not going to be a couple. It was hard for me because we had been close, but she had moved on and there was a new man in her life. Once again I had to accept that people come into our lives and leave our lives at the right time. This was so true of my friendship with Janet. We wished each other well and said our goodbyes So many memories from that short relationship.

That night was hard and I felt alone and empty. I still had a drive from within to have a family of my own. I believed the only way I could be happy was to have a woman in my life. I learned that Ashley's mum had moved on, too. She had met someone she was happy with and Ashley finally had a father figure in his life. I went back to my church again now that I had a car. I asked Pastor Steve, who had officiated at Zoë's funeral, if he could help us with our first meeting. He was only too happy to, so we had a venue. Now all that was left was to ask Colin to put a list together of people to notify who might want to help. Then out of the blue another surprise. Judy told me I was to speak at the Brisbane Advertising Lunch. Apparently I was the second speaker, the first being Cheryl Kernow, a Federal Labour Minister of Parliament. According to Judy, it was an opportunity to address some of the leading business people in Queensland. My time slot was supposed to be for 15 minutes but once again fate took control. Cheryl Kernow had to leave early so I was asked to talk for a little longer.

Standing there I was very nervous. I held my breath to steady myself. As I looked down I noticed Bruce Paige, the newsreader. I started by saying I can see sitting down to my right "Brucie Baby" (Bruce Paige). He had met Zoë during the filming of a documentary about children with Cystic Fibrosis that Anna McMahon had made.

Zoë had a little girls crush on him and always called him "Brucie Baby." It was the perfect lead-in for me. It gave me the steadiness to be able to continue and get through the experiences I had to talk about. By the end, I was emotionally drained but when I received a good ovation I also felt exhilarated because it went better than I had expected. I was shocked afterwards when so many people handed me their cards. They would become my circle of influence. Alan Welsh from the Premiers Department; Gary Ward, the Queensland General Manager of APN (Australian Provincial Newspapers); Lisa Bennetts from Qantas, and more. I was told to leave a note on the table where the General Manager of the Courier Mail sat, so off I went and did just that. The lunch was a huge success and we walked away with a circle of contacts and a few thousand dollars.

Sometime later when Colin approached the Courier Mail General Manager to help us he remarked that what I was doing would not bring my daughter back. I guess he was right about that, but what we were doing was trying to make a difference for other suffering families. It amazes me when people feel they know another person's reasons for doing things. Yes, there was a reason for me to create a children's hospice in Queensland and no, it would not bring Zoë back. It had everything to do with helping other families whose lives were affected by children with life-limiting Illnesses. And just maybe these families would gain enough respite from the grueling routines of their lives to be able to survive in their relationships. That meeting was followed by a smaller meeting at Liberty Church in Loganholme, where I met Dr. Ian Waugh for the first time. He proved to be a wealth of information and a strong believer in children's hospices.

Still unemployed, I was finding it hard to travel around and meet with the people I needed to meet. Then one night as I sat with Colin enjoying a bottle of wine he told me he had applied for a position with a new pay television company, Austar. Since Colin was pivotal to the hospice cause, it sent a shudder down my spine because he would be shifting to Toowoomba if he got the job. In spite of my fears, I told him I was all for him and wanted him to succeed. I continued to make contact with people I met through public and business meetings. Most were helpful and I listened intently to all the advice they gave me. They all promised to be of help once the charity was founded and, true to their words, most of them came on board in some way or another.

I met with Alan Welsh in the Queensland Premiers department who said that there were a few options he could explore. He knew of land that might be available and then assured me that he would do his best to help us achieve our goal. After that meeting I walked down Queen Street full of a good feeling. To say I was on a high was an understatement. For the first time I was starting to believe we had a chance even though it was to be from humble beginnings. Over the next few weeks I stayed with Rod, but it was not the ideal situation so I decided to look for accommodations of my own. Rod and I found a place for me to board at close to the city so I'd have close easy access to the business world, but it was a disaster. One night I got caught in a very heavy rainstorm and when I got home I removed my shoes but forgot to remove my socks. As a result, I left wet footprints on the carpet from my socks. The following morning the lady of the house got very angry and threw my clothes out of the window. When I stepped outside to retrieve my belongings, she locked me out and I lost many personal items, none more valuable than a letter from Zoë thanking me for loving and caring for her.

Sometime after this I received a call from Colin saying he got the position of Manager with Austar in Toowoomba and asked if I would like a job as Warehouse Manager. I was hesitant at first, but Colin said I needed to earn a living to be of any use. Once I arrived in Toowoomba I was able to stay with Colin until I found my own place. For the first time in a long time, I felt a little secure and settled. I had work and a steady income. It was a busy time; Austar was getting ready for the grand opening of the Toowoomba branch. The CEO of Austar, an American named Bob McRann, asked if Colin knew of any celebrities in Toowoomba who should be invited to the launch. Colin took this opportunity to mention what I had done and that it involved crossing America. I didn't realize that Colin had used the walk as a reference regarding work he had done in his community. Community work was something that Mr McRann was very keen to know that his employees had taken part in. Though I didn't know it, my life was about to take a similar turn to that of one of my inspirations, Terry Fox. I was to find a mentor, friend and corporate supporter in Bob McRann.

The day Mr. McRann arrived things were buzzing because we were to meet the CEO for the first time. I was very nervous when he had asked me to join him for breakfast. I knew nothing much about the company and even less about Bob McRann. I did, however, have an opportunity to speak to one of his senior managers who had worked with him in the USA as well as here in Australia. He told me that Mr. McRann had always been philanthropic when he was a Senior Vice President for Cox Cable for 13 years. I went to breakfast a little wiser. I had seen him during the day before and felt that, while he was an impressive looking man, there was a gentle side to him. He said his management style was to walk gently and carry a big stick. I only ever saw the man walking gently.

He asked me to join him that morning and his first comment was, "Did you truly walk across America"? I replied, "Yes, sir". He said, "That's a long way. I know because I have flown it. What is your dream"? His directness caught me off guard, which caused me to ramble on nervously. When I finished he said, "Nigel you need to keep it short and precise and learn it by heart. How can we help you"? For what seemed like an eternity, I tried to think of what to ask for. With little information to base my request on, I heard myself saying, "Four million dollars to build the hospice". He smiled and said, "I cannot do that, but I am going to help you". In the history of the state of Queensland, this was a great moment for the families caring for approximately 3,000 children with life-limiting Illnesses. With help from a hospice they had a chance of surviving the rigors of caring for a child like Zoë. It was hard to fight back the tears at that moment and I would shed a few more tears over the next 18 months due to Bob's kindness and generosity. It was a short conversation but I walked away knowing we had somehow turned a corner.

A few days later I received a call from Bob saying that he was going to make all the resources of the Toowoomba branch office available to me and I could also take time to meet with people in Brisbane. He then added should I need any advice to feel free to contact him. I ran into Colin's office as high as a kite and all I could get out was, "We are on our way"! He said, "OK Nige, settle down, what did he say?" I repeated what he told me and Colin said, "Okay mate, we'll talk this through tonight". It was hard to contain myself; I sat down at one of the staff desks and made phone calls to Erika and all the people who had been at the first meeting. It was great to be able to share this wonderful news. Colin and I decided to work on an approach letter and try to identify some people who had influence and affluence that we could meet with in a bid to keep the momentum going. For the first time we had a major corporate sponsor and the fact Bob was also helping in an advisory capacity gave us some credibility when doing cold calls on prospective supporters.

The road from Toowoomba to Brisbane was beginning to take its toll on my little Gemini. It was taking more oil than petrol, but it was getting me there and back. Around about that time I received a phone call from Erika. She wanted to come up to see me. Colin gave me the use of his car so I was able to go out without worrying about breaking down. He also put fifty dollars on the dashboard. That's the kind of guy Colin could be. In my heart I hoped maybe Erika and I had a chance of getting together again but I was soon to find out that it was the reverse; she had met someone. As she told me about him I had some concerns. He had said he could feel Zoë's spirit at the memorial garden. Before I set off on the world walk I saw how some people preyed on those in grief. I hoped I had this one wrong and my feelings were incorrect. We spent the day talking of how well things were going and how Bob was helping us.

Some days later I met with Dr. Ian Waugh, Erika, Colin, Rod, Judy, Anna McMahon, the Lions District Governor's Representative and the Queensland Manager of Mojo Advertising. We discussed the progress we were making. Ian introduced me to his son, Dr. John Waugh, who was head of pediatrics at Mater Hospital. John proved to be a huge help and at one stage I thought he may take on the project full time, but that was not to be. That evening I suggested that we take the name of Little Bridge House from the hospice in England that I had visited, and call our organization ***The Zoe Reed Little Bridge House Association***. The name received mixed support but I was able to get a win on the night. We then decided to hold a public meeting and see what level of support for our project was out there in the community. Dr. Ian Waugh approached the hospitals and medical professionals. The Rochedale and Springwood Lions Club volunteered to organize the day. We sent out invitations to those business people who had shown interest at the Brisbane advertising lunch. I had my work cut out for me working from Toowoomba, but it was exciting and fulfilling.

One of the people I'd received help from in the past was Greg Carey from 4BC radio. I met up with him in the city and it was good to catch up. I hadn't spoken to him since those lonely, depressed nights when I was en route through England and North America. He introduced me to the station manager, Karen Rasen, and the 4BC business representative, who both wanted to help. I was absolutely overwhelmed by the support coming in from all levels of the community. Then Greg took me to the Kedron and Wavell Service Club to meet with Ken Mogg, the General Manager of 4BC. During that meeting it was decided that they would hold a "Trivia Night" and both the club and the radio station would invite their customers and clients to participate. 4BC would invite sporting celebrities to attend and all the proceeds from the evening would come to our association. Everyone's energy was extremely high as the momentum gathered but I was finding it hard being alone in Toowoomba. Then one day while working in the office at Austar, I received a phone call from Bob McRann. He wanted Erika and me to go to Sydney where we were to meet with Dr. John Stevens, the driving force behind the proposed Bear Cottage children's hospice. My main concern was money. I was not exactly flush with funds but Bob assured me that Austar would pay for the airfares. That was ok although it would not give us much time to visit Dr. Stevens at the Children's Hospital in Sydney. I contacted Erika and she was delighted to be able to come with me.

On our arrival at the Austar office close to the Rocks in Sydney we were greeted by Bob, who was about to go into a Board of Directors meeting. He opened the door to his office and provided coffee to drink. It felt very surreal. Here I was sitting in the boss's office only a short while after finishing the World Walk. This was a very surreal time for me. Like Terry Fox before me, a corporate benefactor wanted to help. I was sure that a big part of the success of the project rested on the level of commitment Bob could make. It was not long before Bob rejoined us and by this time he had ordered a taxi to take us out to Westmead Children's Hospital. The four of us, the fourth person being Bob's personal secretary, took off for the hospital. On arrival I was surprised at how small the team was, especially as they were in some way attached to the hospital. Dr. Stevens was not available when we arrived as he was once again in with the Manly council. We learned from our hostess that this was a regular occurrence. There was quite a lot of resistance to the suggested location of the hospice at Manly Point and Dr. Stevens had to work diligently with the council to get permission to build the Hospice (Bear Cottage). We understood that the land was to be given by a Catholic seminary that was also located on Manly Point. We also learned that, once again, a service club supported the project. For Bear Cottage it was Rotary. The more I learned of the contribution that service clubs make to the general community the more I was amazed.

Fortunately, Dr. Stevens managed to get away from the meeting so we had time to talk about the problems that we might encounter in the pursuit of Queensland's first purpose-built hospice. I remember on the way back to the office Bob looked at me and said, "This is not a small project, Nigel. It will be challenging". It amazed me that Bear Cottage was encountering resistance from the general public. Apparently the general public was not keen to have dying children in their neighborhoods. Isn't it amazing how many people do not understand the concept of hospice? On the other hand, I remembered that there had been very little resistance to Jill Farwell's English project, The Little Bridge House.

On our return to the office Bob decided to take us to lunch at a local Pub in the Rocks. No sooner had we sat to eat than Bob pointed to a table where some people sat. He then said come with me Nigel I want to introduce you to some solicitors. When we reached them and once the introduction was over I knew the company was Freehill Associates. He then told them, not asked them, that they would be helping me by doing our legal work while establishing the Charity. They just nodded in agreement. We had moved along so quickly all I knew was that the value of their services would run into the thousands of dollars. How lucky were we to have Bob as a benefactor?

Back to the office and Bob sprung another surprise. He asked if we were staying over in Sydney and I replied that I had to go to work. He said, "No you do not, I am the boss". Now began the second phase of embarrassment. I had almost no money. He must have heard my sigh as he told his secretary to book a night at the Quay West on his credit card. When would this man's generosity stop? I thought to myself. Erika and I had some time together while they organized our hotel. During our time in a small wine bar Erika said something that shocked me! She asked why I had to be so humble all the time. I asked her what she meant and she said, "Why do you have to call Bob Sir"? It shattered me that she would say such a thing. I called him Sir out of respect. He was my employer and I respected his position so until he said it was okay, I would not call him Bob.

Quay West did not mean anything to me other than Bob had stayed there when he first came to Australia. As we opened the door it just blew our minds. It was a luxury apartment. I wondered what we could touch as even the bed looked out of bounds. It was hard that night. Erika had rocked my boat with her statement about being humble. Eventually I was able to put it out of my mind and focus on how far we had come since I returned home from the walk. We had achieved so much with only a few thousand dollars in the bank.

On my return to Brisbane I continued to undertake speaking engagements, mainly with Lions Clubs. I also spoke at a Loganholme Business Community luncheon, where I met a wonderful lady, the

Queensland Manager of the Funeral Company *White Ladies*, who would go on to become a sponsor as we grew. She put me in touch with two young men who had established the Business Leaders Institute, an organization that allowed business people to network by holding monthly luncheons. This proved to be a wealth of business contacts and an opportunity to tell our story on a regular basis.

I learned that dreams are not made between 8.00 am and 5.00 pm. A tremendous level of effort is required. I found myself working any hour of the day and night. All that work shielded me from my grief, although there were times (especially at weekends) when, if I had nothing planned in my diary, the tears would surface. When this happened I would take myself off to Zoë's school and visit her garden. Many people say that one can feel the presence of someone who has passed away when at a place they enjoyed. All I can say is that it reminded me of the fact that her life had not been a dream. At times our lives are sorely tested by what we are given to experience.

The following week I received another great boost: a phone call from Dr. Ian Waugh. He informed me that his son John had been successful in getting us an office and telephone at the Mater Hospital in Brisbane. I needed to be based back in Brisbane as the little old Gemini was still burning more oil than petrol with each visit I made to the big city. With the help of Colin Walker, the Rochedale Lions and those people Dr. Ian Waugh put me into contact with; we were able to hold our first public meeting. We were fortunate to get Margaret Noonan up from Melbourne Children's Hospice, 'Very Special Kids'. Margaret was a nun who had initially helped two families, the Colemans and the Goods, establish a charity to build Victoria's Children's Hospice in 1984, ten years before Zoë passed away. When we got her agreement to speak and listened to what she had to say, both Erika and I thought about the significance of our decision to put our grief out there in the community and not realizing what the toll would be on both of us. I must be totally honest and say I researched Very Special Kids and I gave a lot of thought as to what had happened to the two families who had started that organization. I believe that they were pushed out of the organization. Both Erika and I had been at an Annual General

Meeting for a local charity in Brisbane where the founder had been voted off and out of the organization that he had started. Deep in my heart I wanted to remain involved in my dream.

It was obvious that few people have the desire to share their grief, time and money to do something that will help other people. Ten years had passed between the start of Very Special Kids and the Zoe Reed Little Bridge House. In a conversation with Colin Walker he spoke of how he felt when, many years after he was the inaugural president of The Queensland Safety House Association, very few people knew who he was and what he had done. He remarked a past president's role could be a lonely one that I might encounter at some time. He also advised me to be careful of people who sit on the fence while we use all our energy and time to establish the organization and then swoop in to take it over. He called it "The Cuckoo Syndrome": People (like the cuckoo) who watch as nests are established and then swoop in and drive the mother and father birds away so they can claim the nest. Cuckoos do not have the wherewithal to start and establish a charity or foundation because they do not have the passion or life experience to make it work. Colin and I had many nights when we would have a few beers (or more than a few beers) and talk about the tail of the tiger we had grabbed hold of and how, on opening day, he just wanted to hang back and walk around touching the bricks with a warm smile on his face. Sadly, Colin was never to do that. I was not sure that was the fate I wanted.

At last it was time for the Inaugural Meeting of Zoe Reed Little Bridge House. It took place in a scout hall at Indorapilly in Brisbane. To say I was amazed at the turnout is very much an understatement. There were people sitting and standing inside as well as people standing outside. Once again, the day's success was due to other people. It taught me that no dream is achieved on your own. We need to surround ourselves with other people who have experience and skills applicable to the cause and who are able to guide us along the path. A successful visionary has the ability to transfer that vision to others who can ensure the success of the team. I also learned that people would have hidden agendas and I needed to identify them as soon as possible. Jill Farwell once told Erika, hold on to the control of the dream at all costs to ensure that the initial vision is never diluted or lost.

That day was a huge success. Although someone from the Royal Brisbane Oncology Unit spoke somewhat negatively about the need for a children's hospice, the positive speech given by Margaret Noone was well received and was reinforced by Professor Pearn, the Head of Children's Services in Queensland. He had extensive knowledge of the hospice movement, which began during the Crusades when monks built places where injured knights could go when they needed to be repaired to face another battle. As with most public meetings, people who have an interest in the proposed project left their contact telephone numbers. It struck me that a number of senior medical people did not leave their phone numbers. After the meeting a group of us, including Margaret Noone, met for dinner at the Crest Hotel, where we had paid for her to stay. At least we had been able to pay for her airfare and accommodations. The Crane family, with whom we made contact at the meeting, described Margaret as a velvet bulldozer. Forceful, committed and focused. I agreed wholeheartedly.

About a week later I had contacted all those interested and was excited at the positive vibes they all gave off. Anna McMahon, Zoë's friend and television newsreader, wanted to put together a documentary about families in need. I contacted the Cranes and asked if they would mind being the family in the film. Without hesitation they agreed. On arrival at the Crane's house, we were greeted by a wonderfully motivated family. Their lives had been drastically changed about 20 years earlier when their two sons were both born with a little-known illness called Battens Disease. Battens is a degenerative illness that causes mental impairment, seizures and gradual loss of sight and motor skills. Sufferers become totally disabled before they die. In the Crane family there were two fully grown males confined to wheelchairs and unable to communicate. If ever I needed proof that we were lucky with Zoë, here it was. She walked, ran and laughed, and she hugged and kissed us. This family had none of that. Although these young men could do nothing for themselves, they were willing to try, by sharing their pain, to help others. Their dad asked me to help put one of the sons into the shower. Never before had I undertaken a task as difficult as to shower someone who could not stand properly and could not communicate with me. I could see the faces of the camera crew and I think they felt as we did; how did this family cope? Once the filming was over, the Cranes smiled as we said our goodbyes and encouraged us to continue with our project. As we traveled home, we all agreed how lucky we were and wondered how, day after day, those parents coped with their lives. They told us they had never had a holiday. Anyone who doubted that Queensland needed a children's hospice could not have considered this family's battle.

Some days later I received a call from Bob. As I picked up the phone the negative side of me wondered what he wanted to talk about. It was not long before he proved once again to be a true supporter of both myself and the 3000 needy families in Queensland. He asked me how much he paid me and I told him $30,000. He then said, "Nigel the work you are doing is worth more than that; we will pay you an extra $5,000". Then out of the blue he said "Nigel, what can I do for you? Not the project, you"! I was blown away with tears running down my face. I thought what do you say when someone asks you that? After what seemed like a lifetime I said my little car is about to fall apart. He then replied, "Get me three quotes and I will see what I can do". It was all I could do to say thank you. I was crying and as I put the phone down I wondered what someone would have thought if they had walked in as I talked on the phone. As requested, I supplied three quotes for a car. Three days later I received a call to pick up a new Ford Falcon. Bob had organized a lease paid for by Austar.

We managed to pull together the inaugural Annual General Meeting with the people we knew were interested in helping our cause. We had a good cross-section of the business and medical communities. I remember a young guy named Chris who was a nurse in oncology at the Royal Brisbane. Both he and his girlfriend were volunteers for Camp Quality. Chris's mate, a training masseur and also a volunteer for Camp Quality, was also there. Dr. Ian Waugh and his son Dr. John Waugh both attended, along with a nurse from the Mater Hospital, the Lions District Governors representative, Anna McMahon, Colin

Walker, Judy Stone, Erika, Rod Ihia and me. I was voted President and Dr. Ian Waugh was voted Vice President. It took some convincing, but in the end Rod Ihia became Treasurer/Secretary. Colin Walker became Chairperson of the meetings as I still had much to learn about meeting procedures. We created a steering committee which included the Queensland manager of MOJO Advertising, a university marketing professor and a social worker from Mater Hospital. The Zoe Reed Little Bridge House Association, Inc. was up and running.

By the middle of April I was impressed with how things were coming together. I had a chance meeting at Mater hospital with a lady who was working as a facilitator and she agreed to facilitate at a brainstorming meeting. We held a few working committee meetings and split into the relevant subcommittees as required: one was responsible for the caring aspect of the organization and the other was responsible for fundraising. As president, I told them that I would not be attending every committee meeting and that I trusted them to keep the management committee informed. They were tasked to come up with draft procedures after making contact with other children's hospices. I was tasked with recruiting the best people I could to raise the funds required. We already had some key individuals and Bob McRann accepted the role of Chairman of Fundraising. What we needed now was a direction and a strategic plan.

Bob said he was working jointly with the CEO of General Electric, Jeff Smith, to organize a Pay Television Golf Day in Sydney. He said he would pay for me to attend and participate when the date was set. We had received Austar's first donation of $25,000 and some Lions clubs were once again donating, so financially we were moving along well. I spoke to the Queensland Premiers business manager at the BAR Luncheon and he told me that he knew of a block of land that was situated out at Mount Ommaney in the western suburbs of Brisbane. Dr. Ian Waugh had been very successful in utilizing his contacts in the health department and we were able to speak to the Minister for Health. During our conversation he said that even if we were successful in obtaining the land, the government would not be willing to provide funds to run a hospice. He said that new charities often came knocking on the government's door when their fundraising fell short. It was stated that we should never receive more than 20 % of the total project's budget from government for two reasons: 1) should the state's economy change for the worse, we could lose that 20% funding and, 2) if that happened, would we still be able to survive without those funds? Personally, I did not want to see the Health Department dictating the type of service that was to be provided and I was sure that if they provided funds they would want some say in how things were run.

At one of the meetings there was some discussion about the name we had picked. *The Zoe Reed Little Bridge House Association* was too long to be good as a marketing tool. I was the first to agree but in my heart I wanted Zoë to be a part of its name because it was her death that inspired me to start this project. Dr. Ian Waugh said children would more than likely just call it Zoë's Place, as in "we are going to Zoë's Place", so we agreed that all marketing literature would use the name Zoë's Place. Marketing said we also needed a mascot. After much discussion with Judy Stone and the MOJO staff, we came up with the idea of a puppy. We created a puppy with "attitude" wearing a baseball cap. Thanks to Judy, we decided to call the puppy Philo because the word is associated with love.

Although things were going very well, getting fundraising functions together was a concern. The success of the project depended on bringing things together as quickly as possible. After talking to the people in Brisbane, I asked Bob if he could come to Brisbane and chair an important meeting that would decide whether or not we should employ the services of a professional fundraising company because we were concerned about the cost. As always, he agreed to come and help give us some direction. His visit to Brisbane was my opportunity to show Bob what we had organized so far and I was hoping he would be pleased with our progress. I was nervous when I collected him and his secretary at the airport, so nervous that as I drove away he asked me if the boot needed to be open. There it was, flapping in the breeze. Nervous was an understatement. I had forgotten to shut the boot! My nerves settled down when Bob told me he was contributing two computers and software to the project. He was in contact with the solicitors Freehills and knew that our constitution was close to being completed.

I dropped Bob off at his hotel and he invited Erika and me to join him for dinner that evening, after the marketing committee meeting. Bob had an opportunity to meet everybody at the meeting. Everything went well and the mood was very positive. When we discussed hiring the services of professional fundraisers, the decision to do so was unanimous. Not one person objected, which was surprising. We still had only the two main pledges and previous discussions on this matter had ended inconclusively. All through dinner Bob was full of praise for what had been achieved and added that the fundraising golf tournament had been organized in Sydney.

The following week I mostly went to meetings and contacted fundraising companies. I invited two of the fundraisers to make presentations to the committee and we agreed on Compton International. The first step in a capital campaign is a feasibility study, which costs about $5,000. I felt okay about the $5,000, but almost choked when we heard that, if the feasibility study was positive, the second stage would cost $100,000 plus enough to fund the Fundraising Manager and an office. Paul Malloy, the Australasian Director of Compton, outlined the feasibility campaign: He would interview all the committee members (as well as influential community and business leaders) to determine how the organization was viewed and whether or not Queensland required a children's hospice. My major concern was how the idea would be received by the medical profession. Would they look positively on a parent offering advice on what help families needed?

Dr. Ian Waugh arranged for me to speak to a group of medical professionals from the Royal Brisbane. I was excited about that and saw it as a chance to put forward the case for hospice. When the day came I felt very nervous for I still did not fully understand the role the medical profession played in the day to day running of a hospice. However, I did know that if I waited until I fully understood everything, I would then find another reason not to carry on until it was too late for the families. My talk went reasonably well but I sensed that it would be a struggle to convince the Royal Brisbane that we could work together toward providing help for families.

BACK TO NORTH AMERICA

Around about this time I received some other good news. I was in contact with many Lions Club members and friends but the work here in Brisbane kept me so busy that I almost forgot that the Lions International Conference was coming up. Pat Hogan, the generous Irish American who had provided me with funds during my walk across America, contacted Erika and me about the two of us attending the International Conference in Montreal and, true to his word, he forwarded the fares and itinerary.

Along with the Richardson Award for Lionism I mentioned previously, I was also awarded Citizen of the Year for Slacks Creek and Citizen of the Year for Loganholme; both suburbs in South Brisbane. Strangely enough, even with all the positive things that had happened to me, when I was alone in my caravan at night I still heard that voice that said I could not fulfill this role and see the project through to completion. I still didn't know how to fight these self-sabotaging thoughts that had the power to overwhelm me.

When it came time to go to the Lions International conference in Montreal, Erika and I were ready. We met Pat and his partner in Chicago. They were a very close, loving couple. We drove with them to Kansas, where we caught up with Owen and Joanne Thero. We also hoped to catch up with some of the guys from Kentucky. We knew that Smithy would be at the conference and I understood Elden from Fairfax was also attending. It was strange driving along the road that I had walked only one year before. I shared some stories of my journey with Erika, hoping that she might have second thoughts about us, but she seemed happy with her new partner.

Next we visited Gary and Melody Sumner. Shortly after we booked into our accommodation, Gary turned up to take us to his home for dinner. We had a wonderful evening reminiscing about our hike up the mountain at Yankee Boy Basin where we had watched the dear play in knee-deep mountain flowers. I never dreamed that I would be back so soon. Pat Hogan was a generous host. He knew that Erika and I had little spare money but that didn't keep him from treating us to a visit to Niagara Falls. It exuded a romantic atmosphere and was everything that the tourist brochures said and more. The drive through the Canadian countryside was stunning. On our arrival in Montreal it was obvious that something big to do with Lions Club was happening. I remembered how the International Conference for Lions that was held in Brisbane had impacted on the local economic community. Here again was a huge collection of committed people from all corners of the world, people who were making a huge contribution to their communities. It had occurred to me while I walked the roads months earlier that the energy of this organization could have such a huge impact on the families that cared for terminally ill children if we could somehow convince them that the most vulnerable families are those who, overnight, become caregivers, physiotherapists and nurses as well as being husbands and wives.

Erika and I were both excited at the prospect of possibly speaking at the conference but Lions chose instead General Stormin' Norman Schwarzkopf, who had recently returned from the war in the Middle East. Owen had lobbied hard on our behalf and was disappointed that Lions International turned down the opportunity to hear a fellow Lion speak on behalf of needy families. We were unable to talk with anyone in a high position but we did speak to someone from their head office that was aware of the Lions' support for other projects similar to ours, in particular the Little Bridge House in Barnstable England. Our hosts were so thoughtful. They allowed us some time alone and we took the chance to walk through the French sector and found a nice café to sit in. As we talked it was obvious that we were both grieving still. It was so hard for me to truly enjoy myself without feeling guilty all the time. I still struggled with punishing myself over my daughter's death and the fact that I wasn't there for Zoë in her last few months. I was glad that Erika and I had been able to remain friends.

We said our farewells at the end of the conference. While it had not been the success that we envisaged, it was great to meet up with some of the people who, without doubt, were responsible for the success of the walk. I shook hands with Pat Hogan and we hugged each other. What a wonderfully genuine and generous man! I felt so lucky to have met him along my journey. Sadly Pat died about a year after we returned from the conference and he took with himself a wonderful generous heart. One of the wonderous things about people like Pat is that they touch so many hearts and leave their footprints everywhere.

REALIZING THE DREAM

On our return to Brisbane we held a meeting to decide whom we would employ as a Capital Fundraiser. It was a unanimous decision that Compton International would be our link to fundraising. I invited Paul Malloy to join me the next day and he outlined how he would undertake the feasibility study, which would help identify people's level of commitment. In a capital fundraising campaign, all the committee or board members are asked to donate money. I supplied Paul with the names of those I had made contact with during my walks. The feasibility study would provide me with an indication of how successful my public relations exercise had been. Prior to Zoë's death we had not achieved a great deal. Now we would see how successful I'd been in establishing the profile and credibility required to initiate a project like a children's hospice. My intention in walking was to develop a persona in the community that would enable me to raise a lot more money in the following years.

Paul and I flew to Sydney to catch up with Bob. Paul wanted to run some ideas past him and see just how strong his support was. After the meeting Paul looked me straight in the eyes and told me how fortunate I was to have such a friend and benefactor. The next step was for Erika and I to attend Compton's International Conference and talk about our dream. Paul said that this would enable us to tap into the collective knowledge of all the Compton Fundraising Managers. One of them was a gentleman who was involved in the building of a children's hospice in Vancouver, Canada called Canuck Place. Here was another story of commitment to hospice. A registered nurse named Brenda Eng, who had worked in Helen House in England, realized that such a place was needed in Canada. She worked hard to see her dream become reality and Canuck Place became the leading hospice of its type across the world.

The people at Compton were positive about our chances and we came away with many ideas. Paul completed the study in about three weeks. At a meeting held at Mater Hospital he told everyone how impressed he was with my impact on both the general and business communities. He presented an Initial Capital Campaign for us to approve so that we could move on to the next step, Entrepreneurial Start-Up. This step was huge and daunting for me but Paul Molloy said that he had never seen a new charity with so many start-up contacts, so much money already pledged and such a healthy bank account. We agreed to hire Compton's and pay for their services out of the funds we raised. We were on our way.

The following Monday I met the Compton Fundraising Manager who would steer us along our path. She was a terrific, positive and very professional lady named Robyn Korst. Robin very quickly set about identifying premises for a campaign office. We quickly found a place centrally located on George Street in Brisbane. Bob and Austar provided us with all the computers and software we needed but I was still nervous about money because we had to hire and pay for both Robyn and a secretary. These costs would have to be taken out of the funds Robyn raised. The golf tournament in Sydney was a huge success making about $15,000.00 and we also formed relationships with many small supporters and sponsors through the Business Leaders Institute lunches but the funds were only trickling in and I was still nervous. I put Robyn in contact with Rod Burbidge, who had spoken about a block of land during my previous meeting with the government. The parcel, which had been earmarked for a hospital, was in Mount Ommaney. Since the hospital plan had been shelved, the Parliament member for that area was keen to see a hospice come to his constituency and started to lobby hard on our behalf. But he was not the only government contact we had. There was also the Springwood representative who met with me when I finished the walk. He had based his inaugural speech on the need to support families who care for terminally ill children and had told our story.

We were now approaching the government from more than one direction but we still needed a patron to coordinate governmental efforts. When I mentioned this to Robyn she immediately suggested Senator John Heron, Minister for Aboriginal Affairs. John Heron had a child with Down's syndrome and was much respected in Australia. He was also a doctor. Robyn drafted a letter and we placed it in the mail the same day. To our surprise, we did not have to wait long for a reply. Dr. Heron said that he would be honored to be our patron, but only if he could work on our behalf. When we later met in his office he asked us to bear with him and he would try to convince some of his influential friends to help. Soon after that, we were contacted by two of his friends, one from each side of the political spectrum. Robyn and I did not want to politicize the project so it was wonderful to have both Terry White (Pharmacies) from the Nationals and Con Sciacca from the Labor Party. Con Sciacca was a mover and shaker as well as being a solicitor. He knew firsthand what it felt like to lose a child, having lost a son to a terminal illness. Con had established a trust to help the community that was similar to our association. I ran everything by Dr. Ian Waugh, who had been busy talking to the medical profession. After my presentation to the Royal Children's hospital he and his son John undertook that side of the campaign.

I told Bob of our success and he decided, as Campaign Chairman, to have a social meeting with all the interested parties. Bob decided we should hold it at the nearest restaurant and it just so happened that there was nice place near our new office. Bob paid for the entire evening and the gathering was very successful. Con offered the balance of the funds from his son's trust. I felt humbled by his gesture. In the privacy of his office some weeks later he said, "Nigel, we are members of the loneliest club in the world, parents who have lost a child". Apparently he had a friend who had also lost a child and they met once a year. I asked him what had attracted him to our organization and he said, "When John Heron picks up the phone and calls asking for help, you respond". During that meeting we learned that Robyn had approached the Jupiter's Trust, which was established by Jupiter's Casino to fund projects like ours. Con pointed out that he knew the chairperson, a very successful woman named Sarina

Russo, and that he would speak to her on our behalf. Robyn had been successful in obtaining funds from other trusts and we felt that with Con and Bob lobbying on our behalf we stood a good chance of getting a lump sum from Jupiter's.

Things were moving along at a frantic rate and I was nearly exhausted. Every day I tackled a full diary of meetings coupled with speaking engagements at night. But everyone's hard work paid off and we secured the largest single donation of that period from Jupiter's Casino. Part of the Compton package was to send me on a one-week course to learn all about fundraising. I mentioned to Paul Malloy during that course that I wondered where this project would take me and he said, "When this is completed you will be in great demand as a fundraiser". During this time the steering committee was busy putting together some rules and procedures. The carers group was very successful in attracting nurses from the Mater and had contacted other hospices they felt would help us in the future. My concern was that I saw both Bear Cottage and Very Special Kids as being too clinical in design, whereas The Little Bridge House was more like a large family home. I was beginning to understand what Colin meant when he said that we had a tiger by the tail and it was dragging us along, a little out of our control.

Later I suggested that maybe this project was one that would appeal to younger wealthy people like Kerry Packer's son and Riley, the owner of Australian Provincial Newspapers. Although the meetings went well, we gained little from them. We still lacked people who possessed influence and affluence, the two things that were required to ensure our ongoing success. Although many people donated in-kind services and goods, and some had made significant donations, apart from Bob and John Heron there were few who were prepared to solicit help from their peers. Instead of getting discouraged, Bob and I went next to Hill's Industries, where we were able to get a donation/pledge of $20,000.00 per year for five years.

The format that we had been instructed to follow by Compton's was happening and we were having a great success with raising funds and attracting support from all sides of the community. I had set a personal goal to make The Zoe Reed Little Bridge House (or Zoë's Place, as we were calling it now), the name that was on everybody's lips and fridge magnets. Dr. Ian Waugh and I generally got on well, but we differed on two things. The first surfaced at a meeting when proposed that any donation over $2 should receive a certificate of thanks. He very quickly strongly objected to this on cost grounds, a point I could understand. However my thoughts were that should a child make that donation, it would make them feel proud and just maybe it would lead to parental donation of a greater value because we took the time to care about their child.

The other disagreement surfaced during a discussion when Ian made it clear that he wanted the hospice to be a centre of excellence with a teaching aspect to it. It seemed to me that the core reason for Zoë's Place was families. Out of the blue Ian said, "You don't think that you're going to run Zoë's Place do you, because you will not". Here I was confronted with a Cuckoo for the second time. I remembered Colin and Bob telling me to beware of people who will allow me to use my energy to establish the hospice and then move in to take control. I was warned to identify people's agendas early. Was this my first major Cuckoo challenge? I asked my volunteer secretary to leave the room and asked Ian what this was all about, pointing out that I had brought my vision to Queensland in 1996 and that *he* had joined *me*. He replied that he had been interested in children's hospices for years before I came along. I pointed out that while he may have had the interest, he had not been prepared to give up his career and pursue the project. When I came along, he had already retired. The conversation continued but I was troubled knowing we had differing thoughts on where the organization should go.

Later that week I drove over to the Loganholme Hospital and spoke to Dr. John Waugh, Ian's son. I asked if he would speak to his father and ask him to calm down. I had no intentions of running the organization but I did envisage staying on as a fundraiser. John said, "Nigel, you need to understand that my father sees this as his swan song". How amazing! His dad was prepared to take my dream away and claim it as his own. We had successfully put together a team of both young and old people and it had been Ian, an older member of the medical community, who had driven a wedge at times between the younger members of the Care Committee. Colin and I had spoken often about the need to groom the younger members of our group like the successful service organizations Lions and Rotary so we could step away and leave it in good hands.

I was still sure that an open approach to management was the best way to operate. I believed in recruiting a complete cross-section of qualified people of all ages and backgrounds to join the organization so that we would have a wide and diverse membership base from which to draw talent and funds. But it was becoming obvious that others did not feel the same way and wanted an exclusive organization. The only reason I could see for this was to protect what they thought was their interest in the organization. Although it was an exciting time, it was also a lonely time. Very often thoughts of Zoë and how we ran along the beach at Byron Bay would surface. Her very infectious laugh would ring in my ears. I would see the determination in her eyes as I chased her and when I caught up with her I would hear her heavy breathing as she fought for sufficient oxygen. As a parent I felt alone. Here I was, trying to help other families like ours, but no one called me after a meeting to see how I was. They would go home to their families and I would sink back into a dark hole, unable to share my pain with anyone.

I remembered something my doctor friend once said when talking about the need for ongoing support in cases like Cystic Fibrosis. He pointed out that when children have cancer they die, get cured, or go into remission after a relatively short period of time. This meant that the level of support stayed very high and intense during only a short period. In Cystic Fibrosis cases, the disease continued to get worse year after year. In most cases, support would dissipate a short time after diagnosis. In Zoë's case, what support we had during her life was little and now that she was gone, it was non-existent. So many people around me understood the need for after-care once the child died but only the ones who have actually lost a child knew the emotion and trauma involved. People who said, "I know how you must be feeling" actually had no idea unless it had happened to them. Sometimes I would lie on my bed and wonder if I had what it took to go on. I just wanted to touch Zoë. I longed to hear her say one more time, "I love you Dad." I smelled her school uniform, hoping to catch a smell of her, but I never could.

We needed a way to reach the greater population of Queensland. In my eyes, we needed to develop a branch network; this was not just a local project, it was for families statewide. In the future we could very well need a second hospice because Queensland is vast. All Queensland families needed to know that they had a place to go when they needed it. On my walks I had also encountered grandparents whose emotions toward their sick grandchildren had worn them out so completely that they also needed relief. All of these people could be our workers on the ground and help us establish a network of supporters. That's when I got the idea to take the message to the people of Queensland by circumnavigating the state the same way I had walked from England to Australia via North America. I wanted to talk to as many local community leaders as possible, as well as doctors and hospital staffs. Surely people would take notice of this type of messenger! But there were a couple of major concerns: how would the Capital Campaign go with me on the road and could I get Bob's approval, since I was still employed by Austar?

I approached Bob about my idea. He had no objections and said that Austar would also act as the major sponsor and that he would speak to the marketing people and would create a marketing plan. I needed a crew, which was difficult to assemble because the walk would take approximately 12 weeks to complete and it was hard for working people to commit to that time frame. My old army mate Tony Boon had retired and was free. Tony had been a good soldier and was good at organizing things. When I spoke to him he accepted without any hesitation so I felt confident that we could undertake the walk and achieve a good outcome. I had coffee with Robyn and Paul to discuss how the project was going. We were all pleased with what had been achieved in such a short time. They felt comfortable with me taking off around Queensland especially as we now had a young Englishman named Jeremy Sparks working for us. He was a wealth of ideas and worked well with Robyn.

Something Paul said truly amazed me. He had been told that the Cystic Fibrosis Association committee questioned my motives for pursuing this avenue of care. When he saw the look of amazement on my face, he said, "Don't worry Nige, if they are attacking you it is because you are succeeding in your endeavour". I could see that as my daughter had Cystic Fibrosis and I was talking about the effect it had on our family, the Cystic Fibrosis Committee would see funds coming our way by speaking about Cystic Fibrosis. They were not hearing that we were talking about other diseases and illnesses as well. But they had not objected when I walked thousands of kilometers for their organization. I also knew some funds had gone to the Cystic Fibrosis Association after me speaking about our issues. Nor had they complained when we allowed our own daughter to be used in interviews for awareness to Cystic Fibrosis. Could they not see how the families needed help? All I was trying to do was complement what they were doing.

The walk came together well. Bob allocated a marketing budget for each Austar branch, and the manager of the branch that raised the most money from their promotion of the walk would earn a holiday to Hawaii. With everything going well with the campaign, Bob also picked up the full budget for the walk. We were very lucky. Tony recruited Jamie, a young friend of his, to come along as a back-up person. Bob decided what we needed was a launch function to be held on the day we set out. He would get Colin and all involved at Zoë's Place to invite as many people as possible, including all subcontractors involved with Austar on the coast. To do this I had to deal with the branch manager of the Gold Coast office. Although everything seemed okay, I felt as if we were intruding on more important issues of the Austar Company. The enthusiasm did not seem to be there at this outlet. But we had put the wheels in motion and we and the team were ready to do our thing.

ANOTHER WALK ANOTHER MARRIAGE

Around this time I met a woman who was already helping families with children with life-limiting illnesses through a church-sponsored group. She came on board to help me in the office. Without a doubt she brought a breath of fresh air to the office. She even invited me to her church. Since my return I had not attended a church on a regular basis. I guess I was finding it hard to come to terms with a God that allows children to suffer. It was the concept that said, "Well he gave his own son to die for us". What always struck me was that we had to have faith that we would meet our loved ones again. I decided to go to her church to seek the spiritual feelings I was sure were there; without a doubt, having a regular day in God's house was good. Some weeks after my first visit to church we were talking about the loneliness and she asked if I wanted to meet a lady. Without hesitation I said yes. In my heart I knew that I needed someone in my life. The void that had been left was still as wide as the Grand Canyon. What was going to be hard was finding someone who understood that this project was my purpose in life. I felt I was making a difference in people's lives. Could I find someone who could accept my relationship with Erika? There was also the question of my grief.

Four weeks before the start of the walk, my secretary arranged for me to meet a lady she knew at Sunday church named Maureen. Maureen was a lovely lady. Even on that first day we seemed to gel. I discovered that she had been married and had three children all over the age of Zoë. There was a part of me that was excited at the thought of maybe being a dad again; be it only a step dad. We went on to meet more and decided that we would like to see each other on a regular basis. Maureen and I agreed that we should keep our relationship pure until we married. I understood that and felt that it would be a good way of building a strong relationship. We talked about my need to continue with the project and the walk. Maureen said that she understood and I felt happy with myself, better than I had for some time. On an evening just before the walk I took Maureen out to dinner at the same restaurant near the office where the committee had met. We talked all night and into the early hours of the morning. I knew it would be hard on both of us to be separated for 12 weeks but I hoped that it would allow us to consider the future and what we were going to do.

The walk started from Southport, Queensland. The kick-off breakfast was packed. We were hoping to jump-start the fundraising with a reasonable amount donated at the breakfast and had donation plates situated on each table. The guests started eating and Bob stood up, said a few words, and introduced me. I said my piece, then Bob finished by asking people to donate by leaving cheques or cash on the plates provided. After a hearty breakfast Bob came over to me and by the look on his face I could see he was concerned about something. He said, "Nigel, no one has given any money of any significance". I said, "Don't worry; maybe it will come later in the day". Outside the club was a convoy of vehicles, some from the Variety Club Annual Rally, plus lots of people to march behind us. Alongside was my wonderful friend Bob. (It would not be the last time that he would be standing on the road with me). Sure enough, later that day the president of a local fundraising group stepped up to Bob and pledged $100,000. We were well on our way raising funds.

It always took a few days for the crew to get to know the routine. It's not the most exciting thing to follow me in a vehicle at seven kilometers an hour. After the second day I already saw the tension between Tony and Jamie. Though I tried to diffuse their differences, it continued throughout the walk. But one thing I learned throughout my walking was that something always happened that brought people back to earth. On the first day we were met by the manager of the Caloundra Austar Branch. They had marketed the walk with point of sale information and although they had not raised a lot of money yet, they had the rest of the walk to raise more. Two days later I had one of those things happen that show you just how special life is and that God does not make seconds when a person is born on to this planet.

We rose early the morning after our walk out of Noosa. As I put on my shoes (that had been provided by my mate Chris Gallagher from Williams the Shoeman), a car pulled up and a lady and two teenage children stepped out. They came over to see me and the lady, who was the mother of the two children, asked if they could walk with me. My immediate response was, "Of course"! We were going to do about 12 km that day and the company would be good, plus we had the local fire truck along with members of the volunteer fire team so the two kids would have some fun with them. When the two introduced themselves and shook my hand, Ashley, the boy, came first. As he held his hand out I instantly felt emotion welling up inside me for he only had a thumb and flesh for a hand. He said, "Mr. Reed, you are my hero". All I could say was, "No, Ashley, you are *my* hero". When his younger sister shook my hand I saw that she had a similar affliction. Here I was in the company of heroes who took what life had given them and still had time to support me. How lucky was I? On any long walk, the blisters are something you just know you have to live with but at the end of this day I was in for a shock. Ashley and his sister both started off with me.

After some distance, the young girl got inside the fire truck but Ashley just kept going. From time to time his mum would tell him it was okay to take a rest, but he declined. He reminded me of Krista Koch, the 21-year old heart and lung recipient who walked with me in the USA, a young body so full of courage willing to go the distance for someone else. If only this type of courage was more evident in our world. About an hour from the end of the day's walk, Ashley finally got inside the fire truck. He had gone farther than what he set out to do and had kept all of our spirits high. At the finish we both sat down outside a little local bush pub with our cans of Coke and started to unlace our shoes. We both took them off carefully just in case it hurt. I knew I had a small blister on my heel. To my amazement as Ashley took his socks off without even a flinch I saw that his feet were also deformed. Where feet should have been he had only big toes and flesh. Walking eleven kilometers for Ashley was more than equal to anything I had done in the past or would ever do in the future. Ashley was most certainly a hero, and I told him so again. Whenever things got tough, remembering that day kept me going. God be with you and your sister, Ashley. Sometimes, just when the journey seemed to be getting to us, God sent along one of his special angels. Very often, when the combination of pain and sorrow were almost too much, a car would blow its horn in support or a beautiful piece of countryside would come into view and I would thank God for the opportunity to help make this place a better world.

I missed Maureen and the guys joked that I was love-struck. It was great to talk to her at the end of each day. We had made plans for the ladies to join us in Townsville and I was looking forward to seeing her. Our spirits were high after our encounter with Ashley and his sister but the next day we were in for a shock. About mid-morning I saw a car parked in the distance. As we got closer, a man wearing a baseball cap back to front got out and walked towards us. To our surprise, it was Bob. He had flown up from Sydney to be with us and update me on how things were going with both the Capital Campaign back in Brisbane and the Austar walk marketing. We had been on radio since leaving Southport and in Caloundra we got to address the local council members. They reacted well and indicated that they would do some research into the number of families in their area.

By the time midday came we found a bush pub where they were having a sausage sizzle. As always with Bob, he offered us something to eat. When the hamburgers arrived, Bob's had a long grey hair hanging out each end. The chef's hair and a beard were as long as Santa's. We just smiled and walked out. Bob's feet were bothering him so he decided to drive to that day's finishing spot. We initially had the impression he would stay overnight with us, but on seeing the accommodation for that night I think he backed out. It was a bush pub, full of good country people but a little the worse for wear, something like the Giru Hotel I stayed at back in 1972. He stayed for a couple of drinks then took Tony to one side and handed him something, waved us farewell and left. He gave Tony $100 for each of us and told him what we were doing was great. One of the Austar branch managers told me that he felt the management below Bob was not fully behind what we were doing and that Bob might need to be informed. My problem, as I saw it, was that as a lower level employee, was it my place to comment on a company's internal politics? After giving it much thought, I chose not to.

For a while, each day along the main highway north was very much like the day before; not the most scenic and littered with unpleasant road kill, but we received a good response wherever we went. Our next big stop was Bundaberg and by all accounts it was a good visit. Once again we were treated to a wonderful display of courage. A few kilometers outside of Bundaberg, we were joined by the manager of that Austar branch and her son. Sadly, the son had leukemia but thankfully he was in remission. She was very enthusiastic and excited about our visit and had planned for us to be in Bundaberg at a certain time to meet with some sick children. Because of the timing, we had to drive a certain distance to make the deadline. During that drive she told me a story that brought tears to our eyes. When her son was first diagnosed with leukemia, he had asked that he be cremated and that his mum would put his ashes in an envelope with a window in it and to keep the envelope on the dashboard with the window facing outwards so he could see and be with her whenever she was driving. I can only hope that when confronted with my own mortality I am so calm and courageous.

The next memorable stop was Giru. We took time to visit the place that had been my home when I first came to this wonderful country. Little had changed. In fact, the son of a local farmer who had become an architect greeted us. He was now the head of the local Lions Club. Once again, Lions Clubs around Queensland were responding by raising funds from their small membership and the local community. That night we stayed in the hotel and memories of my first wife Janet came flooding back. Those were good times, different from anything I had done before, full of adventure and promise. Sadly, it was not for long. I wondered if I would see Janet again. I heard she worked at the gift shop at Marine World. I considered calling in and saying hi and decided to do it if I had the time. We were looking forward to Townsville, where we were going to stay in a good motel and the girls were flying in. I was excited as I waited at the airport. We waited for them to arrive and when they stepped onto Townsville soil we all felt better. The girls stayed for about three days and we went out for meals and did some sightseeing as well as fundraising. Those days were good and it was there that Maureen and I decided to marry. I did catch up with my ex wife Janet, but found that we had little to say after years of being apart.

Fortunately, we were able to arrange for a meeting with the premier to discuss how they could help. In addition, Dr. Ian Waugh organized for us to address a group of medical professionals at the Townsville hospital on our way back from Cairns. Both Townsville and Cairns had responded well to our appeal, but I still got the impression that all was not well at Austar in Sydney. Some staff members told me they had been told not to concentrate too much energy on the walk. All I could do was hope that Bob was aware of it. The meeting went well at the hospital in Townsville with a lot of interest shown in the idea of a children's hospice in Queensland. The major concern was the size of the state and how we would deal with the logistics of that challenge. I said that we would research the problem and develop a strategy that would resolve the issue. I promised to keep them informed and in the loop, for we needed as many ideas as possible. Before Ian left us he said that he felt the meeting had gone well and that he thought we could rely on further help from the hospital. We had a funny night in Cairns. Tony got completely cheesed off with Jamie's snoring and insisted he sleep out on the verandah. Things like this had the potential to cause ill feeling in the crew, but we did our best to laugh it off. It took a while for Jamie to thaw out the next morning, for it was cold in the early hours.

We set off towards our next planned event in Mount Isa, where I had worked when I lived in Townsville. I had also attempted to get a mining job there when Erika and I first came to Australia with Zoë, but I wasn't hired. I was curious to see what I had missed by not working and living in the place they refer to as "The Isa". The mine was in the middle of the town and seemed to be the center of everyone's life. I am not sure that Zoë would have thrived in that environment and was glad we hadn't settled there. The route to "The Isa" was totally different from anything I had encountered before with so many flies. I had never before seen such a multitude of flies. The minute I stood outside the van they came over me like a blanket, crawling up my nose, into my eyes and finding every opening in my clothing. Flies are the only creatures on God's earth I can do without. Their constant need to be in my face nearly drove me insane and I was almost ready to tell the lads we'd skip the walking here and just drive to the next stop. Tony's sense of humour broke the tension. He kept cracking jokes like, "Hey Nige, I recognize that fly from Townsville, he's freeloading on your face".

I was able to get back at Tony later that day. Our staple food when meeting people was sausages and Tony had developed a hatred for the long brown things we call "snags". So I waited until we were near the end of the day, and then said, "Hey Tone just had a text from the local Lions Club and they have organized a sausage sizzle". The look on Tony's face was unforgettable; rather than have another sausage he would have walked backwards to Brisbane. Mount Isa was special in many ways. We stayed at a very regal old hotel and had lovely accommodations. In addition, the Austar branch organized a ball with raffles and prizes that was held at the local nightclub. So many beautiful women turned out all in stunning dresses and gowns. The place was swinging, the night was a huge success and about $12,000 was raised. No other branch came anywhere close to raising that amount and the manager of Austar in Mount Isa won the all-expenses-paid trip for two to Hawaii.

Upon leaving Mount Isa I was informed that we had a date to meet with the Queensland premier, Rob Borbidge, in Brisbane, along with Robin and Bob, so I had to leave the lads for a couple of days and fly back to Brisbane. The local airport was a grassy field with a tin shed whose door was locked and bolted. There was no nicely clad hostess, no booking area or parking arrangements. Where was I to collect my ticket? When would I know the plane was due to arrive and what would the plane even look like? We were about to leave when we saw a vehicle heading toward us with dust billowing up around it. The airport administrator had arrived. He had no knowledge of my ticket, although I had my flight details. Then Biggles in his Sopwith Camel swooped in and landed. The administrator frantically tried to get clearance for me to fly to Brisbane as the pilot prepared to take off. Just as he put on his leather cap and scarf, the permission for me to fly came through and I boarded the plane. Tony watched in amazement as we took off.

The meeting with the Premier was set up by a Mt. Ommaney member. He met us at Government house, keen to organize us and our presentation. What he didn't know was that Bob had already done some role-playing with us to prepare us for our meeting. Although I hated role-playing almost as much as the dreaded flies, it must have helped because all went well. We were guided to a room somewhere in the Corridors of Power. The Premier had only a little time to spend with us and we needed to use it well to convince him of the need for this children's hospice. Upon entering, the member started to make his presentation, and then asked for some words from Bob. I felt that we were not going anywhere and decided to take control of the meeting. I said, "Mr Borbidge, we are not just talking about 3,000 children with terminal illness, we are talking about 6,000 parents, 12,000 grandparents and many siblings. That's a community of 21,000 human beings that need help now! That's the plan for the hospice we would build on this land. Please can you help us"?

The Premier turned to the local member and told him to give us the land and as much financial help as possible. We just stood there, stunned, as he thanked us for taking the time and left. All in all it was over in 20 minutes. As we stood in the elevator I saw the joy in Bob's eyes and he said, "Nigel, I have never had a meeting go so well when negotiating with a government representative. Well done"! He gave me a high five just as I noticed there were cameras in the lift. We all laughed and walked out of the building, much closer to seeing the dream become a reality than when we had walked in. A lot of thanks were owed to that local member who lobbied so hard for Zoë's Place to be in Mt. Ommaney. After the meeting, it was nice to be able to spend the evening with Maureen before flying back to the walk the next day.Dr. Ian Waugh and I were the first to go and see the land at

Mount Ommaney. I had never before felt as I did on that day when we both walked around the block of land. It was now more certain than ever, that we were going to achieve our goal. One day, families in Queensland would benefit from hospice. I felt as I had once before when I received my first promotion in the Royal Dragoons, valuable and worthy of success. My team had worked hard and in only a few months we went from $200 in the bank to a block of land and three quarters of a million dollars in pledges.

I saw when I landed back near Mt. Isa that the boys were happy to be heading towards our next stop, the Walkabout Creek Pub, which was seen in the movie Crocodile Dundee. What greeted us at midday was an empty bar with two young ladies working behind the bar. It was so lacking in atmosphere that I set off to the only other business, a fuel stop servo, to buy the daily paper. Due to the remoteness of the area, it was three days old. We kept forgetting the size of Queensland, which is 40,000 square kilometers. Here we were in McKinley, 250 km east of Mount Isa and approximately 650 km west of Townsville, expecting to find today's paper. A bit of a joke! Sometime around sunset, as we all stood on the steps outside the hotel, we saw headlights in the distance. It looked like a desert movie with bright headlights shining through the golden dust that swirled around the approaching vehicle. We did not have to wait long to realize that these vehicles were making their way to the hotel. We were in for a genuine outback welcome organized by the Queensland Women's Association. What a night it was, with plenty of snags for Tony, beers that came fast and furious and the place full of laughter. We raised a lot of money that night and awoke the next day with hangovers. The place was once again deserted. All the ladies had gone back to their properties, some of which were as big as small nations elsewhere in the world. We collected close to $1,000 that night, which for such a small community was quite exceptional.

The next major town was Toowoomba. I expected a lot of support there since it was the site of Colin's office and our home base. Colin had kept in touch and was excited about families and supporters walking into town with us. When we arrived about 5 kilometers outside of Toowoomba we saw a long cavalcade of supporters. What was even more amazing was to see the faces of the Crane boys in their wheel chairs, with Roger and his wife all set to push them in support of what we had done. I appreciated what it took to get the boys ready to join me: The lifting into the shower, the dressing while one parent held them and the maneuvering of each boy into the transport. It made me feel lucky that Zoë had been so self-sufficient. If I thought that the group walking with us was large, then the group waiting at the park was amazing. There were sideshows, media, and music everywhere. It was a great day with lots of fun for all. Sadly, it was not all good news; Colin mentioned that there were more rumors of a lack of support at the head office. Once again, what could we say? It was disappointing to hear that the Gold Coast branch had not fully supported our endeavor.

I sensed from Tony and Jamie that things were not quite right between them and they informed me that they would like to head home as soon as we reached Toowoomba for a couple of days break. Of course, I agreed; it was not easy staring at my backside for all the distance we had covered. After a couple of days rest, they returned to prepare for the final leg into Brisbane. Tony had some news of his own. Apparently he had been passing blood since we left Townsville. It all made sense now why the atmosphere had been so tense. He was obviously very worried and that's why he had wanted to go home as soon as we got to Toowoomba. Fortunately, it turned out not to be serious and he was able to continue.

On the first day out of Toowoomba we had to walk down the range and I was a little worried that a Mac truck coming down would collect me on its radiator grill and carry me off to Brisbane. Thankfully, I made it to the bottom and plowed on towards Brisbane. About 2:00 pm we saw a car pull up about 100 meters in front of us and we were amazed to see it was Bob again. Here he was baseball cap on back to front, ready to walk with us. This time he'd brought his wife Penny, who was waiting for us at the finish. Cows followed us on the other side of the fence and provided amusement for quite a while. I wonder what they thought.

The Police Pipe Band played as we entered Southbank. My shoulders went back, my chest stood out and my stomach felt tight. We had been on the road for three months and now we were home. Erika and many of my mates turned out. The only person missing was my inspiration, Zoë. It was hard to hold back my tears as I thought of her and the people surrounding me. I would gladly give all this away to spend one hour in her company, to tell her that I loved her and to hear he reply, "Love you too, Dad". But it could never be! I had to be satisfied with knowing in the end all the effort would see other families being helped.

After the thank-you speeches, I glanced through the crowd and watched as Penny and Bob walked away along the river. All I could think was how lucky I was to have met such a wonderful man and how lucky families like ours would be to have a place of shelter for them and their courageous children. That evening Maureen and I met with Bob and Penny. It was a wonderful evening and it was so nice to share my joy at Maureen meeting them. It was great to be home to be able to spend more time with Maureen to prepare for our wedding. We had to take a compatibility test provided by our church. I spoke of my concern about how the children and I would bond; a couple of times, when I had spoken to the girls about their attitude toward their Mum, I had been told not to by Maureen. I was thinking about how my grandfather George may have felt with my Grandmother's family. For me, it was a little like walking on eggshells and though both Maureen and I were pleased to find out that we passed with flying colors, I still felt a sense of concern.

Something happened the day we went to choose the engagement ring that worried me. There appeared to be insufficient funds in the bank when we went to purchase the ring. I said we could wait a week and come back, but Maureen got very angry. I got pretty angry myself. I had just returned from three months away and felt that to wait one week would not make much difference in the scheme of things. I guess she felt embarrassed; I was only earning $35,000 and it cost money to establish myself after the walk. I was not the most cashed-up person, but I had never hidden that fact. In addition, I was having bouts of melancholy and crying on a regular basis. During one appointment, Dr Pearns, Head of Children's Health, said that what I was doing was special and it was all I could do to fight back the tears. A feeling of dread came over me; if anything bad was going to happen it would happen when I was the happiest. The campaign was going well and we reached the one million dollar mark in pledges. Maureen and I were doing great and our wedding plans were coming along nicely when the whole world was shocked by the death of Princess Diana. After church the following Sunday, I overheard some ladies talking as we ate lunch. What they said shocked me: "It's a pity she wasn't born again. She won't go to heaven." I felt so angry! Who were they to judge anyone? If there was a God, would he be so heartless and unforgiving?

The following day I took a phone call from Bob and could not believe my ears. He told me he was leaving the Sydney office as he had been offered a position running another branch in Holland. All I could think was, *it's happening again, someone is leaving.* I then asked Bob if he thought I should go to Sydney and renegotiate the pledge and my package and Bob agreed that would be a good idea. He felt that the pledge might not be honored by the new CEO, John Porter. After I put the phone down I just sat there devastated. We had to find a new campaign manager and we had the annual general meeting coming up. Would we lose momentum? What would I ask for when I met John Porter? Would it be ongoing funding of my position or to keep the pledge intact? My marriage was coming up and I might be losing my job. I honestly believed that without someone working fulltime on this we would not see the hospice built. I informed the Board of Bob's pending transfer and my plan to renegotiate our funding by meeting with John Porter. I felt so much pressure; many families relied on our ability to build the hospice. I flew down to Sydney and almost the moment I walked into the office I became aware that things had changed. The greeting was cold. Was it me or was it the fact that we now had a different type of CEO? I think it was the latter, a change in management style. If so, it did not bode well for me.

When John Porter entered the room I sensed we were not a priority and that the outcome of this meeting may not be what we wanted. There would have to be a trade-off. I remember him saying he would not be playing the same role as Bob and that the company would not meet both pledges. I pointed out that Austar's involvement had seen the company's name in all the local and state media, but I saw that this made not one iota of difference to Mr Porter. I decided that the salary package was the only way to go, as we needed a full time worker to make Zoë's Place a reality. The flight home was not a good one. Things were not as set in concrete as they had been with Bob. The committee accepted the choice I had made, which put my mind at rest a bit, but that didn't stop the feeling of impending doom that I felt when things changed in my life. I started to get teary more often.

Our wedding day arrived and everything turned out great. Friends paid for a brief honeymoon up the north coast and it started so well. However, on the second day I felt the tears again. It was hard to understand. Were they tears of joy or tears of fear? They went as soon as they arrived but they were real. On our return I moved in with Maureen and everything seemed to be going well. Robyn, our campaign manager, was working hard and we were increasing our pledges and meeting our payments to Compton International. Maureen now became even more determined to move into a bigger home. I asked her to please hang on and take it more slowly but she seemed hell-bent on the bigger house and all three of her children moving in. Maureen became aware of my mental state and tried her best to calm me down. I even went to a naturopath but all that did was leave me with a huge bill and a multitude of tablets to take.

There was an incident that did not help. Robyn organized a story for Life Magazine and they wanted to do the interview where I lived, which meant at Maureen's and my home. It just happened to be a Housing Commission house Maureen had before I met her. Maureen dug in her heels and refused to allow the shoot to be held there. Unfortunately, this meant no article. I think Maureen was embarrassed about living in a Housing Commission house; she had been at me for a while to upgrade our housing situation. I couldn't see the sense of this at this point, as we needed to consolidate and take advantage of the cheaper rent. Sure, I wanted to live in a nicer house too, but we needed to wait until my position was more secure. About three months after we married, Maureen and I had a heavy discussion about a house Maureen had chosen and when she left home that day I broke out in a sweat and felt my heart racing. On the spot, I made an impulsive decision to drive to Melbourne to see an old friend. The drive would give me time to think and I valued Mike's counsel. I packed a few things, left a note explaining that I needed to talk with Mike and drove off. One part of me said, "Stop and talk more" the other said, "Keep running".

I cannot remember how many hours I drove, but having to focus on the road helped me clear my mind so I stopped and phoned Maureen. She had every right to be angry but in my emotional state, the words *I am not impressed* were not what I needed to hear. I said: "Nor am I". I threw the phone out of the car window and drove towards Sydney. In my mind I could not see how we could resolve this and, to be honest, I was scared. Here I was, only married three months, running away from issues I could not resolve. Since Zoë's death I'd become frightened of confrontation, frightened of answering the phone, frightened of opening mail. If I didn't have to face things they would go away. If they didn't go away, then I would run away instead.

I found a spot to hide out in a little caravan park in a wooded area. All sorts of thoughts were going through my mind: Should I go back or not go back? Finally, I decided to do what I had done on other occasions—run back to England. I drove the car that Bob had leased for me to Sydney and left it in a car park with a note apologizing and saying I was struggling to make sense of it all. All through the flight I felt positive and in control for a time and then, as if another person took over, I would change my mind and feel awful. I was positive one moment and negative the next. They say that God only gives you what you can handle and what does not destroy you makes you stronger. Well, all I could say was, when does God see that I can't take anymore? I'd had my fair share of sorrow and I felt I was getting weaker, not stronger.

A CRISIS AND HOME TO ENGLAND

I landed at Heathrow with no idea where I was going or what I was going to do. I collected my backpack, walked out of the arrival lounge and saw a bus sign that read Brighton. Brighton was as good as anywhere. I wanted to talk to someone but was too ashamed to call for help. I just wanted to fall into a hole and escape. The voice inside me acted as my conscience, telling me in no uncertain terms that I had done the wrong thing. I wanted so much to do the right thing but I was gripped by a fear of confrontation. I had never been to Brighton so I didn't know what to expect. The in-coach radio reported that there were storm warnings for the coastline around Brighton, so my welcome was cold and wet. When I disembarked from the warmth of the coach I was hit fair in the face by the coldest of winds. I had no idea where anything was situated so I decided to head for the seafront in the hope that there would be a campsite where I could stay for a while until I ran out of funds. Walking along the beach you could hear and see the sea being whipped up into a wild frenzy. There was no doubt that it would be a blustery weekend.

After about one hour of searching I found an information sign saying there was a van and tent ground about 1km ahead so I turned and walked in that direction as fast as I could. When I arrived at the campsite I was pleased to find that there were still plenty of spaces to choose from. Knowing that we were in for a horrible cold time, I tethered my tent behind some bushes and small trees. I had sufficient funds for five days if I ate as little food as possible. With my tent secure, I retired inside my sleeping bag and fell asleep. It seemed as though I had slept for a week when I was awakened by heavy rain pounding my tent and the wind shaking it like a fox terrier would shake a dead rat. The full force of the storm crossed the coast in the early hours of the morning and caught many holiday-makers out. I looked out of my warm tent and saw people franticly trying to secure their accommodations in the pouring rain. It was that time of night when, try as you may not to, you still have to visit the toilet. As I bolted from my tent I felt how drenching the storm had been during my sleep as the ground was already water logged. I was about 20 yards from the toilet block and in the short time it took to sprint over the waterlogged grass I was wet through. I pushed my way into the toilet block only to be greeted by people who had evacuated their tents to find a dry area to shelter. I was fortunate to have chosen my patch of ground well as there were many miserable souls sharing the floor of the toilet block.

Two days later the storm moved on, leaving that part of the coastline well and truly battered. The interior of my tent was damp but it had provided a safe haven almost like a mother's womb. But while I was safe from outside influences, the only way I could leave my conscience behind was to sleep. I was able to survive by eating as little as possible. I got up early in the morning and took a loaf of bread and a bottle of milk from outside a restaurant. I needed to find some help, but having arrived at the weekend it would be 3 days before I could approach the social security. When I did finally pluck up the courage to go to the social security office I discovered that I needed a place of residence to get any help. They did, however, give me a small amount of money for food. It was barely enough. There was nothing else to do but find work as soon as possible so I set off to the employment centre. After much searching I found a position advertised for a night security manager for a small hotel. I went back to my tent and made myself as presentable as possible for an interview. The interview went very well and there was a possibility of accommodation after a month, although the lady at the employment centre had warned me that some of the accommodations that hotels provided were very substandard.

Here was an opportunity to work, but I had no money for food and only two days left at the campsite. Returning to my tent, I lay down and had a conversation with my conscience. It took about 12 hours for my conscience to win. I had to go home and face the music. It was time to act like an adult and not a frightened little boy. I had sufficient funds to at least make a phone call to someone who could help me. It had to be someone I could talk honestly to. The only person I knew that I thought lived close by was Ernie, my old army mate and Zoë's Godfather. He and his wife Sandy had been such good friends to me in the past. I was embarrassed to call them but I had to make the call. Like the true friends they were, Sandy told me to stay where I was and they would drive down and pick me up.

I didn't realize just how far it was from Hull Bridge, Essex to Brighton and it took Sandy a couple of hours. While I sat and waited, the two voices within me kept up their conversation: *Stay. Run. Stay. Run.* The more it repeated, the more I sweated and shook. Sandy and her daughter, Karen, arrived and as we drove back I poured as much of my heart out as I could and asked if I could stay with them a little while. It turned out that they already knew about my situation; Mike Whelton, whom I originally set out to see, had contacted them after speaking to Maureen. I talked about my feelings and what had gone wrong, about how I always believed that things would go wrong or I would make the wrong decision. This time I had hurt someone, and that did not sit well with me. The fear of making a mistake again troubled me.

The day after arriving at Ernie and Sandy's place, I walked along the river Crouch reminiscing about happier times there with Zoë and Erika. I was not sure what I was looking for, but being there heightened the sense of loss. I walked all the way to the antique shops at Battlebridge, where I had bought an antique gold bracelet for Erika, when she decided to start a new life with me. I had stood at this very spot waiting for her to return from Austend with her answer. Now here I was, 17 years later, Zoë gone and me incapable of leading a normal life. Two years earlier, I was the central figure in a walk from England through North America and back to Australia and had established a children's hospice organization. What the hell was wrong with me? Like my school reports had read, "If Nigel had a little more self-belief he could achieve so much more". I don't know exactly when that belief in me disappeared, but it had disappeared like a fog in the night leaving no visible signs that it had ever existed. Was it when Neil Foulds, four years older, beat me up? Was it when I let 11 goals in as goalie for my class? Or was it the battle within, trying to justify my mother for leaving me? I truly do not know.

I was sure that it should not be events that shape our lives, but our reactions to those events. It was here that I went wrong. For too long I made the easy, less painful choice, almost like a coward. When my first major challenge had occurred in 1993, I clearly saw the consequences of choosing the wrong route during a period of crisis. As I mentioned earlier, crisis has two sides: danger and opportunity. The danger was that I would resort to drinking and find myself on the street; the opportunity was to take the emotion and energy of Zoë's funeral and create something of value. Yet here I was, three years later, running from something again.

I finally found the courage to talk to Maureen, although the combination of fear and shame left me sweating and in tears. She offered to come over, but I felt she should not and I told her I would return. In my heart, I was still nervous and unsure of what I wanted to do. I also spoke to Bob McRann, who was in Amsterdam. He decided to travel to London and then down to Ernie's home in Hullbridge to see me. That meeting was on a different level than our other meetings because I felt I had let him down after he had placed so much faith in me, but it was still good to see him. He listened to me carefully and then said he honestly felt that, while it was okay for me to take whatever time I needed to heal, the organization might not want me back when I returned. He also warned me that Maureen might feel that way as well. I could see the truth in both those statements, and I was grateful for his friendship and advice. I still found it hard to sleep and I was unable to make a decision. I started to think about the impact I was having on Ernie and his family. He got angry when I spoke of taking my own life, and he had every right to feel that way. He also said he felt I was running from nothing that could not be resolved.

Ernie shared a story with me that clearly demonstrated how we tend to blow things out of all proportion. Some time ago, a colleague of his had received a letter with a VAT stamp on the envelope and imagined it was bad news. Rather than opening it, he chose to take his own life. In fact, the envelope had contained a refund. It was a perfect example of what can happen when one is confronted with a fear. The adrenalin flows and we find ourselves in the fight-or-flight mode.

The following morning, after our discussion, I left the house and made my way to Southend. I decided to find someplace to stay, get a job, save some money and try to get out of "running mode". I spent a couple of nights sleeping on benches, waiting for the employment and rental property offices to open. I was amazed at the number of people of all ages on the street. Those two nights were very restless because I was worried about the possibility of being attacked for my rucksack and its contents. On Monday, I was very lucky for someone with no home or work. I was able to find accommodation in the form of a small terrace house in Shoebryness and I got a job as a night porter at the Grand Hotel. The Grand was not very grand any more, with holes in the ceiling and many unfortunate refugees from Bosnia crammed into rooms. It was a paying job, however, and it helped me settle.

Before long I had found a better position as a sports club manager. It was short-lived, however, as I had walked straight into a typical club political fight. One day I was misled into divulging that a member of staff had not signed in to work at the right time, and the committee demanded her resignation. Apparently, there was a culture of petty theft and staff signing in for each other long before I arrived. This proved too much and I left the club that night in tears. I felt guilty for hurting another human being, especially as she was someone who had a family. I once again found myself in tears with a need to run away and find a place free of stress.

Once again, I took off with my tail between my legs and no idea where I was headed. While hitchhiking along the coast, I constantly saw the sign for Dover. So Dover it would be! This decision was helped when the guy who offered me a lift said that he was going all the way to Dover. By the time we got there it was getting dark and, as I knew nothing about the city, I had no idea where I was going to find a place to spend the night. All I knew was that Dover had been my port of call when I headed home on leave from my service in Germany in 1966, the day England played Germany in the Soccer World Cup Final. As I sat on the train back then, England scored the winning goal. The screams of joy were comparable to the jubilation of World War two finishing. This time, my arrival in Dover was much different; twenty-eight years had passed by and I was homeless. When we drove over the hill and down into Dover we could see the lights of the two ports, the hovercraft port and, farther along the seafront, the main port of entry into England. The Chunnel between France and England, which was built during my absence, was further up the coast. Dover was the main port for London and, to be honest, it was struggling to cope with the many legal and illegal immigrants that had flooded in since the war in the Balkans. There was also the exploitation of young people, especially in prostitution (controlled by the immigrant hard cases from the Serbian war) and smuggling of contraband alcohol and cigarettes. Young people went over on the ferries and brought contraband back for their criminal financiers. The transfer of goods and money taking place in the local pubs or, blatantly in the port car park was phenomenal.

I got out of the car, thanked the kind person who had helped me, and immediately looked for an indication of where to spend the night. With very little money and no local knowledge, I looked behind me to see a large hill that was part of the cliffs facing France. The hill was well covered in bushes and trees so it would offer me some concealment, shelter and most of all safety. It was a steep and blustery climb and after I climbed sufficiently high to be out of sight from the road I found a large bush area that would allow me to conceal my tent. It took me about 20 minutes to pitch and conceal the small one-man tent that had been home on my charity walk. This time it was a welcome shelter from all my fears. I must have been very tired as I cannot remember falling asleep. Upon waking I heard the sound of seagulls as they swooped along the white cliffs off the coastline. White cliffs that had welcomed thousands of rescued soldiers from the Dunkirk tragedy back to friendly soils. What had brought me to Dover once again and what did I hope it would do for me? Dover was still a place to which many grieving people seemed to gravitate, whether they were disillusioned young men wanting to do the romantic thing and join the French Foreign Legion (only to find later that it is one of the most grueling training grounds for soldiers of any country), or young people who have been robbed of a childhood and are looking for some quick dollars in the hope it will bring long-lost happiness. Me, I suppose I was hoping for some respite, an opportunity to resolve my grief and develop some backbone to return home to Australia and face the music. All I could hope for was that people understood the cause of my breakdown, even though they may not have agreed with my method of dealing with it.

Over the next couple of days I spent a lot of time in the Employment and Social Security offices trying to get some assistance. I was able to get a small loan that was available to the homeless. Because I was living in the tent, I was able to make it stretch for a reasonable time. I also discovered that there was a food van at one of the car parks where you could get coffee, soup and sandwiches. Standing next to the food van gave me a firsthand look at the cross-section of people who shared the same fate as me, ending up on the street living minute to minute; young people who obviously had drug habits and criminals who were making their way out of the country. On the third night, when I was lying in my tent, I heard a gunshot that concerned me. All I could do was lie still and hope they didn't spot me concealed in the bush next to them. Thankfully, they left and I was able to fall back asleep. The next morning I saw that they had just been firing at some bottles, but the incident convinced me to move on. I folded my tent up and stuffed it into my rucksack, then hid the rucksack and set off to find a safer place to sleep. I decided to visit a doctor and talk to him about my predicament. I was able to get in to see one and he arranged for me to meet with the Mental Health Team in Dover the following week. As I left his office he advised me that there was an YHA (Youth Hostel Association) hostel in Dover. That advice was okay, but I had no money so I would have to ask if I could pay when I got my unemployment benefit.

As I walked away from the surgery, I saw a sign that said YMCA. I was a little confused and took that to be the place the doctor had meant. It turned out to be one of those moments in time that I would look back on and ask myself, was there someone guiding me from above. The YMCA stands for Young Men's Christian Association and this one was doing God's work by providing a shelter for those people that found themselves in need of a bed for a night. I walked inside and followed the stairs to the offices where I met the secretary and told her of my predicament. She advised me to come back at 6:00 pm and I would be able to sleep on the gym floor and talk to the General Manager the next day about any help the YMCA and community welfare departments could offer me. As instructed, I turned up at about fifteen minutes to six that night. To my surprise, I saw about eight other people waiting on the steps, some with baggage and others empty-handed. I discovered that they were people who had been there for a few days. The night manager was most certainly not the life and soul of the party and there was a distinct smell of alcohol on his breath and clothing. This, mixed with the smell of cigarette smoke, discouraged one from standing too close to him.

The night manager directed us downstairs to the office (where I had been earlier that day) and took all our details. He then took us into our "bedroom" for the night, where we were issued with a blanket, pillow and foam mattress and told that the security of our personal effects was not guaranteed. Throughout the evening, I saw a parade of people of all types: elderly, homeless, mentally ill, and those who spent a lot of time in the bathroom, sometimes leaving evidence of drug use. When ten o'clock arrived, there were about twenty people sleeping on the floor. To say that I found it hard to close my eyes is an understatement: people smoked and coughed, consumed hidden alcohol and had loud verbal battles. It was enough to make anyone feel vulnerable.

Tiredness overtook me and eventually I fell asleep. I awoke when the door banged open and the night manager yelled at us to hurry up as we had to be out of the building by 8.00 am. We were given a bowl of cereal and tea or coffee, and then sent on our way to return at 6.00 pm that evening. This seemed a little harsh; Dover wasn't the warmest place, with the cold winds coming off the English Channel, but we were left to find our own shelter and food during the day. Intimidating groups of unsavory people always seemed to be standing around in groups. Most of them seemed to be Eastern European and they looked shifty. Isn't it amazing how the unknown scares us to the point where we will run instead of learning more about that unknown? The next morning I waited until the Manager of the Dover YMCA, Alan Sugden, completed his morning tasks and invited me to have a coffee with him. There was something about him that made me feel comfortable and I was able to share in this initial talk some of my past and those things that had worried me sufficiently to see me walk away from a promising future. Over the next week I was able to share more and more of my fundraising background and this interested him. He was keen to show me a project that the YMCA had embarked upon.

The project was in a very old historical building that had once been the Naval College. It was on the other side of the town, on York Street. The project was known as the Prince of Wales Project because it received the funding from the Prince of Wales Fund. It developed from a vision that Alan had for the children of the Dover area, a drop-in centre that would help them develop higher self-esteem and confidence so they could get jobs. It was already obvious to me that there was a big problem in this community with children who lived rough. Many were involved with petty crime and mixed with the professional criminal element in Dover. You could see Alan's pride in getting the project off the ground. He had good reason to be proud as he had been able to convince the government and local jails that young offenders could benefit from being involved. Alan introduced me to Mike Dixon, the hands-on project manager. Mike and his mother also helped the local underprivileged by operating the food van that had provided me with much-needed food when I was sleeping rough. Alan and Mike explained my entitlements and told me where to go to access financial assistance. Alan put me in contact with a lady who was the caseworker for a local government organization that offered furnished flats to young people who had difficulties at home. Although there were none available at that time, she knew of one particular boy who needed a father figure and said I could stay at the YMCA until a flat became available that both of us could share.

Dover had a unique community-sponsored counseling service that charged only what you could afford to pay. It was here that I started to unravel the issues I had carried since childhood. I learned that, as a result of all the unexplained grief I went through in my early years, I lived with the expectation of nothing ever working out for me. It was as if I was doomed to loss and failure. I believed that if people left my life, I was not worthy of their friendship. It seemed that all the people who I relied on for advice, support and encouragement either died or walked away. To me, loss was the only constant in my life. Over the following months I would see first-hand how unresolved grief affects communities all over the world: Young people who chose to live rough after losing their innocence through sexual, emotional or physical abuse; elderly people who lost a spouse after many years of marriage; businessmen who walked away because their business failed. As a middle-aged man who lost his daughter long after losing his father and mother, I could fit right in. And Alan Sugden helped them all by directing them all to the counseling centre.

I remembered that back in 1996, when I spoke to the blood bank doctor in Brisbane about the need for hospice, he had said, "It is impossible to calculate the effect that grief has on the community financially, be it through time lost at work, suicide, homelessness and divorce". It was as if Dover was a vortex that drew these people in. Thankfully, the Dover YMCA staff was there to catch anybody lucky enough to venture in from the cold. The help and support they offered when all other hope was gone was much needed.

Finally the flat became available and I moved in with the 16-year old boy. I was looking forward to mentoring the lad. It proved to be a very challenging situation, he had been beaten by his stepfather and had too many issues for me to cope with. The flats were in blocks and there were other issues like petty theft, drug use and violence that I also found hard to cope with. Try as I did to listen to their calls for help, it always seemed to end with misuse of someone's space and personal items. It saddened me to leave but when Alan Sugden offered me the position of Night Supervisor at the YMCA (which included one of the six rooms upstairs), I jumped at the opportunity to move in.

While living upstairs I saw another effect of grief, the loss of a brother had driven a young man to alcohol. Like me, he'd found himself on the doorstep of the YMCA and Alan had given him a shoulder to lean on. Over the following years he had become Night Supervisor, the role I had just taken on. It was not until he went missing for a while that his true plight surfaced. A few days after he disappeared, a smell started to drift from under the door to his room. It became so bad that Alan was forced to break in. What they found was incredible! Piled three feet high on the floor were empty plastic cider bottles. They were also in the cupboards and drawers. After the YMCA staff emptied the room of bottles, they opened his locker to find many, many more. Thankfully, he was found some days later walking the streets of the next town. He had been a good soldier back in South Africa but the loss of his brother to terrorists had left him a shattered person.

Later, I saw firsthand how a father's abuse of his daughter had left her scarred enough to see her seek similar treatment from her pimp. I will call her Jenny. She showed up one evening at the hostel asking for shelter and, as with everyone seeking shelter, I gave her coffee and bedding then sat and talked with her. It was obvious that she had been beaten by someone. As we talked, she confided in me that she was running alcohol and cigarettes across the channel for a man almost twenty-five years her senior. In repayment, he gave her some money and developed a sexual relationship with her. If Jenny failed to fulfill whatever illegal task he devised he would beat her. She told me this had gone on for over a year. I was able to give her a room. Two days later we heard a noise, a loud thump as if someone had fallen. We ran to the room where she was staying, caught the pimp as he tried to run, and threw him out. We discovered that Jenny had invited him in and he had not only had sex with her, but had hit her when the sex was not to his liking. I asked why, after all the other beatings, she had gone back to him and she replied, "For the cuddles". She said the relationship was like the one she'd had with her father who had sexually abused her, then held her close and cuddled her to keep her quiet.

A few weeks later, a very special man walked into my life. At the YMCA on Leybourne Road I was often introduced to people whose stories were far more challenging than mine. Roger was one of those people. It was about 7.00 pm when two young guys turned up with Roger. He was well, clean and articulate and I later discovered we were born in the same year. It was not hard to like Roger because he was so humble. I was able to give all three guys a space on the gym floor. The next morning, though the other two guys were up fairly early and on the street, Roger made no effort to leave because he was keen to catch up with me and talk. I liked to believe that I made him feel as safe as Alan had made me feel. Roger poured out his pain. Like me, he had walked away from a successful life with a driving school business, wife and family. Since he left everything behind he had not stayed in one place for any length of time but he decided that he wanted to spend some time in Dover with me. It was not long before we formed a strong friendship and I was able to provide him with a room and a safe haven because the street can be a frightening place when you are in your fifties, especially if the young streetwise guys discover that you have a little money. We spent many hours together. He was a patient listener and never judged the people he came into contact with.

One night a month, the YMCA had a disco for intellectually handicapped people. It always made me feel good to see them enjoying themselves but they could be quite a handful. They were very sexually active and inquisitive so one had to be on guard at all times. Over the next 6 months I was able to take stock of my feelings and begin to deal with what I saw as my mistakes. The counseling and prescription antidepressants helped as well. For the first time in a long while, I was in a good space. I was still unable to contact either family or friends in England or Australia but I felt that I was getting closer to being able to face those people I had hurt and left behind. I was still able to believe that in crisis you can take the energy and emotion that accompanies whatever the challenge is and achieve a good outcome. In my eyes, while I had let people down by running away from my problems, I had also been given an opportunity to help others, which allowed me to take away the focus of my own self-pity. In the past, this pity nearly consumed me. Many of the people who inspired me had gone on to have an impact on their communities: Terry Fox, Nelson Mandela, and many others who were lesser known on the world stage.

Dover showed me every day that wherever we are, there are people in need we may be able to help. However, I was upset at the low level of effort put in by some of the YMCA Board of Directors, a group of people led by a member of the local clergy. One morning the clergyman was in the office as I was putting in my nightly report. In a conversation with Alan, he said the people upstairs should be helping themselves a little more. This offended me greatly, for in all my time at the Y not one board member had gone upstairs to talk to the guys. I was sure that they did not know about the highly ignitable cocktail of personality issues that spent each night behind the locked front door. At Zoë's Place, I had tried hard to find board or committee members that understood they were not just there as figureheads to be brought out on parade days; I needed them to take an interest and do the hard yards. Sadly, so many boards just seemed to be there for the kudos. I could see by talking to long-serving YMCA national staff that it would be hard to convince them to change their attitudes on fundraising, etc.

I convinced Alan to let me undertake a feasibility study regarding the public's support of the Prince of Wales Project. After talking to a selection of local business and local government leaders I discovered that, while many people thought the project had stalled they still supported the concept. They knew full well that there was a major problem with the young people in both Dover and Kent. My advice to Alan and the YMCA was to identify a local high-profile champion and then undertake a capital campaign. The building that would become the youth hostel still required a huge amount of work before it would be habitable. At a meeting of local and county staff, it became obvious to me that the organization was set in its ways. Although I worked part time for them I was still one of those who resided upstairs, out of arm's reach. Once people were upstairs, there was no program in place that took their rehabilitation any further. I had spent a fair few hours preparing a SWOT report (Strengths, Weaknesses, Opportunities and Threats), as well as a fundraising plan, but it was never even discussed and I was never given an opportunity to take it any farther.

Twelve months had gone by and I could see that my time at the Y was nearing an end and that I felt more confident to face the people back home. Roger and I talked about me leaving for home and he was a source of great encouragement. We had seen the recruitment of two new board members. One was a young, successful business lady who was focused on helping the guys upstairs; the other seemed intent on replacing the board chairman. Both Roger and I felt that while we could not influence the direction of the Y, we had benefited from our stay. Roger was now able to spend more time in one place than he had before. Without Roger's support and friendship I would not have reached the quieter, stronger emotions I was now feeling. One night while talking to some of the residents I announced out of the blue that I was going back to Australia to face the music as soon as possible. Bob McRann had indicated during our last meeting that when I was emotionally stronger I should contact him, so that night I found myself calling Bob on the office phone. He asked if I was sure of my decision. I told him that after counseling and medication I was sure I could deal with the issues that had to be dealt with. He told me to book the ticket and he would pay for me to return home to Australia.

During my time in Dover I traveled to London in the hope of seeing some of my old military mates, but I was never successful in finding any of them. Then Dover showed it had one last trick up its sleeve. As I walked out of the travel agency having booked my ticket for Brisbane, I looked up and walking through the door was a tall, good-looking guy about my own age. I recognized him as an old army mate, Charlie Brown. I called out, "Charlie, is that you"? When he said yes, I said "It's me, Sack". He looked sad and said he was in a hurry but he gave me his phone number and asked me to give him a call. After all this time, I had met an old mate just as I was returning home to Australia. Sadly, I was never able to contact Charlie and later discovered that he had died. I wondered what life had dealt him since he studied accountancy by correspondence as a young man.

The day before I was due to fly out of the UK, Roger and I spent some time together. We walked around the town and had a couple of pints at our favourite bar. It was going to be hard to say farewell to Roger because he had been a good friend. In fact, I made many friends in Dover. About 3:00 pm we decided to head back to the Y. To my amazement, on our arrival I was greeted by just about everyone who had befriended me. There were decorations and food set out. It just blew me away. Alan handed me a card signed by everyone who had helped me. The greatest surprise came when he presented me with a gold watch engraved with, "From all your friends at the YMCA Dover". Never in my wildest dreams did I expect such a farewell. Many of the people who contributed had been homeless and some were only receiving a pension. Among them was a young Japanese student we had helped who gave half his food allowance, five pounds. I am not sure why, but for the first time in a long while I felt a sense of freedom while I was living in the YMCA. Maybe what I had wanted when I ran away was to be free of my past, to be myself without other people's expectations. As I went to bed that night I knew I would miss these people who welcomed me in and had in no way been judgmental. That night before I left, while I sat watching my last Dover sunset, I noticed an article in the local newspaper about an unfortunate casualty of the Dover drug trade. I had on many occasions seen a guy in his late twenties with a young girl and a dog. As I mentioned before, if you had a dog and were unemployed you received an allowance for your pet. Well, that same young guy was found in a public toilet dead with a needle in his arm.

The following morning, Mike Dixon, Roger and Mike's mate drove me to the airport. It was pouring rain as we drove out of Dover and all I could think about was how many young people like those I had tried to help seemed lost. I remembered the day I sat in a local pub and overheard two elderly men discussing the young people of today as a selfish lot. I took the opportunity to interject, saying that I thought the most endangered species on the planet was children because they

221

were without family life, affection, direction and hope. The boys and girls I encountered just wanted someone to listen to their stories and give them some help. Although I had hurt people through the actions I took during my breakdown, I hoped that I compensated in some way in Dover by working with the homeless. I boarded the flight to Australia not knowing what to expect or where my life was going to take me next.

POLITICS, BROKEN PROMISES AND CUCKOO'S

It had been four years since I flew into Brisbane to see Zoë before she died. That time, I was met at the airport. This time I would most certainly have no one to greet me and I was nervous, to say the least. I had sufficient funds for a few nights in the Youth Hostel Association and hoped that I could access what little superannuation I had to help me start all over again. I wasn't sure if Zoë's Place had survived and did not want to get involved in it. I felt I had no right to be welcomed back, having walked out on everyone and let the families down. I did, however, want to find out how it was faring. I imagined that Erika would have stepped up to be the President.

After booking into the Youth Hostel Association, I made a phone call to the association only to get the answering machine. The recorded voice did not sound familiar. It took a while for me to remember Pamela Barker, the retired nun from the Mater Hospital whom I had recruited after getting the land and setting up the fundraising committee. At the time, I thought the organization should have a spiritual presence and felt that Pamela Barker would be ideal for this. If there is one thing in my life that I regret, it is the fact that I brought this woman to Zoë's Place. She became one of the Cuckoos.

The next day was a Sunday and I decided to go for a walk through Brisbane. I opted to visit the office just in case someone was there. I knocked on the door and, to my surprise; who opened it but Erika. Shortly after I walked into the office the phone rang. It was Erika's partner, Don, and he immediately went on the attack. "What the hell do you want, you left us high and dry" he said. I very quickly went on the attack telling him in no uncertain terms to not talk to me like a dog. I then handed the phone to Erika. It was great to see her;

she looked great and seemed genuinely pleased to see me. She put the phone down and we decided to have a coffee together.

We sat at a coffee shop across the road and talked about how things were going and it was clear that things were not going well. There were two camps and the current president was locked in a battle with Erika. It was a battle that revolved around direction, commitment and accountability. Judging by the tone of Don's voice, I guessed that a Cuckoo had appeared. The battle was between Don, who was the current treasurer of Zoë's Place, and Pamela, who was very controlling. Erika said they were about to have a special meeting to propose a vote of no confidence in the president. She asked if I would attend. This put me in a spot because I had no right to take sides. I had been away for thirteen months and wasn't sure of what was what. If Erika was in the wrong, I could not vote against her because she was Zoë's mum. I was curious now just what was going on.

On Monday I went back to the office to meet with Pamela. She was very pleasant. She asked what had happened and I explained as much as I could without sharing too much. She said that the information they had released regarding me was that I was ill and went home for a rest. It was very obvious that she had no time for Erika and I knew that the feeling was mutual. It was probably due to Don's obvious dislike for the Catholic Church, which he described as a vortex swallowing all that came into its path. He clearly felt that this was what was happening to Zoë's Place. I believed that Zoë's Place should remain independent of any larger body like the Mater Hospital and that it should remain non-denominational. Based on all I had heard from three of the parties involved, I still believed that I should not get involved in the vote of no confidence. I met with the new Queensland Manager of Compton International and she also felt that I should steer clear of any involvement and said to be on my guard when dealing with Erika and Don. I decided to contact Colin Walker and seek council. He informed me that he was going to the Special Meeting and that he would make his decision that night about his vote. I trusted Colin but was concerned about how Erika and Colin felt about each other.

Feeling a little more secure, I sat back and waited for the outcome of the special meeting. Colin had agreed to keep me informed. At this point I had no reason to doubt Pamela's commitment to the project but I contacted one other person whose opinion I valued, Judy Stone. Judy was a good friend and an even better businessperson. She felt that Erika's position was correct. Having been away with no knowledge of events of the last year and hearing several opinions, I just hoped that the members would do the right thing.

Sadly, when Colin came to see me after the meeting he was less than happy about the outcome. The meeting had developed into a slugfest: Don's ability as Treasurer was called into account and Erika was verbally attacked. Concerned about the direction the meeting had been taken Colin asked the patron, Senator John Heron, to take control of the proceedings. I believe that even though he saw that Pamela Barker was wrong, the fact that he was a Catholic prevented him from going against a nun. Surely a person should not allow his or her conscience to be swayed by their allegiance to a particular religion when making a decision relating to the well being of an organization caring for sick children. It seemed that on this occasion it had. Senator John Heron acted as an envoy to Vatican City and the outcome went in favour of Pamela Barker. According to Colin, it had been a complete farce. Erika and Don stepped down and Pamela Barker stayed on as the President.

Over the next two months I attended a few small fundraising meetings to speak on behalf of Zoë's Place. On one of these occasions I discovered why people could not work with Pamela Barker. After the meeting, Pamela said that I was not to include my personal story in any talks, but to focus on what the hospice would do. The next time we met, she asked me if I wanted to be involved with fundraising. Something told me not to take the offer up; that decision later proved to be a wise one. It soon became obvious that there was a move within the organization to distance itself from my family. Pamela said people wanted to change the name, though she mentioned nobody in particular. I contacted a good friend of the family who sat on the board, Anna McMahon, and she said she knew nothing about it.

I started to look for work. One position I thought I could fill was at the Wesley Hospital. However, there was no personal touch at the interview and I got the impression that it was just a big conglomerate taking money from every possible avenue. The interviewing officer asked why I had not approached them with the idea of a children's hospice. I told him I was a novice at building such projects and that I thought that a hospital would not be interested in the idea. The second position I considered was general Manager of a Queensland organization for the blind. I spoke to Bob McRann and told him I was being head hunted by an organization caring for the blind. I gave them Bob's name as a reference and shortly after they spoke with him they invited me to attend an interview. What immediately caught my attention was the fact that it had been started by a blind person, the man sitting opposite me. Like myself, he had stood up and been counted. I was impressed with what had been achieved and they seemed impressed with me. They were concerned about any possible conflict of interest with raising money for Zoë's Place. I assured them that I had moved on and wanted to help visually impaired people.

The next six months were terrible as far as achieving any goals. I soon discovered I was the first sighted person to the position of General Manager and, although I had been hired as someone to manage the team that was already in place, the founder was not ready to let go. Over the following weeks I started to see things that concerned me, things that had the potential to put the organization under close scrutiny. My mental state was also once again somewhat troubled. I decided to resign at the Annual General Meeting that year, but before leaving I pointed out things that needed to change for the organization to survive. During my tenure, I met a gentleman named Bill who had gone blind consuming methylated spirits. His story was typical of many I saw in Dover. He lost a child to cot death in his early twenties and the shock made him walk away from a good position, a home and a wife. For the next twenty years he moved around, living rough, and with every drink got closer to blindness. All I could think was, "there but for the grace of God go I". Tragedy struck us both and created both danger and opportunity: Bill's life was fraught with danger while I had chosen to help others. How lucky was I?

I kept getting drawn back to Zoë's Place. Although I wanted to stay away, others with their own agendas wanted to use my profile. One such incident almost led to the overturning of a committee that seemed more focused on developing good brochures than raising money. One member had been a work colleague of mine back when I sold insurance. I was able to address the committee at their next meeting, which was held on an upper level of a very expensive business address in Brisbane. It shocked me that they all seemed to think that attractive brochures would automatically generate donations. I listened to them approve the brochures and then asked my friend from the insurance company whether he agreed that no matter how good your brochure was, success boiled down to asking for the premium (or in our case the donation). He reluctantly agreed that this was the case. It was obvious to me that the group did not understand their role; the current president had not explained to them their function in the organization. I asked the chairman, John Garnsey, "Sir what do you think the role of this group is"? He replied, "I am the Chairman and this is the Board". When I told him that this was in fact a sub-committee and there is no provision for a board in the constitution, he admitted that he had never read the constitution.

I left that meeting amazed that a group of the most successful business people in Brisbane had not taken the time to read the constitution. What also struck me was that this group of people did not understand their role in the capital campaign. They were elected to the fundraising committee because they had influence and affluence. They were supposed to lead by example and make donations that would influence their peers to donate at a similar level. It was obvious that both the president and the chairperson of the fundraising committee were not prepared to ask their peers to donate. I thought someone like mining giant Ken Talbot, one of the richest people in Queensland, could influence not only individuals but a whole industry by putting a levy on coal per ton. Although Ken gave a small donation of his own, he chose not to use his connections with the coal industry to raise money.

By now the movement to overthrow the fundraising committee had gained momentum, mainly because the current President, Pamela Barker, lacked skills when it came to managing people. Convinced that the group challenging Pamela had the numbers to overturn the current fundraising committee, an emergency general meeting was called to hold a vote of no confidence in the current committee. Although the day was soured by infighting and internal politics, it allowed me to meet Ken Talbot. After Colin Walker, the founding chairman, made his presentation about how the current president had failed the organization, Ken Talbot stood up and basically threatened that if Pamela was removed he would not approach the coal industry for a million-dollar sponsorship. After Ken Talbot finished speaking, Erika and I withdrew our support and the name that the organization traded under and walked out of the room. You could have heard a pin drop. Erika and I waited outside for Colin to join us. When he arrived he surprised us by asking us to return to the table and discuss how we could overcome the problems that had arisen. Like me, Erika was hesitant as we had already gone through too much rubbish over the term of this president. However, we agreed to go back to the meeting. The Committee members had a definite lack of knowledge about the history of the organization but what was even worse was their lack of understanding about how to fundraise. Once again, I explained the basic principle of capital fundraising. Find a chairperson with influence and affluence. Someone who will lead by example by making a large donation, then let him approach his or her peers asking for similar sizable donations. After I had explained all this for the second time I looked at Ken Talbot and said, "Someone similar to you". The only indication he gave of understanding was a sly grin. Another committee member, David Read, said he had a problem speaking to people about Zoë's Place because he had no title that showed he represented the organization. When I told them all that I had raised almost 2 million dollars in pledges and the only title I had was Zoë's dad, it didn't go down well. The outcome of that meeting was that we pledged to work one more time with the current committee.

The following months were basically no different to the previous months. President Pamela Barker did as she pleased and no approach was made to the coal industry as she had promised to do if re-elected. We kept getting the same answer from her, that business commitments kept Ken from fulfilling his promise. As time went by, Erika and I were not kept in the loop so I went along my merry way and tried to come to terms with not having any input. During this period I found it hard to deal with my loneliness and, as before, I was still unable to make a firm decision on the direction I should take. The inner voice was constantly telling me that all the effort required to build a successful life was not worth it. I still seemed to take one step forward and then two steps back.

WALKING FOR MUSCULAR DYSTROPHY

I decided to return to the old format of walking for someone in need and spoke to my friend and supporter, Peter Denham, the CEO of Muscular Dystrophy. I felt that people afflicted with Muscular Dystrophy needed as much as any others and Peter responded well to the idea of me pushing an empty wheelchair from Melbourne to Brisbane. As on other occasions, I was able to call on my mates Tony and Liz to be my back up. I followed up by contacting Chris Gallagher in Colorado for sponsorship. Like on many other occasions, Chris had no hesitation in saying yes and he was able to put together most of the packet. Chris notified Williams the Shoeman stores along the route and asked them to help raise funds, both in-store and in any other fashion they chose.

The start in Melbourne was special because we began the walk at Fred Murphy's house in Croydon. It had been about 29 years since I had last seen Fred and 35 years since he had shared a train carriage as we headed towards Tonfanau in North Wales. Here we were many years later and many miles away from Waterloo station. Tony had also known Fred and served with him in Borneo so it was a great few days we had together. The morning that we started we discovered that Fred had filled every space available in the camper van with cans of beer. He then proceeded to give us cash for the journey. Just before we set off I received the news that I had been selected to carry the Olympic torch. Although it was a wonderful honor, the challenge was that I would be walking somewhere in New South Wales so we would have to drive back to be in time for the relay. Once we were underway, just like on previous walks, we were not sure if each individual store had embraced the event but I was confident that Muscular Dystrophy Association members from associations both in Victoria and Queensland had notified families and the media. In the past, the full potential of the walks was never achieved because little effort was put in by organizations but, to be fair, charities must fight for the dollar when it comes to hiring people so they have to operate on limited staff levels. I was also sure we would again meet some wonderful and inspiring people.

Unfortunately, Tony's spirit quickly faded. I had hoped that he would draw on the fact that he was undertaking something of value. Every family we encountered throughout our journeys could not stop saying thank you, but I guess that each of us is motivated by different things or life events. What mattered most was that he was with us, for I could not be doing this without his help. To make things worse, the first store we visited was a disappointment with nothing at all organized. This had a demoralizing effect on all of us and it was hard to stay positive as we talked at the store.

One of the things that can affect the success of a walk is crossing state borders. Each state organization was protective of both its client base and its funds. This was evident by the lack of attendance at the stores. Two of the stores on route were able to get schools to participate by inviting children to come down so we could talk to them and introduce them to young people who were battling this shocking disease. It was always inspiring to talk to parents and grandparents who were battling to give their young people all the care they needed, especially when they also had healthy children to care for. One of the reasons I wanted to get the hospice up and functioning was to provide sibling support. Very often they were the forgotten ones, as mum and dad had to be so focused on keeping the sick child alive.

When the day came to leave the walk and drive to Caloundra to join the team of people that were carrying the Olympic Torch, I felt an enormous amount of pride. Although I had walked thousands of kilometers, I was not good at running and I was concerned about how running would affect my leg. While we were on the bus waiting to start, we all shared our stories and I realized just how many inspirational people there are in communities all over the world. As I stepped out of the coach, my heart was already pumping away with the exhilaration of the whole experience. Standing on the side of the road I kept a close eye on the horizon. Suddenly I saw the Olympic group approaching and there in the middle was the torch and its carrier. The handover went well. The time flew by and for as long as it lasted I was on an incredible high. Apart from having my daughter, I cannot think of anytime in my life that came close to the way I felt at that time. It made me ask myself how these young athletes felt when winning a medal. You would expect that the things you have achieved in life would be sufficient to drive away the negative voices speak at the strangest of times, but that night my voice was still challenging me, telling me that I should not continue the walk, that I was not going to be successful. Both the crew and I found this walk difficult. The response from people along the route was great but there was little fundraising. I had to go out with collection boxes and ask people to donate after walking and it was hard to stay motivated. Little did I know that there were plans under way to make the finish in Brisbane a success?

The last leg was not that eventful but as we approached Southbank it became clear that something was going to happen that hopefully would raise the spirits of all of us. I was well and truly surprised to see a grandfather with two of his grandsons, both in wheel chairs. Looking at them brought the tears flowing. How lucky Erika and I had been; Zoë had remained able to take care of herself right up till the last day she was with us. Here was a family trying to provide as good a life as they could with two young men terribly contorted through the ravages of muscular dystrophy. When we got closer to the restaurant it was obvious that there was something planned. The next thing I saw was the large frame of my mate Spud. He had flown up to be with us at the finish. In the café San Marco there must have been about 80 people, mostly good friends and supporters. They had also arranged for Andrew Lofthouse to be the compare. The first big surprise was the presentation to me of my torch relay uniform fully framed. Apparently Lizzy, Tony's wife, had spirited it away and had it cleaned so that it could be framed. All in all it was a wonderful reception and I had an opportunity to speak. Although many people commented on how well it went, it was still a challenge for me. It was good to see my mate Adam and all the gym staff that had been behind me all the way but most of all it was a thrill to see my mate Spud from Melbourne.

Not long afterward, Peter Denham approached me to become a fundraiser with the Muscular Dystrophy organization. It was a position I was pleased to accept. For a while things went well, but there were two women there that always seemed to be in competition as to who was meant to be in charge. I found this extremely difficult as each one wanted things done her way. I found it hard to be accountable as I didn't know what was required. Since my early childhood I had found it hard to take criticism. I often felt like I couldn't get things right and was often told I was not up to much. All these years later, the same thing seemed to be happening. It was not long before my inner voice reminded me that although I was encouraged to work on my own, if I made a mistake I would be criticized. It was not long until, after constantly trying to get support from work colleges, I found myself approaching Peter to resolve a particular issue. A couple of statements did the trick: one, that my spelling was not up to scratch; and two, that I spent too much time asking for help. That was all it took to once again shatter my confidence. Another door was closed on an opportunity to develop a future. I walked out.

Thankfully I had my gym work to fall back on. I was okay there for a time, going out and about talking to people about the gym and the benefits of keeping fit. I was then asked to follow a certain procedure to recruit members to sign up for set programs. I was not comfortable enough to ask people to do this when that was not what they totally wanted. Although I am a firm believer in fitness and body well-being, I did not like high pressure sales pitches so once again I walked away feeling down and out.

Although I had my little unit in West End, I was soon to have my world rocked again. The owner of the units was redeveloping and we all had eight weeks notice. I hadn't managed my financial affairs well, due mainly to an excess of alcohol. I had been running with the younger gym crowd and excess was the play of the day. I managed to keep my cherished Olympic torch and framed uniform, as well as my treasured watch given to me by the Dover YMCA. They went in and out of the pawnshop each week just so that I could get by. One time when I went to retrieve the watch I was too late and it had been sold.

I decided to give the Olympic torch and uniform to Zoë's Place to auction at the upcoming ball. Pamela stuck the knife in by refusing to have my name attached to either the torch or the framed uniform. Some time earlier, Pamela Barker told me that the bronze statue of a child that was going to be made for the Zoë's Place garden would not be a model of Zoë. What was it that Erika and I had done to continually have sand kicked in our faces? It was clear, for whatever reason; that Erika and I were to be eradicated from the history of Zoë's Place. Isn't that amazing! Without Erika and me starting Zoë's Place, not one member of the committee had an opportunity to be there. In some ways I suppose it was my low self esteem that led me to hide from confrontation. Heck, I was even frightened of answering the phone. I just let people walk all over me.

STARTING AGAIN

Early in 2002 I went to live in the same caravan park I had previously lived in, which was near the big shopping centre in Brisbane called Garden City. After my last walk in 2001, I was given a laptop by Chris Gallagher. At long last I was in a space where I could sit and start my story. I didn't realize it at the time, but writing became one of the best therapeutic exercises I'd ever done. I spent my days writing and going for walks. It was a time of finding me again. About one quarter of the book was written before I became restless again and needed some company.

A mutual friend found me a place to board with a husband and wife named Vic and Cheryl. I started a new phase in my life in the suburb of Aspley. I still went into West End on a regular basis to have coffee with my friends and it was there that I began to formulate the idea of another walk. Although Zoë's Place seemed to be a stalled project, I still found it hard to separate myself from the organization. The money I raised had provided a block of land, an office, a garden area that included the bronze statue which had been donated and $2,000,000.00 of pledges and donations in the bank. A Volunteer Coordinator had been hired to organize volunteers to do home visits to families to give them some much-needed time out. The Volunteer Coordinator was a lovely woman and was the only person from the organization to acknowledge Erika and myself. On the anniversary of Zoë's death each year, a card would arrive from her. I also learned that this woman spoke to families about how Zoë's Place came about.

I wanted so much for the hospice to become a reality and in a bid to bring this about I decided to issue a challenge to Ken Talbot of MacArthur Coal to fulfill his promise for a coal industry donation of $3 million. What I decided to do was to walk around Australia until he responded. Only then would I stop. Through my local coffeehouse in West End I met a group of very positive young people. I told them of my idea and they committed to helping me. We then made efforts to get sponsors. Philip Di Bella came on board first to provide hotel accommodations in each major city. A camping company provided my clothing and a tent. Collection boxes were placed in each coffee shop. At the same time, the invasion on Iraq prompted a couple of the young guys to demonstrate for world peace by walking to Canberra. This threatened to throw my plans into disarray but, convinced that I was doing the right thing, I decided to carry on.

In April 2003 I started out from Asply but things very soon started to go wrong. I had very little contact with the group, which left me feeling insecure and lonely. As I didn't receive any money from the moneyboxes, I had to organize the withdrawal of my superannuation, which was the last of my financial independence. The further I got up the North Coast, the more I realised that I was developing spasms in both hands which affected my sleep. I decided to visit my old Doctor Tim who had a practice in Childers. It was good catching up with Tim and talking about old times with Zoë, but sadly the news was not good about my hands. He advised me to discontinue the walk, as the condition would eventually cause me to have permanent damage to the nerves in my neck. The backpack I carried was heavy and I was unable to lighten it in any way. I initially decided to give it another go to see if the pains could be managed but by the time I got to Bundaberg I decided to turn around and get the train back home to Brisbane.

To have to call a stop to the walk was soul-destroying; after all the past efforts I felt a complete failure and tiptoed into Brisbane with little money. I found a bed and breakfast and sat and licked my wounds. Where would I go now? I decided to call my friend Cheryl and thankfully she offered me a chance to share their home again, which proved to be a lifesaver. It was not long after that I met another of Cheryl's friends named George. He asked if I wanted work. I jumped at the chance and he told me to front up to a company called Modern Teaching Aids in Strathpine. The distribution manager offered me a job as a packer in the big pack area of the warehouse. He was a little concerned at my age but I reassured him that if I could do all the walks I had done I could carry out my duties as a packer. It was now the end of May 2003. During the early stages of my work for the company it was not the size of the packing that caused a worry but the seemingly endless mistakes I was making. In the end I broke down in tears. Even with my tablet for depression I found it hard to concentrate and I was now getting panic attacks. Fortunately I had a great South African co-worker who had not long before immigrated to Australia with his wife and family. Joe very quietly and deliberately coached, cajoled and trained me back to having a sense of pride and confidence. I then settled into life with a full time job, a roof over my head and a decent weekly wage. It felt good to be stable, which hadn't been the case for a very long time.

I had an old car I had bought from my mate Pete Why. Unfortunately, it broke down in a big way and it took a lot of money to get it fixed. I stupidly got talked into using a backyard mechanic and ended up paying twice when the car had to be fixed for a second time for the same problem. Once again, one step forward and two steps back. Fortunately, I moved into a house in Bald Hills owned by a male friend of Cheryl's that was closer to my job. Prior to Christmas 2003, loneliness engulfed me again and I was longing for the companionship of a woman. I had heard that many people had success with using the internet and I decided to give it a shot. Upon surfing through the sites, it became obvious that many people bent the truth about their circumstances so I decided to be totally honest. My profile said, "If financially secure means broke that's me and if no baggage means no family, that's me. I have nothing but love and adventure to offer." I received a reply from a nice lady who lived on the Sunshine Coast hinterland. We met a few times and it was friendly but she was not the person I was looking for.

A while later I received two replies that I decided to further explore. One turned out to be a non-starter, but the next lady was going to change my life as I had known it and take me on a whole new journey. Our first meeting happened at the café San Marco, the same restaurant where I had finished my last successful walk from Melbourne. I had joked that I would be wearing my bowling whites so that I would be easily recognizable. Although she did not object on the phone, during the hours we spent talking in the restaurant I learned that her parents had been mad about bowls. She was glad I was dressed in something different. We just sat and talked and I felt close to her because she had also struggled through life. As we talked, I referred to her as an angel, something I often did because I am of the belief that we all have the capacity to act like angels and to make people feel special. I could feel a bonding taking place as we had lived almost parallel lives. We even realised that our major relationships had happened at similar times. When the meeting came to an end she explained that she was going out with a friend in the evening and asked if I would like to join them. I had no hesitation in saying yes, although I had very little money.

That night we went to a nice Chinese Restaurant and the Ten Pin Bowling Alley. All the time I was counting how much the evening was going to cost. By now there was no doubt that we were getting along well and I knew I wanted to meet her again. I survived the near financial disaster of that evening and when we left each other that night we agreed to meet again. I knew Jocelyn was going to be special to me and I had to see her again. One thing that my life had taught me was the art of living on my wits. I was still paying off my car bills and, having no money; I proceeded to sell my camping gear. The next date together was great; we got on like a house on fire and I must say the fire was all consuming at times. We barbecued at South Bank, walked up to Kangaroo Point and kissed all the way back. That was the beginning of February 2004. At the beginning of April, Jocelyn and I had a wonderful four days on Stradbroke Island for my sixtieth birthday. It was at this time that we decided to move in together, and a month later Jocelyn and I moved into a lovely unit not far from my job. Jocelyn had a good job with Linfox and I continued to work at Modern Teaching Aids. We didn't have a lot but bit by bit our lives grew as did our house contents.

About June/July, we were drawn into the Zoë's place saga again. Pamela hired a Clinical Manager named Diane. Jocelyn and I couldn't understand this appointment when in fact there was no hospice. We could understand the Outreach Program with its volunteers, but not the other. For whatever reasons, Pamela was soon treating both Diane and the Volunteer Coordinator badly by bullying and being rude. Diane's daughter Jessica asked us to attend a meeting with Diane, her husband Greg, the Volunteer Coordinator and herself. They wanted my help to gain as much historical knowledge as they could about the founding and running of the organization. This was followed by further meetings with Jocelyn, Erika and other interested parties. At the end of August we were asked to attend the Annual General Meeting of Zoë's Place. With all the unrest among the ranks and many of the volunteers becoming increasingly upset, we felt we had no choice but to try again to make a difference. Since only members had voting rights, Jocelyn applied to be a member. There was a fair amount of skullduggery and only people who didn't pose a threat to the organization seemed to be getting membership status.

Jocelyn called Pamela Barker on the pretext of not knowing very much about the organization. She talked about her own experience of hospice, having used a hospice facility in New Zealand when her son was young. She asked Pamela what happened to the founders and was told that Nigel Reed had a bad breakdown and neither he nor Erika wanted anything to do with the organization. Jocelyn thought Pamela was disrespectful for disclosing my medical history and felt it was outrageous that she lied about Erika and me not wanting to be involved. Was that okay for a nun to lie and disclose confidential medical knowledge?

Although it took a few phone calls and quotes from the constitution, Jocelyn gained her membership the day before the Annual General Meeting and was able to vote as well as stand for the position available on the board. At the Annual General Meeting Jocelyn was successful in gaining the board position, nine for her and five against her. However, Pamela chose to use her nineteen proxies and voted Jocelyn out. Another new member gained the vote to the board as the proxies could not be used twice. But procedure was not followed for this vote. It was supposed to be done in alphabetical order and the person who gained access to the board had a surname starting with *D* whereas Jocelyn's surname started with G. The board broke the rules to manipulate the vote by voting for Jocelyn first.

In the October of that same year Jocelyn took me on a trip to New Zealand to meet her friends, family and see some of the most beautiful scenery in the world. This was my first experience of being with someone who was terrified of flying. Jocelyn was so frightened that she spent most of the flights crying, not eating, not wanting to leave her seat and generally being in an elevated state of anxiety. When we arrived back from New Zealand, we also gave up on the old Mitsi, bought ourselves a reliable Ford Falcon and started looking forward to our first Christmas together.

We attended a couple more meetings with the hospice action committee and it became clear that it was going to be difficult to change anything at Zoë's place. The present board formed a company with a different constitution and was awaiting authority from the Australian Tax Department to transfer to them the charity number that was given for Zoe Reed Little Bridge House Association. It was clear that this Board was maneuvering the situation to be able to stay in control. It became more and more apparent that the staff members and volunteers were being bullied and treated badly. A case was brought against Pamela and Zoë's Place by past employees and volunteers who provided statements about the way Pamela treated them. I also gave a statement on the subject and I believe two employees won their battle against Zoë's Place and were paid compensation. During this time Jocelyn became aware that I continually allowed myself to be drawn into the politics of Zoë's Place. For a group of people whose main daily work was caring for families, they seemed unable to grasp the pain they caused me. My heart was with the families so I was always unable to say no. Jocelyn, like many others, could not understand why the two founders were kept from playing an active role in the organization.

About this time there was a televised protest at the Mount Ommaney property. Protesters wanted to know where the money had gone and why there was still no hospice. Out of the woodwork surfaced Terry Boyce, a well known Queensland lawyer who had been disbarred. He spent some time talking to a television reporter, then left. I believe he had attended a volunteer training program and had become a volunteer. I believe his participation spurred Pamela Barker and the board into action because they soon decided to construct an administration building. Everyone wanted a hospice, not an administration building, but Pamela felt that if an administration building was built the families would at least know that something substantial was there. However, I remembered that the fundraisers had said not to build until we had the funds *to build and to run a hospice for at least the first year.* I knew there was insufficient capital in the coffers to run the hospice for the first year. According to financial records that we had seen of the previous four years we knew that not very much money had been raised since I had been uninvolved.

I started to drink on a more regular basis, a bottle of wine a night. Zoë's Place ate away at me. Needy families were not being helped because the volunteer program was no longer running and there was only the odd volunteer still visiting a family or two on their own. That in itself was dodgy; since there was no longer a volunteer coordinator, and there was no public liability insurance. Jocelyn and I learned that Zoë's Place was close to folding, which greatly concerned us. I believed that the ruling for charities is that if they fold they can either be taken over by a likewise organization or be closed. So, to provide a safety net for needy families, we bit the bullet and created another charity known as Promise House Children's Respite Services Association, or Promise House. As before, we had no money to start.

We needed to get public liability insurance quickly in order to have fundraising functions, so I wrote to Bob McRann again. Lo and behold, he came up with $2,000.00 and on January 1, 2005, Jocelyn registered the charity with the Australian Tax Department. The ball started rolling. We had a founding meeting and formed a committee with me as the president and Jocelyn as secretary/treasurer. Luckily, Jocelyn had an extensive administration background and she was able to deal with all the government departments and negotiate our insurance policy. All in all, it took about four months to set ourselves up and get our Australian Taxation Charity Number. In the early stages of Promise House, a past employee of Zoë's Place brought along the disbarred lawyer Terry Boyce and Shay Zulpo to one of our meetings. Shay offered to put together a weekend "think tank" and give us a price on it. We told her that we had no money for such luxuries and she was taken aback; apparently she thought that we could fundraise for it. I naively thought it would be about $2,000, but when the costs came in it was $25,000.00 which was far too much for us to consider. Shay also offered to write our constitution, not knowing that Jocelyn and I had already started working on it on our own. The thing that shocked me was that Shay immediately tried to suggest I was not the person to run Promise House and that I should be the Patron. I nodded, listening, then suddenly I saw Terry Boyce outside talking to the ex Zoë's Place staff member. The hairs on the back of my neck stood up. What was the game they were playing? Shay did eventually come up with a constitution but it was the very same as could be got from the internet on any site dealing with such matters. After all that was what we had done and modified the document to suit our needs. After that we heard no more from them and it came to pass that Terry Boyce ended up on the board of Zoë's Place and Shay ended up as the Chief Executive Officer. Here was another cuckoo ready to swoop in after the hard work of setting up an organization was done. It was decided that the proceeds of Promise House would be spent supplying weekends away for parents that had children with life-limiting illnesses. We were able to work with a hotel at South Bank to supply the best deal as well as supply the odd treat for the parents. By fostering a relationship with a company in Woolongabba, we also provided large family portraits for those families who were going to lose a child. They would always have a great portrait of when their families were whole.

Amongst all this, Jocelyn and I decided to marry and were busy organizing our wedding. Jocelyn would have been happy to go to the Registry Office and then for a meal on the River Queen but I wanted our marriage to be a celebration with our friends. A friend of ours, Rod Ihia, had a lovely older Queenslander home that was offered to us for the day. It was a wonderful day. Colin Walker was my Best Man. Rod cooked the traditional Kiwi Hangi and taught the guys to do the All Blacks Haka. We decided to use the wedding as a fundraiser for

Promise House in lieu of gifts. A couple of guests insisted that we use their donations as honeymoon money so we spent one night in a motel in Northern Brisbane and a further four nights at Harvey Bay. The Promise House donations from the wedding came to a little over $1,000.

After we returned from our honeymoon, Jocelyn and I were busy doing fundraising for Promise House. At Modern Teaching Aids the staff got right behind all of our efforts and each week the ladies organized some form of fundraiser. Jocelyn came in occasionally taking leave from her job and did lunchtime Sausage Sizzles. All in all, over a period of six months, the staff raised over $5000. We also carried on with other fundraising and managed to get money boxes into many De Bella coffee houses (as well as a few others in different businesses).

We enjoyed a great Christmas. Jocelyn's son Matthew visited from New Zealand. At times Matthew's disabilities were a handful, but on the whole he was okay to be around. In January 2006, Jocelyn and I organized a breakfast fundraiser. Having organized a lot of raffles, we were able to get two bands to play for free. All in all it was a great success and confirmed Jocelyn's belief that she was able to do fundraising on the scale required to run a successful charity.

The building at Zoë's Place was coming along and we heard through the grapevine that Shay had dismissed Pamela Barker. I guess this was made easier by the fact that Pamela never drew a wage for the work she did. I am not sure if Pamela had a place on the board but in the past she seemed to have a lot of sway with any decision that was made. Soon after this Bob McRann came to Brisbane for an overnight visit. We collected him from the airport, booked him into his hotel and later took him to see the progress of Zoë's Place. Like us, he was more than pleased with the fact that something was finally happening. We met Shay there that day and she told us that they were turning Pamela Barker's administration block into a four-bedroom hospice as well as an office block. This seemed like progress and we went away prepared to give the new administration the benefit of the doubt. The rest of 2006 was spent fundraising and helping families through Promise

House. The workers at Modern Teaching Aids continued to show their generosity and their families helped create one-off fundraisers. Jocelyn and I continued to be the masters of the Sausage Sizzles which, incredibly, bought in quite a bit of funding.

In May 2006 Jocelyn's daughter Tara gave birth to our first grandchild, a little girl named Chontaé. This was fantastic for me because, with the passing of Zoë, I thought I would never know the feeling of having grandchildren. When Chontaé was five months old Jocelyn went back to New Zealand to visit her new granddaughter. She came back with many photos and happy memories. This was a great time for Jocelyn. Tara and she had not been together a lot over the previous five years and the birth of Chontaé cemented their relationship.

From time to time I had meetings with either Shay Zulpo or the board. At one board meeting that Erika and I attended, my first question set the cat amongst the pigeons. I asked, "well guys, what money have you raised and what have you done since you have been here"? The disbarred lawyers got all high and mighty and said that he was not going to have me walk in there and challenge them. I told him not to raise his voice to me just because we had "history". I took one look at Shay's face and knew that she knew what I was referring to. The Promise House meeting at our home where they tried to muscle in on what we were doing. I turned to Erika and said, "they don't need our help, let's go". As we got up to leave, we were called back but we knew that it was only lip service on their part. Erika and I continued to attend some of the functions but Jocelyn chose to stay away a lot of the time because the disrespect that Erika and I were shown made her extremely angry and she was never sure that she would be able to hold her tongue.

During this period, Zoë's Place needed a Fundraiser. I took my CV to Shay Zulpo and the Board and offered to work for the wages I was already getting at my job, about $30,000. I never heard another thing about it until we went to a fundraiser and met the young lady they hired sight-unseen before she returned from England. The event we attended was organized by another member of the staff, a nurse's aide, and it raised $7000 toward the purchase of an all-purpose van for Zoë's Place. Sometime later, I spoke to Shay about fundraising and she made a remark that answered a few questions that Erika and I had. She said that she would not let any one family run the organization and I guess that meant Erika and me as well. On another occasion when a Race Day was being organized on the Sunshine Coast, Shay asked that the solicitor's name not be mentioned. We knew why as his indiscretion resulting in disbarment had taken place there.

At the end of 2006 it was decided that I would do a walk for Zoë's Place to once again get the message out to all of Queensland that the hospice was there and funds were needed to run it. Usually these walks were able to collect $30,000 to $50,000. We began this walk in April/May 2007. We started from Port Douglas to walk down the Queensland Coast and back to finish at South Bank, in Central Brisbane. Once again, my mate Tony Boon, a guy named Bill and an employee from Zoë's Place named Tony were with me. The vehicles and some of the food and clothes were sponsored. Fortunately, one of the main sponsors was Athlete's Foot, the chain of shoe stores.

A big fundraiser was organized for the start of the walk at Port Douglas. On the eve of the walk we boarded a boat for a wonderful dinner and evening cruise. About $10,000 was raised on that first night, which gave us a tremendous boost and made us look forward to the rest of the month with renewed enthusiasm. Unfortunately, not much else was prearranged. I would often don the mascot Philo suit and parade around towns shaking the collection buckets. By the time we got to Cairns it was evident that Tony Boon was not doing well. We got him to the doctor and it was not good news. Tony was advised not to fly (because of his condition) but told to get home and see his own doctors as soon as possible. Tony, being Tony, defied orders and flew home. He later had an operation and has been free of the complaint ever since. Tony's departure left us in a dilemma because we were using two vehicles, so we left one vehicle safely housed in Cairns and continued on with the camper van only.

This made it even more difficult to organize fundraisers along the way. The shoe stores were supposed to organize fundraising events, but in the end not many participated. All in all, we raised about $30,000, but the highlight for me was being joined by the young girl and her mother who had joined me on my first walk. The young girl was a baby in a pushchair the first time around and the mother told me that she wanted her daughter (now a teenager) to know the man who gave so much for others. I was so humbled and I thanked that person from the bottom of my heart. These are the people that make charities possible. Shay Zulpo worked hard all through 2007 to secure some funding from the government and in 2008 they received funding of around $700,000 for one year only. I believe it was on an invoice system per patient and was due to run out in June 2009. I thought it would give management the time to find alternative funding. It was also a great coup, as when Zoë's Place was given the land, I was told not to go looking for any more Government funding.

Sometime in 2008 Erika was approached by Shay and asked if we would be able to secure the attendance of Lisa Neuman, the Lord Mayor's wife, at a fundraising luncheon. Erika thought it would be a good idea to take me as well to talk about all the walks and fundraising I had done. We left knowing that Lisa was on board and she was only too happy to attend the luncheon to support Zoë's Place. Erika and I were over the moon because Lisa already had her set charities and now she was agreeing to help Zoë's Place. We both felt good that we could do something for Zoë's Place. The date was set but due to a lack of marketing for the event, only about 20 tickets were sold and the event was cancelled. Apart from the Zoë's Place emailing/mailing list of supporters, most of the advertising for events was focused on the Mt. Ommaney/Western Suburbs area. For some reason the management seemed to be reluctant to branch out.

On many occasions I tried to get them to understand that Zoë's Place needed to run both a Capital Campaign and a Regular Running Cost Fundraising Campaign. It would have been easy to hire a person or a firm that took commission only and whose sole purpose was to raise the required funds. If this was not done, they could very quickly lose sight of the original project and it would never get finished. Once again, they all nodded their heads in agreement but nothing was ever done to form a Fundraising Committee or to hire someone for that sole purpose.

Toward the end of 2007, we were led to believe that Zoë's Place was doing reasonably well and, as Jocelyn was starting to have health issues while still working a full time job, we decided to close the charity Promise House. We no longer felt that Zoë's Place needed a likewise charity to be there for any closure. The committee agreed and Jocelyn proceeded with all the closure paperwork. Jocelyn and I by now had moved into another house big enough to house our daughter and granddaughter but sadly that did not eventuate. For whatever reason, our daughter found it hard to leave New Zealand, even though we were prepared to help financially to get them to Australia. Unbeknown to us at the time, she was getting caught up in a lifestyle that would lead us all on another journey; one we never imaged.

Jocelyn left working at Linfox on the Mobil Contract and went to a mining company in the city. She found the mining company to be too corporate for her liking and went to work for South East Queensland Fuels, now under the umbrella of Caltex. Her pre-employment physical showed that she had emphysema! So once again, here was another shock to shatter the system. The prognosis was fairly good and Jocelyn was told she could look forward to another 20 years of life but we were just not sure of what the quality would be in the long term. Jocelyn's life had been full of such challenges with not being able to have babies and her daily struggle with curvature of the spine. Jocelyn has two adopted children who have had their own challenges in life now this! It seemed that there was no end to our challenges.

About a month after Jocelyn's diagnosis I faced a challenge of my own. I very suddenly developed double vision. I was unable to drive and walking was extremely hard as I could not judge the heights of the kerbs or distances. I had to see a specialist who did all manner of tests and a brain scan was ordered. We were told that there were only two reasons that this would happen: Either diabetes or a brain tumor.

Since we knew that I didn't have diabetes, it had to be the tumor. I set about getting all the required tests and, while awaiting results, I was given special lenses to attach to my glasses to help normalize my vision but I still could not drive. What a time it was! Thankfully, when the test results came back they said I didn't have a tumor which left the doctors mystified but the specialist was sure that the condition would right itself over a period of about six months. That is precisely what happened, although over the recovery time I had to have varying types of special lenses made to help my sight as my vision adjusted back to normal. After a few months my eyesight came back to normal and Jocelyn and I came to terms with her health issues. Life seemed pretty good and we organized and paid the deposit on a camping holiday down the New South Wales Coast. Once again we were optimistic for the future.

In October/November 2008, we received phone calls from our daughter Tara and discovered that she had problems, but we didn't know exactly what those problems were. The only way to find out was to cancel our holiday plans and go to New Zealand to see what was happening. When we realised that our daughter's problems were quite serious, we extended our holiday and spent a great deal of the time in a motel de-toxing her. We went back to Australia naively thinking that things were back on track. Six weeks later she nose-dived again and we realized that we had to return to live in New Zealand to help our daughter and granddaughter. This was not what we had planned for the next two years, but in our hearts we knew there was no other decision to be made. I knew that had this been Zoë I would have gone at a moment's notice. Our final six weeks in Australia was a very intense time with both Jocelyn and I often breaking into tears. We went through the process of working out our notice at our respective jobs, selling the furniture and car, shipping off the dogs and our personal possessions, cashing up our super, saying goodbye to our dear friends and my wonderful sister-in-law and boarding the plane back to the Land of the Long White Cloud. It seemed like what could go wrong went wrong. I had to increase my dose of antidepressants as the worry was great. Could we survive? Could we find work? What about the dogs? What would happen with our visas and pensions? Were we going to get there in time to help?

Before we left I wanted just one more visit to Zoë's Place, a chance to "touch the walls" as Colin, the founding Chairman, had said. Through a chance contact with my old Lions club I decided to invite a great supporter of the walk from England, Greg Nothling. He agreed to join Erika and me on our visit. I felt it would be nice for the club to see what their support had been converted into. By the time Erika and I got there Greg, was already in attendance and he was stunned by what he had found. As we walked around we saw three ill teenage boys being cared for. In my eyes (and I am sure Erika's, too) we had left our marks and Zoë's life had achieved a lot. My last gift to Zoë's Place was a brass plaque that we had once left on the lighthouse hill at Byron Bay. In memory of Zoë it said, "Every Ending Has a New Beginning". We said our farewells and it was over. We had lost the love of our lives. Like the plaque read, our new beginnings came with the end of a journey. I had reached my destination. The fact that Erika and I could stand there together made our message one of hope. When the day came to say goodbye to some of our friends, even though I felt sadness and a concern about the future, I was happy. It was a strange feeling as I entered the plane. I was going to live in another country. I felt good! If someone had told the little boy that never believed in himself; that his life would pan out this way he would never have believed it. Jocelyn and I had seats in separate locations for the short trip. As I sat back in my chair and did up my belt, I saw an old black dog looking at me through the window, followed by a voice that said, "Are you sure you can handle this challenge? What about all the mistakes you have made Nige"? I looked back out the window but he had gone, if he ever was there anyway. All I could say to myself was, "I will give it my best shot". The engines roared and we were off. As we flew over those red roofs of Queensland I was proud I was leaving it a better place than when I had arrived in1973. I could hear my little girl saying, "My dad The Walking Man did that".

A NEW LIFE, FRESH CHALLENGES: WHAT DOES THE FUTURE HOLD?

I didn't think that I would ever again be confronted with problems associated with Zoë's Place, but then about 6 weeks after arriving in New Zealand I received an email from Erika informing me about complaints of bad management and poor treatment of children. Talk about the wind being blown out of my sails! I just could not get my head around it. Apparently, a nurse had made accusations that the level of care was something from the past and that management had not acted on complaints in a timely manner. It would have been easy to rant and rave but it was too late for that. Erika and I both had offered to help knowing that passion was the secret. I'd even offered to work for my cleaner's pay. But they went ahead and hired a person unseen with little or no previous experience.

If I thought I was in control of my depression, I was wrong. The more I thought of what Queensland had lost, the deeper the hole became. I spoke to Erika to see what was truly happening and she informed me that information was hard to come by but she had heard that the parents were devastated and were prepared to approach the journalist who had interviewed the accusing nurse. All in all it was hard to know what to do. Maybe somehow our move to New Zealand was predestined to protect me from the day-to-day pain. Many mistakes had been made on all sides, mistakes that could have been avoided had the board and management only been able to work together. Alas, that was never to be, for whatever reasons. My heart goes out to all the families that are now without support.

Jocelyn and I talked about it and I felt a need to speak to someone who had played a role during the years I was kept out. So I spoke to one of the board members. I had no hesitation at laying some blame on a board that had not taken the time to ask Erika and I what the dream was, or how we had been able to obtain the level of pledges and donations that we had. I was amazed when he said, "You sound upset". Upset! I was bloody angry! Jocelyn spoke with the same person and was accused of stating untruths. Amazing how people's memories can think of a situation in such different ways. As on many occasions, I spoke to Bob in America. He was quick to point out that in most cases, when an administrator is appointed the business goes into liquidation. However he made the comment that I had done the best I could and that I could not be held responsible for others' failures. I wanted and needed to hear someone else reassure me that I had done my best. Over the next few days it began to unfold and the final straw was the withdrawal of funds from their major sponsor, Queensland Teachers Credit Union. Had there been a reasonable size pool of funds in the bank, maybe they could have survived the loss of one such sponsor.

There was only one other person to tell and that was Colin, who was up in Cairns on his boat with his wonderful wife Carmen. He, like all of us who had been involved in the early days, was angry. Like Bob, Colin reassured me that we had left the association in a good state. After discussing what we may be able to do, we both came to the conclusion that it was all too late. Colin told me he was off to work on a prawn trawler. At his age, 62, I was worried, but the last time I saw Colin in January 2009 he looked terrific and both Jocelyn and I told him so.

The day finally came when the gates of Zoë's Place closed for the last time. Never again would a family pass through them knowing that they would get some relief from their daily struggles with their terminally ill children. Twenty years of walking the highways, influencing people to support the cause of respite care, were all gone because others thought they knew it all or were better than the people who started the project. I was so empty all day it was surreal. When we had stood in the entrance of the hospice, we'd been reassured everything was OK. Now I asked myself how many people were aware of the failed state of affairs and how many people had lied to Erika and me.

With hindsight, Jocelyn realised that the person we saw at Zoë's Place seemingly in charge was properly the receiver.

The next few weeks went by fairly quickly. Things and home life was going well when once again the calm was interrupted by a phone call from Carmen telling me Colin had something he wanted to tell me. As soon as I heard his voice I knew something was wrong. I said, "Hi buddy how are you"? He replied, "Not too good, my old mate. I have come home off the prawn trawler and, after investigations; I have been told I have pancreatic cancer". I just felt as if I had been hit over the head with a cricket bat. I was stunned! The guy who had looked so well on his last visit was battling cancer. He was a mate, a mentor and the closest person to a brother I have ever had.

As always, he was positive and felt they had got it early so he stood a chance of beating the cancer. I was stuck for words as here I was in New Zealand and my mate was facing his greatest challenge. We had gone through so much together helping each other. Over a bottle or two of red wine we had solved many of the world's problems. After a few minutes we both wished each other well and I reassured him I would keep in contact. As many times before, someone close to me was ill with cancer. Having lost Stanley, Maurice and Barbara I was very upset at the thought of losing Colin to that dreaded disease. The constant loss of people in my life was responsible for my depression. How would I deal with this new challenge? I was a little better prepared for this particular challenge as I had been receiving counseling for my depression and unresolved grief.

Over the next few weeks, Jocelyn and I spoke to both Colin and Carmen, often shedding our tears. I became hesitant to talk, so Jocelyn spoke to Carmen. We all felt positive until Carmen told us that tests had shown that the cancer was on the move and was now in his lungs. Also, the chemotherapy was not making any difference and the level of pain medication he was receiving told us that all was not well. Sometime during this period, Colin asked me to read his eulogy and I assured him I would. I also said I wanted to see him one last time. He was concerned that some people thought he was a bit of a waster and he wanted me to share some of the truth I knew. How could I say no? About a week after his tests he started to deteriorate very quickly. So bad was he that Carmen called and asked if I could make it to see him. They had given him two weeks to live. We knew I couldn't travel twice and with work commitments we asked Colin if he wanted me there to visit or for the funeral. He chose to see me and I wrote the eulogy to be read by another at the funeral. Although Jocelyn and I had little money in the bank, I said I would get there as soon as possible. We immediately obtained an overdraft and booked a flight.

The night before I flew I stood on our verandah and looked back on a 30-year friendship. It was truly the end of an era. I knew I would miss him, for his mentorship had supported me through many personal hiccups. I was glad he was able to get his boat and his boson's ticket. He had lived three years of his dream to sail and live on a boat. I thought of the first day we met. Terror, his Labrador, had dashed across the road, dived into my house and pinched one of my socks. Colin had looked up and seen his adventurous puppy coming out of our carport. He dove to his right and was able to retrieve the wet sock. We struck up a conversation and the rest is history.

I made it to Cairns and was able to hold my mate and tell him of my love for him, but looking at him was hard. He was nothing short of a skeleton covered with skin. Over the next days I saw that although his body was being devoured by cancer, his heart was still as strong as ever. On one occasion his son James held him while putting him back on the bed and Colin looked across at all of us and smiled as if he was dancing with him. Later that day he struggled to look at me and asked, "well my old mate, do we have anything to settle"? I replied, "no my mate, I am just here to be with you".

The next day I had to leave and by this time he was in a poor state and I felt he would not be with us for long. As I said farewell to Colin, although he had not spoken for most of the previous day, he replied with what sounded like a grunt and for me it was enough. The tears flowed and I rushed out of his room to the waiting car. Before Carmen's son Jason drove me to the airport, I was joined by Colin's two great kids. We held each other and vowed to keep in contact. Finally, Carmen hugged me and we assured each other we would stay in contact. Colin died the following morning at 2:00 am, just a short time after I had arrived back in New Zealand. Colin had been the person who helped put the world walk together and he was like a brother. He also was the person who had told me, "Beware the Cuckoo, the bird that watches other birds build their nests and then swoops in and claims the nest as it own". To anyone who dares to dream of establishing something of value to the community, beware the human cuckoos as they will be watching. But you must not let them stop you from becoming a visionary.

What now? Every ending has a new beginning. We came to New Zealand to help family and that is working very well. A lot of what has happened here is still very personal, but what I can say is that our daughter Tara has been well for well over a year now. We know that there is still a lot of support required to move through the process of recovery involved in our family. I have a part time job which adds to our aged pension and Jocelyn is not working in order to give the family support as it is required. Jocelyn has also worked really hard with writing, rewriting, editing and getting this book ready for publication. We know that there is going to be a lot of hard work ahead of us to put all of our lives back together and to unite us back to being the family we once were.

We have a wonderful son Matthew, a beautiful daughter Tara, and an amazing granddaughter Chontaé. We have a house filled with love and much laughter and we all have a keen sense of humour. It doesn't get any better than that.

REFLECTIONS OF AN ORDINARY GUY

As I look back on the first 65 years of my life it is easy to say what if:
What if my father had lived?
What if my mother had stayed?
What if someone had explained it was not my fault?
What if any other one of my marriages had survived?
What if Zoë had lived?
What if! What if! What if!

Yes, my battle with depression goes on but maybe, just maybe, my life would have been different and besides, what the heck? I believe I made a small difference, even though I still have the black dog as my companion.

LAYING TO REST MY DAD

In March 2010 I received a letter from Ministry of Defence in England telling me what they knew of my father's passing. At long last after 65 years I now know what happened and I can finally put to rest all the ghosts of not knowing and wondering. This was a major constant for the whole of my life. Now I feel that a huge weight has been lifted and I am able to focus on a future instead of dwelling on a past. The not knowing as always is the worst.

This happened quite by accident by playing around on the computer and typing in my father's name looking for information. It appeared that others were trying to find out what had happened to my Dad and were able to give me the process with which to follow in order to receive information. I followed this advice and the following scanned letter is what I received.

From: Flight Lieutenant M Hudson MA BA
The Air Historical Branch (RAF)
MINISTRY OF DEFENCE
Building 824 RAF Northolt West End Road Ruislip
Middlesex HA4 6NG

Telephone	(Direct dial)	0208 833 8162
	(Fax)	0208 833 8170
	(Military)	95233 8162

Mr N Reed
26 Luculia Drive Bay
Fair Mount
Maungaui
Bay of Plenty
NZ 3116

Your Reference

Our Reference
D/AHB/8/27
Date

12 March 2010

Dear Mr Reed

Thank you returning the completed Certificate of Kinship relating to your request for information about the circumstances surrounding the death of your late father, Flight Sergeant F E Reed. I have now consulted our casualty records and have found the following information:

Your father was the Flight Engineer onboard Stirling EH945 of 620 Squadron which took off from RAF Chedburgh at 19.55 hours on 27 September 1943 to take part in an attack on Hanover. RAF Chedburgh was a satellite station of RAF Stradishall and was near Bury St Edmunds in Suffolk. No 620 Squadron was formed there on the 17 June 1943. The attack was the 2nd of a series of 4 made on Hanover by the RAF between 22/23 September and 18/19 October 1943. On the night of 27/28 September the bomber force comprised 678 aircraft (312 Lancasters, 231 Halifaxes, 111 Stirlings, 24 Wellingtons and 5 USAAF B-17s). Out of this number 38 Bomber Command aircraft and 1 B-17 were lost. Sadly your father's Stirling was amongst this number.

Stirling EH975 was shot down and crashed on the railway embankment of the Hanover-Celle line at the Birkenweg Crossing at Krahenwinkel. There are 2 reported times of the crash, one is given as 23.15 hours and the other as 22.45 hours. The aircraft did not explode and there were no signs of bombs amongst the wreckage but it did catch fire. Your father was found alive but badly injured and was taken to hospital by the Germans. The Germans reported to the International Red Cross Committee (IRCC) that 3 of the crew had been killed and that 2 others were prisoners of war but gave no further information regarding your father. Numerous requests for information were made by the Air Ministry and others to the Germans through the IRCC for news of Sgt Reed. An enquiry to the IRCC made at the end of October 1944 elicited the following response from the IRCC in December "Berlin replies that Frank Reed was in September 1943 Reserve Lazarett 1, Hanover. No further information as documents of Lazarett destroyed". Lazarett is a German name for a hospital.

Your mother was informed of this news and told, that since no further information had been received it was sadly concluded that Sgt Reed had lost his life when the Lazarett had suffered damage during the heavy raids on Hanover. A particularly heavy raid took place on the night of 8/9 October 1943 when 504 Bomber Command aircraft attacked Hanover very accurately. Local reports described extensive damage in the centre of the city and many other parts except the western side. The German reports said that 1200 people had been killed and 3,932 buildings were completely destroyed and more than 30,000 were damaged but no individual buildings were named. The German authorities informed the IRCC that the Reserve Lazarett 1 was completely demolished by enemy action but gave no date.

The Air Ministry Casualty Branch informed your mother that your father had been classified as missing and that formal steps to presume his death would be taken. In January 1945 the Air Ministry wrote to your mother to tell her this action had been taken and that Sgt Reed had been presumed to have lost his life on 9 December 1944, this being the date of the cable from the IRCC forwarding the news from Berlin.

When aircrew were listed as missing it was the job of the Casualty Branch to find out what had happened to them, by the end of the war some 38,700 RAF personnel were listed as missing in Europe. The RAF established the Missing Research and Enquiry Service (MRES) to determine the fate of these missing personnel. MRES units operated between the last years of the War and the early 1950s and were active in all the theatres in which the RAF had operated. One such unit was instructed to undertake a search for Sgt Reed and other members of his crew. The search was undertaken in September 1948. The investigating officer went to Krahenwinkel and interrogated a number of witnesses. The investigating officer found that a 4 engined bomber, later identified by the Luftwaffe as a Stirling approached the village of Krahenwinkel at 22.45 hours on the night of 27 March. The date was clearly remember by the witnesses as a large scale raid on Hanover had taken place that night. Because it was dark and there was no moon the aircraft was not seen only heard in the air prior to the crash. The investigating officer said that the crash occurred at exactly 22.45. On impact the aircraft caught fire but did not explode. The crew who were killed in the crash were found in the aircraft and were buried in Limmer Cemetery by the Luftwaffe who also removed the remains of the aircraft. The witnesses also said that one of the crew was found alive but very badly injured. He was given First Aid and was taken to hospital but the witnesses did not think he was strong enough to survive the journey there. However, the German reports indicate that he was admitted to hospital and he would therefore have been a prisoner of war.

Very sadly it must be concluded that you father either died of his wounds or was killed when the Reserve Lazarett 1 was hit by the RAF bombers, probably during the attack on the night of 8/9 October 1943.

The investigating officer then searched the Limmer Cemetery but he reported that he had failed to find any trace of Sgt Reed's grave. However, in October 1948 the Air Ministry wrote to your mother seeking her assistance in the identification of some dental evidence found in grave 1886 in the Civil Cemetery at Hanover as a German grave marker had been found on it which read "Reed Officer September 1943". Her domestic circumstances were such that she passed the letter on to Sgt Reed's mother, and requested that she dealt with the matter. Your grandmother replied to the Air Ministry that she had been unable to get a response from the civil dentist at the practice your father had attended prior to joining the RAF. Although corroborating evidence from the dentist was not forthcoming from the dental information supplied in the Air Ministry letter your grandmother felt that everything seemed to point to the remains in grave 1886 being those of her son, Sgt Reed, and our records would indicate that she passed this belief on to you as it would seem that you visited the grave whilst you were stationed in Germany. However, the Air Ministry, advised by the MRES, did not accept that there was sufficient evidence to place the identification of the remains in Grave 1886 beyond reasonable doubt. Sgt Reed was therefore listed as having no known grave.

The Head of the Air Historical Branch has decided that the casualty records appertaining to the loss of Stirling EH945 should be reviewed as we have had a number of cases relating to the Hanover-Limmer Cemetery. This review may take sometime but you will of course be informed of any outcome.

In the meantime I hope that the above information will be of assistance to you.

Yours sincerely

Mary Hide

BUCKINGHAM PALACE

The Queen and I offer you our heartfelt sympathy in your great sorrow.

We pray that your country's gratitude for a life so nobly given in its service may bring you some measure of consolation.

George R.I.

Mrs. F. E. Reed.

A SPECIAL THANK YOU

While compiling this "Thank You" list my only hope is that I do not forget anybody. If this is the case I would now like to extend my thanks to all the good and kind people I have met along my travels. Your deeds may have been small but you will be indelible in my memory.

Colin Walker you will be my brother/friend forever and a special thanks to your dear courageous wife **Carmen (Mencar)** who nursed you to the end.

Bob McRann. Words are not enough for the impact you have had on my life. Whenever I needed you, you were there. Many thanks for believing in me when nobody else did. Thank you to dear sweet **Penny** for the editing help with the book and being there for Bob.

Jocelyn Wijs-Reed. This lady is my steadfast rock as she says I am to her. It is hard to quantify what love and effort this lady has given to me and others.

Tara Otto-Reed. A big thank you to our daughter as without her technical abilities with the web site we would have been completely at a loss.

George & Ethel Sharpe. My Grandparents/Parents. Thank you for giving up part of your retirement to love and care for me.

Stanley, Maurice, Fred, Betty and Joyce. Thank you for being the best Uncles, Aunts/Brothers and Sisters in my time of need.

Pete Why. Thanks mate for being the nemesis that I kept trying to beat.

Tony & Lizzie Boon. Thank you both for the years of unwavering love and friendship. Jocelyn and I both miss the Sunday morning coffee visits.

Erika Reed Thank you for being Zoë's Mum and being able to remain friends with Jocelyn and me.

Sandy & Ernie Arnold and Mike & June Seven Words are not enough for the times you were there for me.

Pat Hogan & Edwina Bogacki. Pat and Edwina made sure I had money every month of the American walk and paid for Erika and I to go to the Lions Conference. They also took us on endless sightseeing adventures.

Fred Murphy. This is for believing in me Fred

Staff of Modern Teaching Aids, Brisbane. Many thanks for the endless fundraising efforts.